SPANISH
LESSONS

DEREK
LAMBERT

SPANISH
LESSONS

BEGINNING A NEW LIFE IN SPAIN

Broadway Books   New York

BROADWAY

Broadway Books titles may be purchased for business or promotional use or for special sales. For information, please write to: Special Markets Department, Random House, Inc., 1540 Broadway, New York, NY 10036.

BROADWAY BOOKS and its logo, a letter B bisected on the diagonal, are trademarks of Broadway Books, a division of Random House, Inc.

Visit our website at www.broadwaybooks.com

Library of Congress Cataloging-in-Publication Data
Lambert, Derek, 1929
Spanish lessons: beginning a new life in Spain/
by Derek Lambert.—1st ed.
p. cm
1. La Jara (Alicante, Spain)—Description and travel.
2. Lambert, Derek, 1929—Homes and
haunts—Spain—La Jara (Alicante) I. Title.
DP402.L143 L36 2000
946'.765—dc21   00-021185

FIRST EDITION

Designed by Nicola Ferguson

ISBN 0-7679-0415-X

00 01 02 03 04 10 9 8 7 6 5 4 3 2 1

For Ray and Julie Livett

and their daughters, Zoe and Maria,

who came, saw, and conquered

CONTENTS

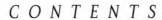

ACKNOWLEDGMENTS

Heartfelt thanks to:

My agent, Al Zuckerman, president of Writers House in New York City, whose industry, remedial talents, and marketing panache gave this book liftoff.

My typist, Carol Outram in Denia, Spain, maestro of the word processor, who has worked so patiently on the project that she could now recite it chapter, verse—and author's corrections!

My old friend Doddy Hay for helping me in absentia with his succinct, informed, and superbly written book, *The Bullfight*.

AUTHOR'S NOTE

The Spanish village in this book is based on La Jara (the J is pronounced *ha*) or, in Valenciano, the regional language, much more distinctive than a dialect, La Xara (the closest I can get to the X is *zh*). It lies about two miles inland from Denia, a vibrant town on the stretch of Mediterranean coastline known as the Costa Blanca. In the interests of personal privacy and the narrative flow, I have changed some locations and names of establishments and people.

SPANISH
LESSONS

O N E

A Taste of Oranges

The two civil guards wore black tricorn hats, capes, and olive-green uniforms. And although mounted on angular bicycles, they looked as sinister as their predecessors had in the civil war that tore Spain apart in the 1930s.

It was late December, and the citrus trees that covered most of the plain separating the Mediterranean from the mountains on the Costa Blanca of Spain were heavy with oranges, lemons, and grapefruit. The trees looked so beguiling that Diane and I stole a couple of oranges. We were eating them, juice trickling down our chins, in our venerable, chocolate-brown Jaguar, when the two *Guardia Civil* stopped beside us.

Maybe pinching oranges was a heinous crime in Spain. Tales were still rife after the death of the dictator General Francisco Franco of foreigners being imprisoned for years without trial for unspecified offenses. I imagined us lying on straw mattresses in fetid cells miles apart, while rats snatched food from our eating bowls.

Or perhaps we would be deported and declared *persona non grata,* a preferable scenario but nonetheless depressing, because it would mean that the vision we had shared when we first met in Africa would be aborted before it even got off the ground.

Diane, a Canadian airline stewardess with blond hair and eyes the color of the sea before a storm, had told me on our first date in Nairobi that having experienced a couple of scary landings, she wanted to quit flying and start a new life. So did I. I was a journalist in my forties, a foreign correspondent, and I wanted to become a novelist: our meeting was convened by the gods.

But supposing the gods had now turned against us, snitched on us to the *Guardia* . . .

Diane offered the two of them a brilliant, please-fasten-your-seatbelt smile while I stuffed incriminating orange peel into a plastic bag. "What can we do for you?" she asked. She had been brought up in Paris and Rome, had studied Spanish, and in any case picked up languages as easily as children catch measles.

One of the *Guardia,* young with a downy mustache, dismounted. "Are you lost?" he asked in English, peering into the aristocratic but doddery old Jaguar as I tried to back-heel the plastic bag under the driver's seat.

"No," Diane said, "we're just admiring the view."

It was worth admiring. Lizard-gray mountains on one side of the citrus plantations, the sea beckoning in the cold sunlight on the other. Here and there a field of leafless grapevines; almond and olive trees and carobs with trunks like fairytale witches.

The *Guardia,* who seemed to have exhausted his English, produced a creased booklet from beneath his cape and read from it: "I am so pleased you are admiring our territory."

Diane tried a few phrases in Valenciano, the regional language that confuses tourists who have studied orthodox Spanish, but he held up one hand and again consulted his phrase book. "Please, I do not understand, I am from the north." His colleague, a sad-looking *cabo,* a corporal, who looked like a long-ago Hollywood actor, Adolph Menjou, joined him.

"Do you have any papers?" he asked—"papers," a disturbingly general term that could embrace anything from a visa to a last will and testament.

Diane told him in English: "We might settle in the area."

True enough—we were looking for a village so ordinary that it would bring us into contact with people remote from the clichés of Spain—flamenco, sangria, and bullfights—and would define the changes that had taken place since Franco's death in 1975, so that I could write about them one day.

Her statement perturbed the *cabo.* He spoke with one hand, flapping and clenching it. Endless complications, his hand said. Bureaucracy, papers . . .

Diane searched for some sort of ID in the chaotic contents of her purse. Ballpoint pens, lipsticks, coins, a comb, a chocolate bar . . . The *cabo* suggested that we get out of the car. A preliminary to being frisked, handcuffed?

Diane found her passport and handed it to him. Fishing rights in international waters hadn't yet exacerbated relations between the two countries, and a Canadian passport still commanded respect. He flicked through it, handed it back, and saluted.

He stabbed a finger toward me. "Your husband does not speak too much."

Conceding that Diane was better at placating irate policemen, I had kept out of it. Not only that; she was much more fluent in Spanish than I was, and although I was studying manfully I preferred to converse in English even with any Spaniards who spoke only on the level of "Me Tarzan, you Jane."

"He's very shy," Diane said, and burst into helpless laughter. Reticence had never been my strong suit.

The younger officer, thinking perhaps that she was weeping, laid a hand on her shoulder. The *cabo,* suspecting that he was in the presence of an unstable neurotic woman and a deaf-mute, took a step back.

"In the orchards," he said in English, "one person one orange is allowed. More"—he cut across his throat with one finger. "If you want to eat a good meal this place is very pleasing." He handed Diane a grubby visiting card and both men pedaled away, capes flowing behind them.

We embraced, our visions of a home here still intact. We drove to a village perched in the hills and gazed beyond the citrus trees to the sea, fishing boats perched on its rim. The church clock tolled and the chimes rang through narrow streets that smelled of whitewash and grilling sardines. Hunger stirred. We each drank a glass of rough wine in a bar so dark that I couldn't tell whether I was being served by a man or a woman—at five pesetas a glass, who cared?—and headed for the restaurant recommended by the *cabo.* In my experience, policemen anywhere in the world knew the best establishments in which to take on ballast.

When we reached the address on the card, a shack with a cane roof beside a sandy beach ankle deep in seaweed, it was shut. We decided to hang around. After a while a door opened, a bead curtain parted, and a woman in black, wearing slippers, bunched cheeks squeezing her eyes, confronted us.

What did we want? She had already paid her rent and she didn't want to buy a carpet or an encyclopedia from traveling salesmen, her tone implied.

"We're very hungry," Diane said in English.

The woman's face softened. The period after the Civil War and

World War II, when Spain was ostracized by much of the world because it was ruled by Fascists, was known as the Years of Hunger.

"Are you American?" she asked Diane. So many families had fled to the United States and Britain after the Civil War ended in 1939 that, happily for me, a grasp of English was not uncommon.

"Canadian."

The woman shrugged. What mattered was that we were foreigners and could not be turned away. "The restaurant is closed for the winter," she said. "But I can give you lamb chops and rice." My stomach whined.

After she had poured us a pitcher of beer at the bar, she rolled up the slatted blinds. Sunshine lit a faded photograph of a football team and a statue of a madonna with a chipped face. A skinny black cat wrapped itself around my legs. White plastic tables and chairs covered with a patina of dust stood where they had been abandoned at the end of summer.

As the smell of the chops grilling reached us, an orchestra played in my stomach and I drowned it with beer.

Watched through slitted yellow eyes by the cat, a canary sang in a cage.

The woman placed hunks of toasted bread on the table and we fell on them, spreading them with *alioli,* a thick sauce made from pounded garlic cloves, egg yolks, olive oil, and lemon juice.

Faintly we heard the swish of modest waves unfurling on the seaweed.

After we had wolfed the chops and saffron-yellow rice, she served coffee and walnut cake.

Then a middle-aged man appeared in the kitchen doorway behind the bar. He looked familiar. "It was good?" he asked.

His voice sounded familiar, too.

As we nodded vigorously, the woman said: "This is my husband, Pepe. He is a *cabo* in the *Guardia.*"

And suddenly I realized that the corporal who had stopped us was a man of parts. Policeman, tout for his own restaurant, and chef.

I peered into the kitchen: the *Guardia* with the downy mustache was peeling potatoes, presumably for a private meal.

Pepe winked and began to clear our table. Diane and I exchanged glances. Such devious charm was difficult to resist.

We paid the bill, linked hands, and walked toward the Jaguar. An old man wearing a hat with spaniel ears was collecting firewood on the beach; gulls floated on the milky sea; behind us the mountains were beginning to retreat into the winter night.

We found the rest of the walnut cake on a paper plate in the front of the car. I squeezed Diane's hand. She squeezed back. Without speaking, we knew we were in the area to stay.

We found the sort of unassuming village we were looking for inland from the apartment blocks, hotels, and beaches of the Costa Blanca, the White Coast. It didn't possess any historic landmarks, unless you counted the bubble-blowing public wash house; no castanets clicking, not a pitcher of sangria in sight.

Located at sea level deep inside the citrus groves halfway down the Mediterranean coast, La Jara was equidistant from the cities of Valencia to the north and Alicante to the south, sixty miles or so either way.

We came across it by chance when our decrepit car broke down with a sigh and a hiss on the road skirting its boundaries. It had transported us in its dotage across France from England and limped around Spain for five days while we inspected prospective homes.

While a mechanic in a small garage coated with black grease examined its engine, we wandered around streets lined with nondescript terraces of whitewashed cottages and hole-in-the-wall stores. The streets were flat and paved, and yet I imagined them in a turn-of-the-century painting, rutted with mud. Perhaps it was because the people seemed still to be lodged in that epoch, scowling women in darned black dresses, men wearing collarless shirts and tight jackets, faces engraved by sun and wind.

What we didn't yet know was that on the outside, Spanish villages smile only in the mornings and evenings and we had arrived just before lunch. Inside, they laugh most of the time.

We found seven bars, a church with a spire like a space rocket, an open-air cinema, four groceries, a bank, three hairdressing salons, a school, and a combined newsstand and tobacco shop becalmed in eternal dusk. All this for a population of one thousand.

But the village possessed a few delicate attributes as well, brass door knockers polished wafer thin, courtyards where old ladies in the ubiquitous black weaved lampshades, roses painted on ceramic tiles outside doorways to keep summer a prisoner of winter.

Finally we adjourned to the Bar Paraiso into a wall of noise—the steamy roar of a coffee machine, the bark of impassioned debate over coffees and brandy, tobacco coughs, the smack of dominoes on plastic tabletops.

A dusting of last night's cigarette ash lay on the pool table, which bore a stain the shape of Australia. A diminutive barman was fanning a smoldering vine root in the grate. The hands of a wall clock that, we discovered later, occasionally went backward, stuttered erratically.

We ordered a couple of beers and sat at a table. We were joined by a balding priest, his soutane hemmed with dust, and a carpenter who said: "My name is Emilio."

Emilio had arms as thick as most people's thighs, curly hair threaded with silver, and a voice as rough as the rasp of a saw. Like many Spaniards whose families had fled to the United States in 1939—he had been born there and didn't need any prompting to volunteer his family history—he spoke English with an American accent.

His father had reopened the family's toy factory in the nearby town of Denia when he came back from New York, but the market for wooden toys had declined and he had retired. Emilio had been left to make doors, window frames, and coffins in an annex here in the village.

"Are you going to settle here?" he asked. When we said we might, he thumped the table with a mallet fist. "Let me be the first to congratulate you. I know just the place for you to buy."

I assessed him cautiously: in my experience, back-slapping extroverts were often con men, and I'd learned to be wary of the twinkling gaze, the knuckle-crunching handshake. But Emilio's hustling was so outrageously transparent that it was disarming.

"First," I told him, "we'll look around by ourselves."

He nodded understandingly. "In your position I'd do the same. But it doesn't matter, because nothing you'll see will compare with the property I will show you. It only came on the market this morning, God must have guided you to me."

We adjourned with Emilio to the garage to find out what was happening to the Jaguar. Its body was raised on a ramp; parts of its engine lay on the greasy floor like the components of a stripped gun.

A voice issued from the pit. We were lucky: the fault had been located. "When will it be ready?" I asked.

"*Mañana*"—tomorrow. A bowlegged mechanic, his cherubic face daubed with oil, climbed out of the pit. Meanwhile, he could lend us a Seat 600, Spain's ubiquitous little workhorse in the 1970s.

We left Emilio behind and drove the car, little more than a battered toy, to the village bakery, where we bought four big crusty rolls for *bocadillos,* jaw-straining sandwiches stuffed with fillings such as tuna, cheese, *chorizo* (a relative of salami), or ham. In a grocery we bought Manchego cheese, strong as saddle soap, smoked ham, tomatoes and olive oil, plastic knives, forks, and cups, and a bottle of red wine from Navarra.

The purchase of these small items made us feel proprietorial toward the village, like pioneers in an undiscovered outpost.

We drove along a dirt road to a clearing in a citrus grove where orange pickers had left the remains of a fire, the hub of their *almuerzo*, their mid-morning snack. We stirred the still-hot ash and pale flames danced in the embers. Diane slit open the rolls, spread them with olive oil, and crammed them with cheese and sliced tomatoes.

On one side of us, grapefruit lay rotting on the red earth beneath the trees, no longer a fashionable fruit, we had been told.

A herd of munching goats passed by, accompanied by an ancient shepherd with a gooseberry chin and cloudy eyes. A burst of what sounded like machine-gun fire threw us into a panic while on our second cup of wine—merely fireworks marking a private fiesta.

When we got back to the garage to check out the car again, Emilio was waiting for us. The number of engine parts on the floor had multiplied, and the mechanic was standing in the pit staring gloomily at the chassis.

Emilio said he had taken the liberty of booking us into a hotel on the main Valencia-Alicante road, but now there was just time before it got dark to take a look at the property he had set aside for us. He would take us there in the Seat.

Why not? We were free spirits.

I thought I caught a flicker of clandestine understanding between the mechanic and Emilio. Were they in cahoots?

Emilio squeezed his bulk behind the wheel of the little car and we took off.

"Is the mechanic a friend of yours?" I asked.

"The house is just around the corner," he said, overtaking a motorcyclist who wobbled to a stop and raised one finger at him.

"I asked you if you were friendly with the mechanic."

"He is not just a friend." The Seat skidded to a halt outside a pair of wrought-iron gates. "He is my sister's husband."

At the end of a short driveway stood a white *casita,* a small house, with barred windows, moldering roof tiles, and an exterior circular staircase with a rope handrail leading up to a terrace. The garden was hedged by tall cypress; a dozen or so citrus trees grew on one side of the driveway which continued down the opposite flank of the building, presumably to land hidden from sight at the rear. A single chimney rose like an imperious finger from the roof—incongruous on such a self-effacing building—and creeper covered the wall facing us.

We waited for Emilio to unlock the gates.

"We will approach from the rear," he said.

"Why not the front?"

"I haven't got the keys—I left them in my house." He slapped the pockets of his blue dungarees.

"Well, let's go and get them."

"By the time we get back it will be too dark to see the place."

"So we'll come back in the morning," I said.

"By then it might be sold."

"Overnight? Don't push your luck, Emilio."

"This property is very special."

Special? In the fading light, the house looked more apologetic than prepossessing. And yet it beckoned as though it contained small mysteries that might one day become familiar to us.

I shook off such fancies. Why had Emilio chosen this predusk hour to show the place to us? Was he a charlatan preying on vulnerable foreigners, or was he motivated by genuine pride in his adopted village? After all, he was a relative newcomer too. Maybe he longed to share it with other dewy-eyed newcomers.

As the air turned colder and the outline of the house sharpened against the darkening sky, his voice grew conspiratorial, and an alarming possibility occurred to me: maybe he was crazy, armed with a hammer or a screwdriver sharpened to a point.

He shepherded us to the Seat, drove a few hundred yards and parked on the roadside. Then he led us through a grove of neglected lemon trees, creepers entwined in their ragged branches. A couple of stars sparkled frostily, bats flitted overhead.

He stopped at the foot of a drystone wall about eight feet high shoring up one of the former agricultural terraces built centuries ago by the Moors to retain the soil. He pointed at the top of it. "There is the end of your garden."

Diane said: "You mean we've got to climb the wall?"

"Paradise lies up there," Emilio told her.

"Paradise lost, if the *Guardia* see us," Diane murmured.

Some prescient instinct told me that this moment could decide our future lives. It might be no more than the ignominious ascent of a crumbling wall; but surely fate, a geriatric Jaguar, and a Falstaffian carpenter had combined to offer us something more grandiose than the humble edifice we had seen through the wrought-iron gates.

"Okay, let's go," I said to Diane.

"Are you sure?" she asked. A rat or lizard scuttled along the wall. "We don't want to make any decisions we'll regret—we've got all the time in the world."

But Emilio was already climbing. Stones tumbled around us. A car stopped nearby for a moment or two, its engine idling, but then it took off again.

Diane, who was wearing jeans, shrugged and found a foothold. I steadied her, she found a second ledge, and grasped Emilio's down-stretched hand.

I followed, and rolled onto the grass at their feet.

Ahead stood fifty or so citrus trees. Beyond them, water glinted in the first light of the rising moon.

We approached stealthily, snail shells crunching under our feet. The water turned out to be a swimming pool, a breeze shaving the moonlight on its surface into pieces of silver. Beyond that a lawn and a *naya,* an arched terrace. The arches were framed with bougainvillea; a tiny extension with a sloping roof stood to one side of the main building.

Emilio flung wide one meaty arm. "Well?"

The house looked mysterious, enchanted, in the moonlight. But it was small and we had our son, Jonathan, and friends from long ago who would probably resurrect our friendship when they heard we had bought a place in the sun. I almost hoped that the interior would be dripping with beards of moss, because there is nothing like rampant damp rot to put paid to an infatuation with a house.

"It looks interesting," I told Emilio, "but we would like to see inside."

"Of course." He mounted the steps to the arched terrace and pointed through a barred window. "There!"

I pointed at a massive wooden door. "Haven't you got the key to that, either?"

"Keys, you are always talking about keys. What you need is heart."

"For God's sake, Emilio," I said. "We've got to have a look around. Maybe it's rotten inside. Maybe there are squatters in there. A body, a skeleton . . ."

And maybe you are a fraud.

Peering through the windows I could just make out an open grate beneath a copper hood and the charred remains of a fire. The floor was covered with ceramic tiles. No beards of moss.

I imagined cushions scattered in front of a blazing log fire, Diane and I lying on them gazing into its glowing caverns.

"The house is cozy," Diane said, "but far too small."

Emilio chuckled. "Small? What is size? We will build a dining hall, you and me." He gave me a rib-cracking hug. "Another fireplace, great beams, a gallery . . ."

I imagined myself smoking a churchwarden pipe in an inglenook, waited upon by a serving wench wearing a low-cut bodice, rosy nipples visible to the discerning eye.

"I'll think about it," I said.

"Think big, *hombre,*" Emilio said. "And think quickly, because tomorrow it may be gone."

T W O

First Night, Second Thoughts

After Diane and I had decided to quit our jobs in Africa, my newspaper sent me to Moscow. And as the prospects for gathering material for thrillers were glittering, we stayed there a year. Initially, the Russian consulate in Canada had refused to grant Diane a visa, but when I announced in Moscow that her absence would blight my dispatches, a KGB contact made one midnight phone call to Ottawa and she got her papers the following day.

After a year in Russia I finally quit, and we lived in Israel, the United States, Canada, Ireland, and Gibraltar while I worked as a freelance journalist to muster funds to enable me to write THE NOVEL about the Soviet Union.

I did make one abortive start. Seduced by stereotyped visions of Ireland—soft rain, salad-green pastures, bottomless wells of Guinness, and the wayward charm of the Irish—we rented rooms overlooking the ocean in the village of Ballycotton near Cork. There Diane developed a talent for painting and her neat, resolute figure, fair hair bright in the occasional sunshine beside her easel, became a landmark on the cliffs above the pounding Atlantic surf.

We loved Ireland with unbridled passion and got married in Dublin—I had been married once before to an English girl but, like many others, the marriage had foundered on the treacherous rocks of journalism—but then our savings and my creative inspiration ran dry and we moved to Gibraltar, the isthmus on the southern tip of Spain that was bristling with news stories waiting to be plundered.

One summer day, we crossed the border into Spain and knew that we had found our future homeland. We drove to the highlands of Galicia in the northwest and drank a firewater called *crujo,* and to the Pyrenean mountains spiking the border with France; we toured parade grounds of vines, plantations of silvery olive trees, and gasping ochre plains in the interior; swam off the shimmering beaches of the Mediterranean and skirted the wetlands of Doñana in the southwest. We stopped at cities as elegant as grandees and villages as threadbare as beggars.

But because we were still poor, we had to wait another couple of years, sojourning in Canada and the United States, before, with a publisher's advance for my still unwritten novel in my wallet, we finally drove to Spain in the 1970s in our chocolate-brown chariot, determined to put down roots. We also had a small son, Jonathan, whom we left temporarily in Montreal where he had been born, while we searched for the Elysian fields.

I was awakened at one A.M. by shouting in the hotel that Emilio had found us. I shook off dreams of the house in the moonlight and the ragged lemon trees, struggled into the molting bathrobe that had served me well in luxurious watering holes and bug-ridden flophouses around the world, and strode out of the room. I held only a few commodities to be precious and sleep was one of them.

Down the corridor outside an open door, a naked man was slapping a fully clothed woman around the face. Remembering my headmaster's final injunction—"Always treat the fair sex chivalrously"—I grabbed him by his shoulders and shoved him through the doorway.

As he came back at me, bald and overweight but burly, I slammed the door in his face, grabbed the key from the woman, and locked it.

I handed the key back to the woman, a plump bleached blonde, one eye slitted in swelling flesh. She spat at me, stuffed a wallet down the front of her rhinestone blouse, and ran down the corridor.

Other men and women in various stages of undress appeared in doorways; a small man with strands of hair plastered from one ear to the other whom I took to be the night porter approached.

I asked if he had called the police.

"Why should I?" He looked perplexed.

"Because a woman just stole his wallet," I said, pointing toward the door the prisoner was battering from inside the room.

The porter shook his head patiently. "He *is* the police," he said.

The porter put our minds to rest marginally when we paid the bill at seven-thirty A.M. Yes, we had been staying in a brothel; no, we needn't worry about the policeman. When the hooker had realized the identity of her client from the contents of his wallet, she had returned it to the front desk.

But I had assaulted him, I pointed out. The porter shrugged. This was a macho country; no police officer would admit he had been ripped off by a prostitute and tossed, naked, into a bedroom by an *extranjero*, a foreigner. In any case, he came from far away.

The Seat was waiting for us under a stuttering neon sign CLUB. What we hadn't realized last night was that "club" was often a euphemism for brothel.

We stopped at a café for breakfast, ate toasted hunks of bread spread with olive oil, washed them down with *café con leche,* then drove to the garage.

The Jaguar was still mounted forlornly on the ramp. Emilio stood outside, gold teeth reflecting sunlight in the depths of his smile.

"You will, of course, make an offer for the house," he said. "Never pay the price anyone asks—they will think you're *loco*. In shops, always ask for *discuento*."

"We haven't made up our minds," I told him. "And why did you book us into a whorehouse?"

"The owner is a cousin of mine . . . But never mind, we will go to the Bar Paraiso and discuss finance."

"Emilio, stop trying to railroad us. We don't even know the asking price. Or the name of the owner."

Emilio tapped the side of his nose. All would be revealed. "Come."

"First, we're going to look at other properties," I said. "And tell the owner of your house that whatever price he's asking it's too much."

"But *Señor* Derek, even I don't know what price he's asking."

Odd, we agreed as we drove away. If Emilio was a scout who found properties and charged a commission on their sale, then surely he should know how much they cost.

We called on several real estate agents two miles away in Denia, a fishing port kneeling beneath the walls of a ruined castle, its main, tree-lined street leading from a self-effacing square to a harbor with crab-claw jetties reaching into the Mediterranean, rocky inlets to one side, sandy beaches to the other. The agents showed us half a dozen "desirable properties" with views of the sea—if you stood on the chimney.

A few were pleasant enough, with swimming pools and orchards and negotiable prices, but they were too close to the specter of tourist Spain, with its gift shops, tacky bars, and currency bureaus. And in any case, I was haunted by a picture of a small moon-lit house waiting to have a timbered dining hall added to it.

Later that morning we drove back to the house, approaching it circumspectly in case Emilio might be lurking there. We again climbed the terrace wall and wandered through the orchard. Oranges lay on the ground, a blackbird sang.

The rear terrace was tiled in black and white squares, the white walls looked sturdy. Peering through all the barred windows, we saw high ceilings, webs left by generations of spiders trailing from beams, tiled floors, but, miniature annex apart, only two bedrooms. Never mind, we would be able to sleep an army in the dining hall. This hall, still only a figment of Emilio's capacious imagination, already dwarfed the rest of the house in my mind.

Diane read my thoughts. "We don't know the price. We don't even know if it's for sale. And I don't like the kitchen, it's too poky, like the rest of it. And supposing Jonathan falls in the pool."

I made a mental note to call Diane's parents in Montreal and ask them to arrange swimming lessons for four-year-old Jonathan.

We climbed the spiral staircase to the roof terrace. Jasmine sprawled across it and the view was awesome. Ahead stood Montgo, a small mountain with a broad brow. To its left lay a handful of white-washed cottages and a lane winding through the dense, dark-green citrus orchards hung with oranges, lemons, grapefruit, and mandarins, to Denia in the distance. To its right, at the end of a road through the orchards, stood the village itself, sun-faded terraces clustered round the space-rocket church spire.

Behind us stood the wrought-iron gates of the driveway we had seen the previous evening. They led onto a narrow road and a high, drystone wall encircling the grounds of a deserted mansion, once the home of a citrus baron, according to Emilio. The grounds encompassed a chapel, a line of swaying umbrella pines, and a coach house containing a landau that, according to legend, so Emilio said, took to the road on Midsummer Eve.

We made inquiries from a couple of neighbors about the availability of *our* house.

It had been on the market for a year they said—a far cry from Emilio's call for swift action to secure it. It belonged to a property developer in Denia, and Emilio had no authority to sell it.

So he was a flimflam merchant. And yet . . . There was a naive quality to his enthusiasm, as though he were deceiving himself as much as us. Even if he was out for a fast buck, he stood little chance of getting it if he didn't even know who the owner was.

Then one of the neighbors, a plump, middle-aged woman who was painting a picket fence green, told us that Emilio, devastated by the collapse of his father's toy-making factory, often talked about building a minstrel gallery. "You know, one of those platforms with wooden rails near the ceiling where years ago musicians used to play."

I *heard* mandolins, lutes, clavichords, troubadours singing ballads.

"Emilio loves music," the woman said. "He wanted to play classical guitar but his fingers were too thick."

A minstrel gallery above an inglenook in a timbered dining hall! Emilio wasn't a Mr. Five Percent: he was a dreamer who saw Diane and myself as the instruments of his fantasies. He was the blacksmith who dreams about shoeing the prancing Lipizzaner horses at the Spanish Riding School in Vienna, the house painter haunting the galleries of the Prado in Madrid.

Even if he had booked us into a brothel!

That evening we booked into a functional hostel in Denia from where we could hear the throb of fishing boats returning to their berths. After we had settled, we went to an old bar, Benjamin's, hung with posters promoting long-ago bullfights and calendars with photographs of naked girls with big breasts.

We drank Ricard—the bar had acquired a Gallic ambiance from French Algerian émigrés who came to savor the cheap booze and the calendars—and discussed Emilio and the house.

"A dining hall needs a minstrel gallery," I said.

"Why?" Diane poured water into her Ricard and watched it cloud.

I changed tack. "Emilio is a craftsman. Those toy soldiers . . ."

"Those coffins!" She also changed direction. "If I tried to cook a chicken in that kitchen, the two of us would be a crowd."

"We could extend it."

"Using what for money?"

She had a point: the advance for my as-yet-unwritten novel was modest in the context of dining halls, minstrel galleries, and kitchen extensions.

"If the book does well," I said, "we'll even be able to afford another bedroom."

She finished her Ricard and laid her hand on mine. "I'm not doubting your ability, not for one moment. But you haven't even started the book yet. We don't want to do anything rash, let's sleep on it."

I had, in fact, begun the novel in Ireland, but that was long ago, before Diane became pregnant, so I would have to begin all over again. Could we blow the publisher's check and our savings on a mirage among the orange trees? No, Diane was right, we should be cautious.

After all, we already had enough problems, one of which was the book itself, a thriller set largely in the icy wastes of Siberia, which I would have to write as the heat gathered in Spain.

We left the Algerians gazing wistfully at the bosoms on the calendars and went back to our hotel to sleep on our options: house with gallery, house without, no house at all.

THREE

A Guardian Angel
in the Garden

We tracked down the Spanish developer who owned the property to an office in Denia. He was a dashing entrepreneur with sleek black hair and endowed with extravagant charm. He showed us the inside of the house; no obvious structural faults, no corpses.

Having decided to put any decision on hold, I asked him to keep us in mind in case our cash flow changed direction. He agreed and rented us a small house on a hillside overlooking a valley on the outskirts of Denia.

We broke the news to Emilio that we were keeping his pet project in mind. He stared into his beer in the Bar Paraiso in the village. When he stood up, we stood up with him. He shook my hand and kissed Diane on both cheeks.

Then, head bowed, he left the bar without saying a word. As he walked down the street I noticed that he had crossed two fingers of one of his big hands.

The garage was closed for lunch. When I went there in the evening, the Jaguar was standing outside, freshly polished bodywork gleaming in the light from a street lamp. The mechanic switched on the engine and it purred.

I took out my wallet. "How much?"

The mechanic wagged one finger from side to side. "It has been taken care of," he said.

I tried to write the book, blaming the absence of inspiration on lack of marital support when Diane flew to Montreal to collect Jonathan, blaming it on their intrusive presence when they both returned.

But I was deceiving myself. I knew what the real problem was— I had found an ideal workshop, the house in the orange groves, and the creative juices would remain uncorked until I moved there.

I managed to stick it out for another week, typing a few rambling sentences, staring into space, chatting maniacally in the garden with stray dogs. Finally, I told Diane that we had to buy the house.

She said, "I know. You've been unbearable and I've made an appointment with Miguel Ferrer for tomorrow." He was the developer.

We made an offer and the paperwork began, mercifully straightforward, because Miguel was an honest man and journalism had alerted me to the pitfalls of property deals. We signed a few papers in his office, a modest establishment for one of the first big-time developers in the area, and then walked to another office in the tree-lined main street where we appeared before a notary like disobedient students in front of a professor.

The notary, gray-haired and spruce, read out the deeds sonorously and we embarked on more signing—the lawyers' signatures an art form in their own right, complete with scrolls, curlicues, and kiss curls. I scrawled my name once more—on a check—and the house with its phantom dining hall was ours.

By lunchtime we were installed among the oranges or, as Diane put it, "embryonic marmalade." In the bright midday sunlight, the house suddenly looked vulnerable, hairline cracks in its white walls, a loose shutter creaking in the breeze, and we wondered if we had done the right thing.

Jonathan, Nordic blond hair like a halo (deceptively so), whooped round the garden, picked a bag of oranges, almost fell in the pool, and punctured his football on the spike of a yucca bush. Diane and I patroled at a more leisurely pace, wonderment expanding at what we had done.

Rain earlier had distilled the perfume of the new orange blossoms already growing alongside the fruit. We walked to the end of the orchard. Fresh scents reached us from the gardens of the nearby cottages—thyme, rosemary, mint, and sage. We held hands: afternoons had never smelled like this in Montreal or London.

We were awoken at dawn by birdsong. I padded through the living room to the kitchen in my bathrobe and squeezed our first jug of home-produced orange juice, as fresh as dew, and made tea in an earthenware teapot—no more teabags. Diane boiled brown, free-range eggs and we ate toast spread with honey.

I took over the cramped annex and made it my office. Diane reigned elsewhere in the house. She swept and mopped, snared cobwebs with the head of a broom, lit fires with cut-offs from a timber merchant in Denia, charmed bureaucrats into switching on the water and electricity, unblocked the sink, ordered three of the butane gas canisters that fueled the basic stove and heated the water, and bought two sleeping bags that proved to be a serious handicap to spontaneous passion—on one occasion the zipper on mine jammed, and by the time I had fought my way out of it, Diane was asleep in front of the dying embers of the fire.

What impressed me most during the following weeks was her seamless transition from serving packaged meals and duty-free booze on aircraft to primitive expediency. She was the stuff of which the adventuresses of history were made. More Amelia Earhart than stewardess.

While I typed and retyped the first page of my novel, she kept house and cooked, producing gourmet meals from a Mickey Mouse stove with the aplomb of a magician producing rabbits out of a hat.

She bought her provisions in one of the stores in the village but, deciding that we had virtually been camping under a roof for long enough, she insisted on driving to a department store in Valencia sixty miles away to buy makeshift furniture such as plastic tables and chairs to use while the dining hall was being built.

We also bought a king-size bed. No more zipper-crippled lust. With a triumphant mating call I hurled myself onto the mattress and snapped the wooden frame of the bed on both sides.

The garden, a rectangular acre of rampant fertility fenced off from the undulating citrus trees with chain link, was my territory. Or so I believed.

I hadn't anticipated Ángel. Either Emilio had advised him that I was fair game or he assumed that writers were dysfunctional. Whatever, he was as quirky and persistent as Colombo and convinced that I was in dire need of his services as a gardener.

Ángel was a fey young man from Andalusia in the south with a pale poet's face and a wiry, long-distance runner's frame, who appeared to communicate with the clouds, glancing skyward when confronted with a difficult question. He wore a straw fedora that looked as though it had been nibbled by mice, and soon made it plain that he considered the house to be a mere appendage to the grounds. I told him I would consider his services, because the house was indeed lost in an acre of well-kept orange, lemon, and grapefruit trees, plum, apricot, and almond saplings, yucca bushes with their swordlike leaves—I blunted them with a pair of shears—jasmine and hibiscus that we hoped would soon bloom with red trumpets, one palm and one fig tree, a few flowerbeds sprouting with wild asparagus, separated from the house by a small lawn, a swimming pool, and a barbecue with a sink and a bar. The ground beneath the fruit trees was carpeted with Bermuda buttercups, yellow clover-leafed flowers with long stems which children picked to suck the sweet-sour sap. The land extended in an escarpment to the top of the drystone wall we had climbed during our first reconnoiter.

But could I cope with it by myself? Spray and prune the fruit trees, plough the land between them with a cultivator. Tend exotic blossoms that I had only encountered on my travels. Sow and nurture and reap. I told Ángel to come back later and agonized long and hard over this my first decision as a property owner in a foreign land.

I discussed it with Diane one cold and brooding afternoon. The trees, heavy with citrus, suddenly looked intimidating, the fruit as menacing as grenades. We wandered through their silent depths and noticed a sticky white blight on the leaves. "Can you get rid of it?" Diane asked.

"Ángel would know how to," I said.

We reached the end of the garden and looked down on the overgrown lemon grove below. The trees were woody with dead twigs, stifled with creepers. That was how our orchard would degenerate if we didn't have professional help. We looked at each other and nodded.

"Ángel is selected unopposed," I said.

"For a trial period," Diane said. "I get the impression that he's a prima donna. You'll have to be firm with him."

So I had made an executive decision. Replete with power, I picked an orange, peeled it, and bit into it. It tasted as sweet as honey.

We shared the garden with a colony of tree rats, nursery-book creatures with gray fur and white bellies, which lived in the tall, dark cypress hedge; they ate the rind of lemons, leaving the pith, and ate the pith of oranges, leaving the rind. They were as graceful as squirrels and as disarming as chipmunks. Ángel, who took up his duties with alacrity, said they were pests but we didn't believe him.

The garden was also home to hedgehogs, field mice, voles, grass snakes, quick green lizards, and geckoes that scuttered across the white walls of the barbecue, which, with a roof and chimney, was as big as an alpine shelter, and to blackbirds, goldfinches, and a hoopoe, a clownish bird with pink plumage, black-and-white wings, and a crest that it raised indignantly when disturbed. Foxes and owls took over at night

On his first working day, Ángel beckoned us to the detached garage in the driveway, built at such an angle that it required a six-point turn to drive the Jaguar into it, and pointed at a tiny wooden box with a hole in one side nailed to an interior wall.

He lifted a flap and told Diane to look inside. She approached warily and, standing on tiptoe, peered into it. And screamed.

I steadied her as she stumbled back. "What is it, for God's sake?" she asked.

"A bat hanging upside down, it's only a baby," Ángel told her. He spoke reasonable English acquired from other employers.

When she had disappeared into the house, Ángel lifted the box off the wall. I peered in; the bat was little more than a winged scrap of tissue and it was indeed hanging upside down.

"Where are you taking it?" I asked him.

"To the pump house behind the barbecue, she'll never find it there." The pump house was a hut which housed the pump for the pool and the vacuum for cleaning it. "In the spring there will be lots of bats flying over the pool and drinking from it. But don't tell the *señora*."

The tenor of the future relationship between Ángel and myself was established by a packet of marigold seed. I had been fond of the yellow-and-gold, daisy-like flowers ever since I was a child in North London, when my father embroidered our small patch with them and my mother relieved the pain of bee and wasp stings by rubbing the petals into them. I wanted to grow them here. Ángel didn't.

He removed his straw hat, poked one finger through a hole, glanced at the packet of seeds and said: "Some weeds are pretty."

He stuffed the packet into the breast pocket of his denim shirt, which he wore above baggy blue trousers, and sandals with soles made from automobile tires.

"When can you sow them?" I asked him.

He gazed toward castles of cumulus cloud on the horizon. "It is too early."

Maybe it was, but judging by the pitying expression on his pale face, the packet would remain in his shirt until the seeds germinated and flowered there if he had his way.

"And I've bought some morning glory," said Diane, producing a packet bearing a picture of the blue climbing flowers, as fragile as poppies of the field, that bloomed at dawn and died at dusk.

Ángel laughed indulgently.

"What's so funny?" Diane demanded.

"Gardeners spend a lot of their time trying to kill them and *you* want to grow them."

"I think they're beautiful," Diane insisted.

So did I. I had often admired blue waterfalls of them tumbling from hedgerow and fence in Africa, and they had become part of the backcloth of our vision of a new life here. I wasn't going to let Ángel trample on that.

"Ángel," I said, "you and I are going to have a good working relationship if you agree to one condition. I know you're one of the best gardeners in the area." Neighbors had told me this. "And I will accept most of your decisions."

Ángel frowned. "The condition?"

"That you do what I ask you to do." I tapped the packet of seed in Diane's hand. "Plant them, Ángel."

"But—"

"Please."

Crooning an Andalusian lament, he headed for the garage where he kept his tools. While Diane made coffee I followed him and asked him why he had left his home in the south. Because, he said, he had met his future wife there when she was on vacation in Granada two years ago and she had invited him back here. Bewitched, I supposed, by his youthful assurance—he was only twenty-six—and his fragile looks. Indeed, there was an enigmatic charm about him that I would have to treat as warily as Emilio's exuberance.

"There is also more work here," he added. "I work on the land as well."

Town dwellers apart, most of the people in the area lived off the land, growing vegetables, oranges, olives, almonds, and *nisperos,* a yellow fruit with big slippery pips.

They dropped tools during fiestas (national, regional, and parochial holidays), got boisterously drunk, and let off cannonades of fireworks that during the day struck fear into the hearts of tourists and at night smeared the sky with color.

I asked Ángel how this part of Spain compared with Andalusia. For me, the greenery around La Jara and the cheerful fatalism of the people, augmented by a streak of guile, gave it the edge over a region that had been fashioned by travel writers, its cities clasped to their images like brooches.

Ángel thought differently. He honed a scythe with a stone. "It is not as refined as Granada or Córdoba," he said.

I tried to imagine Ángel wearing a sharp suit in one of the smart cafés near the Alhambra but the image was short lived.

I wanted to grow the sort of crops that were piled high in Spanish markets. Eggplants with polished purple skins, red and green peppers, *habas* (broad beans) with bulging pods, *acelgas* (chard) with celery-like stalks, carrots as small as babies' fingers, parsnips with roots long enough to strike oil.

I envisaged them growing in verdant rows hemmed with the yellow flowers of pumpkin and cucumber, melon and marrow.

I explained this to Ángel. He nodded wisely. Just as he would have planned it. Diane and I were driving to Madrid for a couple of days and I gave him the go-ahead.

When we returned, I found he had built a miniature POW camp 80 by 20 feet, beside the two almond saplings at one side of the orchard, occupying about a tenth of the whole plot with concrete posts and chain-link fencing chest high. All that was missing was a watchtower manned by SS guards.

"Why, Ángel?" I asked. "For God's sake why?"

"To keep out thieves," he said.

"But anyone can climb over that," pointing at the chain link. Anger surfaced; it was the Irish in me—my father was a Londoner but my mother was born in Dublin, the daughter of a reprobate who had abandoned his family and fled to the United States never to return. I thought my modest furies had gone into retirement but here they were straining at the leash, rekindled by an eccentric gardener.

"Foxes can't climb over it," Ángel said. "Nor can cats or dogs or rabbits or small children."

"Hostia!" I snapped, invoking the Host, the most common profanity in Spain. I stormed back into the house.

That evening, sitting in front of a log fire watching sparks chase each other up the chimney, Diane and I debated Ángel's behavior. My feelings had hardened: I wanted to sack him; Diane, who wasn't dealing with him directly, was more compassionate.

"Why does he always stare at the sky when I ask him a question?" I demanded. "I pay his wages, not Messrs. Cumulus, Cirrus, and Nimbus."

"He's a contemplative person," Diane said. "His head is in those clouds. You wouldn't understand that."

"I don't understand why a contemplative person would build a prison yard in my garden."

"He means well."

We agreed to leave Ángel's future in abeyance, but secretly I determined to replace him: I wanted a gardener, not a mystic.

A solution presented itself a few days later in the person of Rodrigo. Bowlegged and overweight, he arrived at dawn and said he had come to prune the fruit trees. He added that he had done so annually for the past ten years and was due to start again now.

To test his prowess I put him to work on an ancient lemon tree outside the kitchen.

A devious idea occurred to me as, on one of Ángel's days off, he attacked the tree with a small ax. Could he, I asked, manage other types of gardening? He spread wide his arms: the Garden of Eden if necessary.

"Rodrigo may be our man," I confided to Diane over breakfast. A strange mixture of relief and guilt washed over me—Ángel *had* meant well when he barricaded the vegetable plot.

"Our man for what?" She sipped tea, incapable of articulating thoughts before her first cup of the morning. From outside came the steady thud of Rodrigo's ax on the lemon tree.

"To take Ángel's place. Of course, we'll have to get references for him."

Mopeds sputtered along the road past the wrought-iron gates. A yellow crop-spraying monoplane visible through the windows skimmed the orange plantations while Diane absorbed the fact that I intended to sack Ángel. Finally she said: "How can you be so two-faced?," picked up her cup, and disappeared into our bedroom, slamming the door behind her. Flakes of plaster from the wall fell to the floor. Impetuosity and passion were engraved on her heart, leavened by a sense of the ridiculous.

Alone on the terrace, I tried to rationalize. Ángel had built a stockade I didn't want, Rodrigo seemed to be a hard worker and not so temperamental.

At that moment Ángel arrived unexpectedly in his van. I wondered if he had been tipped off that a pretender to his throne had infiltrated the garden.

He came onto the terrace. "What is Rodrigo doing here?" he asked.

I told him Rodrigo claimed he always came to prune the trees at this time of the year. "Do you know him?"

"I have seen him drunk in every bar in the *pueblo*," said Ángel, who was a teetotaler.

"But you don't mind him pruning the trees?"

"Murdering them." He inspected the lemon tree outside the kitchen while Rodrigo ate his lunch in the garage. "He's certainly killing that one. He's removed the wrong branches, cut them at the wrong places, and used a blunt ax."

"Doesn't Rodrigo come every year?"

"Impossible—the trees are still alive!"

"You could do a better job?" His presumption was getting to me.

"Better than that," Ángel said pointing at the lemon tree. He turned on his heel and drove away in his van.

After lunch a truck backed into the driveway and deposited a large mound of horse manure.

I asked the driver who had authorized the delivery. "Ángel," he said and took off, tires screeching.

When Rodrigo started his afternoon shift, I diverted him from pruning and asked him to shift builder's rubble that had been left under the cypress hedge to a garbage collection point at the end of the street where it joined the road to the village.

His first accident happened almost immediately. I heard a cry of pain and raced to the spot where he was working.

He was sitting in the shade of the hedge, balding scalp beaded with sweat, unlacing one of his rope-soled shoes. He told me he had dropped a brick on his foot. If he had known he was going to shift rubble, he said, he would have worn boots. Was he planning to sue for damages? I wondered. I inspected his foot but there was no outward sign of injury.

An hour later he knocked on the door of the annex where I was working on my book. Could he drive into Denia to replace the handle of his *azada,* the tool like a large hoe, with which Spaniards perform much of their manual work on the land? "It snapped," he said, "when I was clearing weeds in the area where the debris was."

He was away for two hours. At the end of his stint, he told me he had lost a hundred-peseta-banknote; it must have fallen from the breast pocket of his shirt when he was dumping rubble at the end of the street.

I walked with him to his van. One of the tires was flat, a jagged wound below the tread. As he began to change the wheel I noticed dark clouds gathering on the horizon. Had Ángel summoned malevolent spirits?

Half an hour later a dozen sacks of chemical fertilizer were dumped in the driveway by the same deliveryman. A few spots of rain fell.

"What are we going to do about the pile of horse manure?" I asked Ángel when he made another guest appearance. If it rained heavily, it would be swept into the house.

"It will be better damp," he said. I suspected this was his way of telling me he had no intention of shifting it until Rodrigo was dismissed. He drove away in his van.

So I was stuck with an accident-prone malcontent and an eccentric with a penchant for chain link. I stacked the plastic sacks of chemical fertilizer into a neat pile.

I had just shifted the last sack when, with a flash of lightning and a crack of thunder, rain sluiced from the clouds—and the pile of horse manure began to disintegrate, moving on a malodorous tide down the slight incline of the driveway toward the kitchen door.

I grabbed a shovel and tried to stem it before it flowed under the door. Diane found three sandbags in the garage and tried to make a dam. The rain fell harder, the smell of dung became more pungent. I had covered floods as a reporter and knew how ineffectual sandbags could be against an inexorable current of water; if we didn't take decisive action the kitchen would become a stable.

Inspiration visited me. I dragged the sacks of chemical fertilizer from the side of the driveway and, cursing Ángel, laid them in the path of the oncoming tide. It lapped the bags, faltered, then changed course and flowed down the driveway toward the lawn on the other side of the house.

At dusk we locked up and sat down to supper—Diane pointedly sitting at the end of the plastic table, as far away as possible from the faint aroma of the farmyard, which the two showers I had taken hadn't totally dispersed. I slept in a sleeping bag and dreamed I was drowning Ángel in a barrel of liquid manure.

In Britain, America, or Canada, or any other country where the customs were more familiar, I would have acted with more expediency—sacked Ángel for refusing to shift the manure, paid off Rodrigo when I realized he was a malingerer, and found someone else to do their work.

But, being a foreigner, I had to proceed with caution. Feelings could easily turn against us if we acted autocratically. And that would be unfair to Jonathan, who would soon be starting school and trying to adapt.

And in any case the overall perception here was more benevolent than it had been in the cities where Diane and I had lived. The village was more a family than a community; crime hadn't entered its portals (except for regular bank robberies in which money was handed over amicably); old people and children were cherished; bureaucracy existed to be outsmarted.

It was up to us to adjust, and some foreigners I had met elsewhere in Spain who didn't try should never have left their native shores. The greatest challenge was language; the Dutch coped brilliantly because, as practically no one else spoke their language, they were used to getting their tongues around other people's; British, Americans, and Germans often struggled—they mostly succeeded, particularly the women who did the shopping, but a few gave up and went home.

I woke at dawn, put on a bathrobe, and went outside. The rain had stopped, the jigsaw-shaped paving stones of the driveway had dried, and the flow of manure had stopped short of the lawn.

The crop-spraying aircraft was making an early start. I waved at the hedge-hopping pilot, he waved back.

Everything seemed to be back to relative normality except the problem with Ángel and Rodrigo and Diane's opinion that I was a hire-and-fire overseer from a sweatshop.

The crisis began to resolve itself a couple of hours later. Rodrigo didn't show up for work; instead a small and belligerent girl knocked on the door. Rodrigo wasn't well, she said, and could I please give her the money for his work yesterday, bearing in mind that he had lost one hundred pesetas and hurt his foot.

"Is he coming back?" She shook her head vehemently. *Not to work for a perfidious foreigner like me.* I experienced a surge of relief—one problem solved, one to go.

I paid her Rodrigo's wages plus damages. She grabbed the money and ran away to remove herself from my malign influence as swiftly as possible.

When Ángel reported for work he scraped up the drying manure with his *azada*, loaded it into a wheelbarrow, and took it to the vegetable garden. As he dug it in he crooned a lament, lightened, it seemed to my untutored ear, by a few triumphal notes.

I told Diane he could stay—for the time being.

FOUR

Who Said Anything About Snow?

Work began on the dining hall early in February. All we had wanted initially was a sun-warmed house steeped in character, remote from tourist traps with their thumping discos and whiffs of tanning oil. Now we had a house and suddenly an extension was the heart of the matter. High-raftered, baronial, redolent of orange-wood smoke in the winter, ventilated by breezes from the distant mountains in the summer. A massive timber door, old terra-cotta tiles, an inglenook, Emilio's minstrel gallery . . . Slyly it had insinuated itself into the vision Diane and I had shared for so long. If my book was a success, then we would add a patio, an adjoining studio, and a kitchen extension.

The dining hall was designed by Peter Pateman, an old friend and bon viveur. A bearded Englishman and entrepreneur, he had been a lumberjack in Canada and a TV cameraman in Britain, and had converted a warehouse by the harbor in Denia into a medieval inn.

He obtained our building permit—a relatively easy procedure because we owned more than the minimum amount of land required and subcontracted the construction work. The contract between the two of us was a handshake, payment for labor and materials to be made as work progressed. Paperwork was the scourge of Spain, but common sense could cut through it as cleanly as a laser beam.

Jonathan had returned from Montreal with Diane, unsure whether he was Canadian or Spanish, but willing to give either or both a try. One windswept day the three of us stood together like a family group waiting for a Victorian photographer to take our picture, to witness the symbolic laying of the foundation stone, a humble cinder block.

The foreman of the eight-strong building team laid the block in a bed of soft cement and I squeezed Diane and Jonathan's shoulders, the euphoria of the moment marred a little by doubts about the wisdom of what we were embarking upon.

Could I afford the dining hall? Supposing the book failed; could we adapt to the clash of cultures? Were we right to impose our wishes on Jonathan?

Emilio, who had been accepted by the foreman as a casual worker—his talents, it seemed, now encompassed brick-laying, plastering, and dispensation of advice on all aspects of building—applauded while Ángel fingered the holes in his straw hat. They had known each other for about a year, but their temperaments were so dissimilar that they were bound to clash.

Ángel, who had decided with my consent to work five days a week with shorter shifts, and Emilio both kept arriving progressively earlier; if they continued to try to outdo each other, they would eventually be arriving at midnight or, worse, not going home at all.

Once, on my daybreak trip to the bakery to buy warm bread, I found Emilio asleep in his van on the roadside. He had set his alarm clock an hour too early and decided to take a predawn nap; as I roused him, Ángel swept triumphantly past and parked in the driveway.

Ángel now worked as close as possible to the dining hall, so that he could issue instructions, usually contrary to Emilio's, to protect the garden from excavations.

Emilio was expansive when it came to foundations. He told the foreman: "You'll have to extend the wall here by half a meter to make it safe."

Ángel intervened. "Over my dead body."

Emilio to the foreman: "While you're at it dig a grave."

At nine A.M. the whole team adjourned to the garage for *desayuno,* breakfast—*bocadillos* followed by oranges, peeled with the delicate application of manicurists, washed down with beer or red wine diluted with *casera,* weak lemonade.

They were all hard workers, but sometimes ferocious debate, tempered by bursts of hilarity, prolonged the meal. While we ate breakfast in the house, we could hear the accents and occasionally some of the regional languages of Spain, which Diane did her best to interpret for me.

Among the workers was Jordi, as stout as Friar Tuck with a monkish fringe of hair, from Barcelona, the capital of Catalonia, the sprawling, prosperous region in the northeast. He ate two *bocadillos* to everyone else's one, poured wine down his throat as though he were filling a gasoline tank, and referred to Catalonia as a separate country. "Barcelona is the true capital of Spain," he would announce and wait for outrage to erupt.

The dissent was led by Chimo, a sunken-cheeked Madrileño, as skinny as Jordi was corpulent, his sleek black hair as shiny as new paint. Madrid, he said, was more than just the capital of Spain: it was the capital of civilization. And, even more provocatively, Real (Royal) Madrid was the inspiration for all world-class football clubs (Real Madrid and Barcelona were sworn enemies). Sebastián, a young and dour Gallego with Viking-blond hair, said that football apart, they were both talking rubbish: Galicia, the mountainous land in the northwest where he was born, was the most influential part of Spain because hardship had dispatched waves of immigrants from its shores to the United States and that was the only true superpower in the world, wasn't it?

He had a point, said Iñaki, a granite-faced Basque who wore a flat beret, the male headgear of his homeland, which straddled the French border, where ETA terrorists waged a campaign similar to the IRA's in Ireland. "We speak our own language, and we were the original inhabitants of Europe."

"So?" With one syllable Emilio's voice was unmistakable.

"So? Were you in America so long you left your brains there? Europe is the center of Western civilization, we made it so," Iñaki said.

Regional differences and football apart, they debated village gossip, sex, and politics. From time to time Ángel inserted his own peculiar views.

After breakfast, work accelerated. One wall of the original dining room was knocked down; the driveway became a builder's yard; choking dust filled the house.

The new walls of the dining hall rose roof high and even the weather collaborated. Frost sparkled on the lawn beneath arctic-blue skies, a cloud of almond blossom bloomed in a corner of the garden, yellow winter jasmine flowered close by. Diane fed crumbs to robins and glossy-haired carpet salesmen unrolled their wares beside mounds of sand and bags of cement. I worked on my book in the annex, wax plugs in my ears to isolate me from the din.

Diane hired a languorous beauty named Maria to help her with the housework. She worked dreamily, accompanied by Julio Iglesias on her cassette player; we substituted a Rolling Stones tape and she jumped around like a Keystone Cop. And everything might have proceeded smoothly enough if it hadn't snowed.

Estimates varied about the length of time since the last snowfall. Some pundits reckoned it was twenty-five years, other sages—there was no shortage of them in the village—said a hundred.

Snow had occasionally dusted the top of our small mountain, Montgo, but this was serious stuff. It capped the citrus trees with white millinery; the branches of olive trees snapped under its weight; motorists drove blithely into drifts of it.

By midday it was nine inches deep in the village. Cats pawed it suspiciously, small dogs disappeared in it. The school closed down to let children touch it, taste it, throw it. Women swept it from the sidewalks with futile industry; in the Bar Paraiso there was dark talk of ruination.

But it was our roofless dining hall that really concentrated it, funneling it into a blizzard. It climbed the walls, spilling out of glassless windows, and dispatched the builders into the garage where they played cards.

I asked Ángel how long he thought it would snow for.

"Until it stops," he said.

It continued to snow well into the afternoon. We lit two portable fires fed from canisters of butane gas to supplement the log fire and the house crackled with heat. Jonathan, who was staying with a friend, phoned and said, "Spain isn't so different from Canada, is it?"

At four o'clock the phone rang again, the owner of the building company asking to speak to the foreman.

Five minutes later a truck arrived. The workmen piled into it. The foreman explained that they were going to finish interior work on a house on the beach near Denia. Time was money, he said.

"But the snow will be gone by tomorrow," I said. "This is sunny Spain, isn't it?" He shrugged. *"No pasa nada."* Don't worry, the phrase that encompassed all life's tribulations.

A couple of workmen jumped out of the truck, collected tools from the garage, and with ominous finality handed them to their colleagues. The truck drove away, taillights fading in the gathering dusk.

Normally I loved first snow, particularly at this time of day when it was bladed with cruelty and lighted windows beckoned beneath white bonnets. Not this evening. All it did was add another desolate dimension to the mounds of sand and heaps of bricks and cinder blocks and the skeletal silhouette of my folly, the dining hall.

An hour later I realized we were marooned, our food supplies reduced to a loaf of bread, a few potatoes, and a bottle of vinegary wine.

Ángel, who had been in the garage stripping and sharpening canes to be used as garden stakes, offered to drive me to a grocery, but I didn't trust his van—cars and trucks had already been abandoned on all the roads around Denia. Snow was pouring from the sky as he drove away.

As I walked back to the house down the driveway the lights in the house and the village went out.

I tried to make a phone call: the line was dead. I found a flashlight: the batteries were dead.

I piled logs onto the fire and sat beside it opposite Diane.

"I'm hungry," she said.

"My mother used to make potato cakes with mashed potatoes and bread."

"Your mother isn't here," she pointed out. "And the stove's broken."

"Then I'll put on a Sinatra tape and we'll go to bed and make love."

"All night?"

"If music be the food of love . . ."

"I fancy steak and chips. First," she added.

"I'll go into the village and get food. You stay here and prepare for a gourmet meal—sausages grilled over the fire and potatoes baked in their skins in the ash—and a night of debauchery."

"Don't forget the wine," Diane said.

She was lighting candles as I trudged along the driveway, knee deep in snow, wearing rubber boots, sheepskin jacket, and a knitted hat. Behind me the kitchen and living room glowed cozily in the candlelight.

It wasn't far to the village along the route Emilio had taken us on when we first saw the house, but now the road was in total darkness; the snow had thickened into a blizzard, there was a deceptive fork in the road and an irrigation ditch to one side of it.

I passed a couple of abandoned cars. Somewhere ahead lay the crossroads on the road from Denia. They were perilous enough in normal driving conditions, and I worried about what they might be like tonight.

Five minutes passed and there was no sign of the intersection. Maybe I had taken the wrong fork. I took a few more steps—and plunged into the eight-foot-deep, snow-filled irrigation ditch. Pain leaped up my left leg.

I tried to haul myself onto the roadside but fell back, cracking my head on a protruding boulder. My skull filled with cold and pain. I lay still for a moment, part of my reeling brain anticipating headlines.

SUN-SEEKING AUTHOR DIES IN BLIZZARD
BODY FOUND CLOSE TO NEW HOME

And the first paragraph: *A would-be author who was trying to write a bestselling thriller about Siberia died yesterday in Spain in a Siberian-style snowstorm.*

Ludicrous. I heard echoes of well-meaning friends' voices from the past. "Writing a thriller in Spain? Get back to the real world." If I was shipped back to England as a corpse, they'd be exchanging hindsight wisdom all the way to the morgue. I had to get out of the ditch.

I tried once again but its sides had been cemented, and they were sheathed in ice. I waded through snow, pain shooting from shin to thigh. I felt blood seeping from the wound.

A tractor passed, thick-ribbed tires gripping the surface. I shouted. But the tractor trundled away and was lost in the veil of snow. Panic set in, and yet Diane and a blazing fire were only a few hundred yards away . . .

I encountered another boulder protruding from the cement. I got one foot onto it, but the sole of my rubber boot was as slippery as the ice and I fell back again.

Further on the ditch became more shallow. I managed to scramble onto the roadside and lay there for a few minutes. Hypothermia next! Even more ridiculous. I stood up. My head ached and my leg was numb but as far as I could make out there were no bones broken.

But where was I? On the way to the crossroads or on the other branch of the fork? I decided to retrace my footsteps, cautiously, as though I were making my way through a minefield.

Then, like the sound of a tank in a war movie, I heard a metallic clatter. The beams of headlamps peered through the falling snow. I waved and shouted. A van with chains on its wheels stopped. And Ángel climbed out!

I grinned stupidly.

As he drove toward the village, he told me that when he had reached home after leaving our house, he had fitted the chains on the tires. When the lights had gone out, he had driven back to our house to see if he could help.

Diane had told him that I had set out for the shops. I asked him where the chains came from. "When I lived in Andalusia I used to drive in the Sierra Nevada mountains," he said. And why had he taken what I now realized was the wrong fork? "Because you took it."

I had been contemplating firing him. And I would probably contemplate it again when he perpetrated some unfathomable trans-gression in the garden, but there was a lot to be said for his inscrutable logic.

He took me to a *practicante*, an upmarket nurse, who stitched a six-inch gash on my shin, painted it with antiseptic, bandaged it, and gave me aspirin for my aching head.

I bought black *butifarra* and pink *chorizo* sausages flavored with paprika and garlic and a bottle of red Rioja wine.

After Ángel had dropped me at home, Diane grilled the sausages over the fire. I buried four potatoes in the glowing ash and opened the bottle of wine.

Never had a fire been more embracing, never had a meal been so appetizing. Through a gap in the drapes I could see falling snow fill-ing the night.

I wheeled a heater into our bedroom, placed a candlestick on a saucer on a bedside table, and climbed into bed.

Diane joined me and said: "So what about the debauchery?"

The thaw the following day was as abrupt and dramatic as the bliz-zard had been. Water swept from the grounds of the haunted man-sion across the road, depositing earth and gravel in our driveway; the lawn became a lake; the branches of the orange trees shed dripping loads of snow that thumped onto the ground.

The sun jeweled the melting snow with diamonds; the garden filled with the music of running water and birds sang along with it.

There was no sign of the builders. But Emilio and Ángel reported for work, although until the thaw finally spent itself, there was nothing for them to do. Both displayed the extremes of their characters: Emilio, singing robustly, stored parts of the minstrel gallery, wooden steps, balustrade, and floorboards, on the covered terrace, Ángel wandered around the garden humming plaintive melodies from the south.

In the afternoon a gale sprang up, spattering the outside walls of the house with mud and sand. Surveying the mess, I was once again plagued with doubts. I was crazy to want a beamed dining hall in the middle of plantations of Diane's "embryonic marmalade."

I drove to the coast, to a beach deserted except for a man with a beard throwing a stick for his dog. Leaning into the wind, I watched the rollers breaking into spray on rocks out to sea before spilling themselves on the sand.

When the wind had blown away some of my doubt I returned to the house.

Emilio was hosing down the walls of the house, and Ángel was staring dreamily at a patch of exposed earth between wings of snow melting in his stockade.

He pointed at the wet soil. Green snouts were pushing their way through it.

I frowned. "What are they?"

"New potatoes," he said. "I planted them when you were in Madrid."

I patted him on the shoulder. "Well done, Ángel, you're a genius."

He nodded: no need to orally confirm the obvious.

I walked back to the house. Lamb chops, green peas, *and* new potatoes in the dining hall before spring? It sounded good to me.

A Plague of Pigeons

A fine day, a false spring day, the sort of day when echoes of childhood abound. Poinsettias raised their dying petals, clumps of wild freesias and narcissi bloomed among the Bermuda buttercups in the orchard, silver snail trails laced the driveway.

But the day was flawed: the dining hall wasn't finished—the walls were a mere six feet high—a stark reminder of the follies foreigners could perpetrate.

What we needed was a diversion. And we got more than one: a flock of birds with feathers as bright as jockey silks, a precociously amorous puppy, and two cats, one with four legs, the other with three.

The puppy arrived, unseen at first, while we were eating lunch on the terrace at the rear of the house. *Empanadillas*—small pasties filled with tuna fish, tomato, and peas or spinach—avocado salad, slices of cold potato omelet, and a bottle of white wine.

Despite the voices of spring, birdsong, and murmur of insects, Diane and I ate a despondent meal. Although we had cajoled and threatened Tomás the builder, sturdily built with unevenly chopped black hair, on the phone that morning, we had extricated nothing but vague promises, the opening chapters of my novel were being sabotaged by worry and the weather—while I was describing a sweltering day in Moscow, here it had snowed, now while I was approaching Novosibirsk on the Trans-Siberian Railroad in a blizzard, here the sun was shining; Jonathan's first day at kindergarten in Denia had been disrupted scarily by ghosts and skeletons (visitors from a neighborhood carnival) and at the moment he was vehemently pro-Canadian. I watched him kicking a football by himself in the garden and knew he needed more than just his parents to shepherd him through what lay ahead.

Halfway through our meal, Ambrosio, a muscular young man with a roguish smile, strode down the driveway to service the blue, rectangular swimming pool—clean the tiles with a vacuum attached to a suction hose that writhed like a stricken python and preempt the formation of algae with liquid chlorine.

Ambrosio was honest to a fault, often telling me I paid him too much. But I didn't reduce the payments, because I had already overstepped my modest budget so comprehensively that a few hundred pesetas wouldn't affect bankruptcy proceedings one way or the other.

When water stopped gushing from a pipe at the rear of the pump room—the backwash to clear muck from the filter—I gave him his money and a beer. He drank slowly, frowning.

"What's the matter, Ambrosio?"

"You could do the pool yourself," he said.

"Don't you want the money?"

"It isn't that." He wiped a mustache of foam from his lip. "I shouldn't be taking it."

The prospect of operating the mysterious controls in the pump room while simultaneously plotting to kidnap the Russian president on the Trans-Siberian in my thriller made my head ache.

"Don't let it worry you," I told him.

"All right," he said, implying that if I wanted to continue throwing good money after bad that was my business. The phone rang and Diane went indoors to answer it. Ambrosio finished his beer but he didn't look as if he was going anywhere.

In the ensuing silence I heard yelping from the direction of the driveway. I walked around the side of the house with Ambrosio, whose frown was now knotted between his eyes.

The yelping came from inside his van. Sheepishly he opened the rear doors. Three khaki-colored puppies with paws the size of a Great Dane's lay among the pipes and brushes.

Ambrosio said: "So, what do you think?"

"What do you mean, what do I think?"

It was a well-established practice to dump unwanted animals on foreigners, and it was not uncommon to arrive home to find a litter of kittens outside your door. I didn't blame the owners: many of them couldn't accommodate pets in cramped homes and they dealt with them as best they could.

Ambrosio claimed he had found the puppies on a rubbish dump and taken pity on them. He had brought them to the most *simpatico* foreigners he could think of. His roguish smile wavered a little under the impact of the last transparent fib.

He took the puppies out of the van and arranged them at my feet. They were well on their way to maturity, part boxer, part ridge-back, part donkey.

"You need guard dogs," he said.

"Que no!" We had owned a boxer in Ireland, an escapologist who

could have climbed the walls of a prison; he had died prematurely from a rare liver disease and I didn't want all that grief again.

The puppies sat down and, brown eyes staring at me, wagged their tails.

It was as if they had been trained as accomplices by Ambrosio, archexponent of a brand of charm that derives from exuberant humor, compassion, and manipulative prowess. I knew he was deceiving me, he knew I knew, and yet we both went on sparring.

"No, thank you," I said addressing Ambrosio and his canine cohorts. "No puppies."

"They like you."

"I'm honored, but no."

"Dogs are no problem," he said.

"Unless you're a cat."

"Just one?"

Well, come to think of it taking walks wasn't much fun without a dog . . .

Ambrosio, sensing doubt, pounced. He picked up a puppy and handed it to me.

"Not that one." It was a female, and I shuddered at the thought of more big-footed, khaki-colored puppies being born in the future. "Maybe that one."

He handed me the puppy I was pointing at. It lay on its back in my hands, unquestionably male.

Ambrosio picked up the other two, put them in the back of the van and came back to me. "You'll never regret it," he said. He smiled. "We understand each other, you and me."

He made off at great speed in the van just as Diane emerged from the house.

She pointed at the puppy in my arms. "What's that?"

"That's Jones," I said. To this day I have no idea where the name came from.

"You haven't—"

Yes, I said, I had.

"But we agreed . . ."

Had we? I couldn't remember. "We need a guard dog."

"To guard against what? The orange groves aren't exactly teeming with rogues and vagabonds."

"And I need a dog to keep me company on walks."

"I'm not good enough?" We had walked hundreds of miles together, in upstate New York when we had rented a house at Tomkins Cove on the Hudson River and in the birch woods outside Moscow when I was a newspaper correspondent there.

"I'll take both of you with me," I told her.

"You'll feed it?" We had a four-stomach family now.

"Of course."

"Clear up its mess?"

"He's too small to make much."

Which was when Jones began to pee copiously.

When we returned to the terrace we found to our astonishment that we had also acquired a cat. It was an overweight tabby with a white blaze on its chest and it was sitting like a buddha on the step while Jonathan stroked it.

I put Jones on the floor and said to him: "For crying out loud, where did that come from?"

"It was just here," Jonathan said.

"Well, it can go back to where it came from."

"Maybe it hasn't got a proper home," Jonathan said.

At that moment Jones began to advance on the cat, which was blinking in the sunlight, monarch of all it surveyed. The cat spat at him. Unperturbed, Jones continued his approach.

The cat feinted with a left dab and let fly with a right hook, bloodying his nose.

"Obviously," I said, "we can't keep both of them."

"Why not? The cat can be mine, the dog yours." He stroked Jones, who was whimpering.

I knew that eventually I would succumb to his persistence. A cat washing itself in front of a blazing fire helped make a home, and a home, not a residence, was what we needed. I also realized that for Jonathan to come home from the kindergarten to two animals would smooth his transition into his new life. The son of a Canadian mother and an English father with Irish blood in his veins, growing up in Spain in a region where a lot of locals spoke another language, Valenciano . . . Difficulties in finding an identity lay ahead. Blond hair among children who were predominantly dark wouldn't help either. Luckily he had inherited his mother's charm and he loved sports, invariably an asset in male company in Spain. I imagined him, puppy under one arm, standing among a group of children urging on the players of the Denia football club.

So both animals stayed. I named the cat Ethel after a rotund aunt who used to get drunk on chocolate liqueurs and stay for extended weekends at my parents' house until my father gave her the taxi fare and sent her home.

That afternoon Jones, dropping the pretense of extreme puppy-hood, burrowed under the cypress hedge and dug up several rows of seeds in a neighbor's garden. The neighbor, a young six-foot woman with a deceptively shy manner, called at the house and told Diane: "I'm going to call the dog catcher."

The previous day I had seen the dog catcher, a wizened predator, snare a black-and-white stray with a loop of wire on the end of a stick, bundle it into his van, and drive it away to be destroyed.

The neighbor, it transpired, was the Avon representative in the village, and Diane appeased her by buying a bottle of body lotion and a jar of face cream. She served manzanilla tea and biscuits to clinch the deal and Jones's neck was saved.

Jones soon emerged as an energetic lover, frequently being caught *in flagrante delicto* with any accommodating bitch. On one occasion I parted him from a scruffy mongrel with a bucket of water.

Bitches apart, he loathed all other dogs and loved all humans with the exception of Eduardo the woodman. For some unfathomable reason the woodman, squat and saturnine, infuriated him, and when he delivered logs for the fire, Jones had to be locked in an improvised pen where, teeth bared, he hurled himself against chain link.

A friend of ours, a sassy New York painter, Beryl Kranz, lived nearby in a converted farmhouse where she painted nudes in her studio. Eduardo offered to pose for her but pulled out when he heard that we often brought Jones there. A pity, because the vision of Jones chasing a naked woodman round her studio was appealing.

On the day Jones and Ethel joined the family, Emilio was working alone in the half-finished dining hall. A longtime adversary of his, Jesús, who delivered the canisters of butane gas, arrived while the two animals were sparring on the terrace, Ethel with regal aplomb, Jones in fits and starts.

Jesús wore orange overalls, and had developed a callus on one shoulder from carrying the heavy canisters from his company truck.

Young and sleek, he intimidated and infuriated Emilio. Vociferous in debate in the village, Emilio was politically right of Attila the Hun until anyone admitted he might be correct; then he would have bought Lenin a drink if he'd walked into the bar. In fact, he hated verbal accord on any subject, so Jesús made a point of agreeing with him on all topics.

To attract the attention of Jesús on his rounds it was necessary to display an orange flag, in our case a dust cloth on a broom stuck between the bars of the gate. When Jesús walked down the driveway from his truck that afternoon, orange canister on one shoulder, Emilio emerged from the dining hall.

"You're late," he shouted.

"Very," Jesús said.

Emilio clenched his fists.

Jesús dumped the canister outside the kitchen door, asked for a glass of water, and joined Diane and me on the terrace. Emilio followed.

"You foreigners love your pets," Jesús said in a mixture of Spanish, Valenciano, and English, pointing at Jones and Ethel.

"We don't have a choice," I said. "You leave them with us." British, Americans, and Dutch were the favored recipients.

"Do you like bull fighting?" Jesús asked. A provocative question, because he knew many foreigners condemned it.

"I have no strong feelings," I said diplomatically.

"No strong feelings?" Emilio smote his hands together. "How can anyone not have strong feelings on such a topic?"

"You're an *aficionado?*"

"I prefer football," he said.

"So do I," Jesús said.

Emilio glared at him. "But I do like to see a true *torero*. Manolete, now there was a man," he said, referring to the legendary matador who was goaded out of retiring by the public and killed by a bull named Islero in 1947. The death of the sad-faced bull fighter at the age of thirty encompassed all the double-bladed qualities of the *corrida*—the futile bravery of the bull, the educated courage of the matador, the fickleness of the *aficionados*, the fans—from the opening parade with the three matadors marching abreast in their glittering suits of lights to the *Suerte de Matar,* the act of killing. Manolete's crime was that, having established himself as a purist and maestro of his calling, he was weary. His health, sapped by whisky and a capricious mistress, was failing, and all he wanted to do was cut the pigtail, bull-fighting speak for calling it quits. But the *aficionados,* having become much taken with a handsome *torero* named Luis Miguel Dominguín, whose name was linked with the film star Ava Gardner, accused him of cowardice. This he could not take so he agreed to fight one last season.

In the southern city of Linares he faced Islero, a Miura bull, the breed known as the Bulls of Death because they realize quicker than others that the enemy isn't the *muleta,* the heart-shaped red cloth attached to a baton, it is the man holding it.

Manolete entertained the spectators with his usual repertoire of refined passes, then went in for the kill, considered perfect if the sword plunges into the base of the neck above the bull's lowered head, severing the aortic artery. For a moment, as he takes his weight on his left leg, the matador's right leg is vulnerable to the horn of the exhausted bull if it suddenly makes a thrust. Which is what Islero did, severing Manolete's femoral artery in his right thigh, the wound dreaded by bull fighters.

Both man and bull died and *aficionados* throughout the land who had sent Manolete to his death mourned guiltily.

"What right have you to criticize bull fighting?" Emilio demanded. "Bulls bred for battle have a wonderful life and a glorious death and all you foreigners do is fatten them up for *rosbif.*"

He had a point. I didn't understand the intricacies of the *fiesta brava*—the art of the banderilleros who thrust long frilly barbs into the bull, the matador's sequence of passes known as the *faena*—but I did know that after a picador on horseback has thrust a lance into the bull's muscle at the back of its neck, it is an unequal fight.

And I did know that the aftermath of a bungled kill—dispatch with a shorter, substitute sword through the spinal cord and a final stab with a dagger by an assistant—was a degrading spectacle.

Emilio was getting into his stride now. "In Britain men and women on horseback chase one small fox and stand back while dogs tear it to bits. What about the Grand National horse race? Do you really have to shoot the horses when they break their legs? Would you expect to be shot if you broke your leg?"

I went on the defensive. "I didn't say I was against bull fighting."

"What about your old people?" He was diversifying wildly. "What do you do with them? Stick them in nursing homes. We keep them with us and they die among their loved ones."

"Emilio is right," Jesús said, staring at the distant mountains.

"About what?" Emilio demanded.

"Everything you've said."

I intervened, looking for genuine common ground. "But you're both fond of animals, aren't you?"

They waited, willing each other to make an admission. Jesús broke first: he didn't have much choice because he was stroking Jones. "I have nothing against animals."

"As long as they are kept in their place," Emilio said.

"What's that supposed to mean?" I asked. "Keeping dogs chained up all day and night?" It was an uncalled-for remark because I had only seen one chained up in a farmyard, but I was incensed by his accusations that the British were hypocritical about animals.

"I have heard," Jesús said, "that in the north of England they still bet money on cock fighting and dog fighting."

A chill breeze heralding evening sprang up and Jesús and Emilio departed. A *carro*, a small covered wagon drawn by a pony with bells jingling on its harness, passed the gates.

We lit a wood fire in the living room hearth and switched on the secondhand television we had recently acquired. A series of cabaret routines from South America appeared, introduced by a young man who seemed to have more teeth than most people.

It was so boring that we let the fire burn itself out and at seven-thirty drove with Jonathan to a nameless restaurant nearby, which we favored because the steaks were Texan-size and the owner was so outrageously rude that we respected him. It was late for Jonathan. In a country where children sometimes stayed up to midnight and beyond, he was normally in bed by eight. But it was Friday, no school in the morning.

The restaurant was stark, a few tables and chairs gathered

around an open fire. The owner, a Basque named Aitor, was waiting at the door, the scowl on his face a permanent fixture.

He was tough and insular like many Basques. As far as I could ascertain they had every right to be: their homeland, set among misty green hills in the north on the border with France, was unique. They spoke euskera, or "eskara" according to their dialect, a language like no other; they were descendants of Europe's aboriginal inhabitants, pre-dating migrants from Asia three thousand years ago; they were taller than their neighbors; as well as the ballgame pelota, they enjoyed esoteric sports such as woodcutting and stone-lifting; they ate and drank hugely; their reputation for chivalry to women, real or romanticized, pre-dated Women's Lib by centuries.

Their autonomous region is known in Castilian as the País Vasco and consists of three provinces, Guipúzcoa, Álava, and Vizcaya. Tragically the struggle for separation was still being waged in blood by ETA terrorists.

Aitor pointed at a table covered with a red-and-white-checkered cloth, the only concession to civilized eating, and gave us a pitcher of red wine from Jalon, a small town fifteen or so miles away. It was a heady brew liable to put you to sleep before your meal arrived. We ate hunks of toasted bread to damp down its fumes and watched him prepare two steaks, each the size of an elephant's ear. There was no menu, just steaks.

First he pumped the log fire into life with a pair of cracked leather bellows, then he waited until the flames had died down and mounted a grill across the embers. He tenderized the steaks with a carpenter's mallet, seasoned them with salt and pepper, and threw them on the grill where they sizzled and spat, drops of fat flaming in the ash.

"Turn them when they're ready," he told Diane, handing her a toasting fork.

He made his way, still scowling, from the dining area, deserted except for the three of us, to the crowded bar. Customers were said to come from miles around for the privilege of being insulted by him.

We finished the bread, the produce of a bakery in a nearby village where a soulful girl with flour-gloved hands wrapped *barras,* Spain's answer to France's baguettes, while she gazed into the street for a glimpse of a shy young man who was trying to pluck up courage to ask her to go to the movies with him.

Diane approached the fire and flipped the hissing steaks. "Do you think I should serve them?" Jonathan was going to share the steaks with us—neither Spaniards, nor Basques for that matter, minded parents getting three meals for the price of two.

"I'll ask him." Aitor was said to keep a gun under the bar and I felt that protocol should be observed.

I told him. "I think the steaks are ready."

"So? Eat them."

As Diane speared the steaks and dropped them on our plates, he emerged from the kitchen carrying dishes of French fries and canned peas.

"If you have complaints," he said, staring at me through bloodshot eyes, "let me know."

"Don't worry," I said. "We will."

Every restaurant and hotel is obliged by law to keep a book in which dissatisfied customers can record complaints, which are supposedly read later by bureaucrats. When asked for these tomes by clients who claim they have been fed salmonella with their salmon, proprietors often discovered to their astonishment that they have mislaid them.

When we had finished the steaks, Aitor said: "Well, do you have any complaints?" his tone implying that they were as rare as truffles in the desert.

"The steaks were a little overcooked," I said, looking at his muscular forearms and wondering if he was a stone-lifter or a woodchopper.

"Your wife cooked them." He stared at Jonathan. "What did you think of them?"

"They were a little tough," said Jonathan in Spanish—he was fast becoming bilingual, a great asset in the future.

"Tough, were they?" Aitor rasped his finger on his unshaven, Rocky Marciano chin and went back to the bar. To fetch his gun maybe.

When he returned he gave Jonathan a handful of boiled candies, each wrapped in silver foil.

"You'd make a good Basque," he said.

What could have been the ghost of a smile flitted across his face. I later reported this phenomenon to shopkeepers in the village who knew him but they said I must have been hallucinating.

Diane went on the offensive. "I might have cooked the steaks," she said, "but you were in charge."

Aitor turned to Jonathan. "If you say the steaks were tough then they were tough. Steaks shouldn't be too tender. How's the candy?"

"Good," Jonathan said, munching.

"Anyway," I said, "we'll be back."

One of Aitor's reddened eyes twitched. "Don't hurry," he said.

The three-legged cat arrived several days later.

To be accurate it was a three-and-a-half-legged cat. One of its front legs had been severed halfway up, probably by a trap set to catch foxes in the orange groves. It had a ring of black fur around one eye in an otherwise white coat, and sported a piratical air—a feline Long John Silver.

It came in the arms of Emilio, supposedly archopponent of domestic animals' rights, while Diane was picking up Jonathan from kindergarten.

I was amazed at such a display of tenderness but apprehensive that he hoped to off-load the cat. "Where did you find it?" I asked him.

"In the ditch outside your house."

"Are you sure?"

"Have I ever lied to you?"

I didn't bother replying. "What are you going to do with it?"

"I thought you might—"

I told him I now owned a house that looked like the set of a disaster movie, a chair-chewing dog, and a pregnant cat. A three-legged cat didn't fit into my scheme of things.

Emilio shrugged his shoulders. "Okay, I'll take it to the vet." To have it put down, he meant. I was appalled.

"Okay, let's have a look at it."

Emilio laid it gently on the floor. It sat up and tried to wash its stump. The wound had partially healed but blood still seeped from it. Perhaps it would it be kinder to have it destroyed painlessly. It looked at me, tried to raise its other front paw and fell on its face.

Emilio fondled it behind the ears. "What are you going to call it?"

"Hoppity," I said. "What else? But that doesn't mean I'm going to keep it—Jones would have it for breakfast. Why don't you keep it?"

"My wife is allergic to cats." News to me. "But in any case they can take care of themselves."

"Not three-legged cats."

But I had an idea. I asked Emilio to drive into Denia and buy some electric lightbulbs to get him out of the way.

When he had gone I found a short length of kindling wood and took it to the garage where he kept some of his tools. I sawed it in half, whittled it with a razor-sharp chisel, and cut a wedge from one end. Then I sandpapered my handiwork and went back into the house.

When Emilio returned, Hoppity was wearing a wooden leg attached to his stump with a bandage and adhesive tape, the bandage threaded in between prosthetic limb and open wound. (I later made a canvas harness that girdled his shoulders and chest.)

After Hoppity had made a couple of unsteady circuits of the living room, I brought in Jones on a tight leash to test his reactions to the cripple. Hackles raised, he went into the attack mode that had so far brought terror into the lives of nothing more ferocious than insects and small rodents.

Watching him superciliously, Hoppity sat in front of the fire and began to wash his whole front leg. Jones whined, lip curling. When he was within sparring distance, Hoppity unleashed a haymaker with his wooden leg that caught Jones on his already abused nose. I released him onto the terrace where he continued to repel voles and beetles.

I tapped Hoppity's new leg. "So what do you think of my handiwork, Emilio?"

"Not bad," he admitted grudgingly.

"Couldn't have done better yourself?"

"Maybe not."

Such an admission was a victory of sorts for me so I offered him a sop to his pride. "If you like I'll say you made it."

"You'll tell Jesús and Ángel that?"

I nodded.

He punched me on the arm and left without saying another word.

The birds flew in a week later. A flock of them with plumage so vivid, purple, scarlet, and emerald, that they looked as though they had arrived from an Amazonian rain forest. Or had the rough red wine from the bodega at the end of the road affected my perception?

The birds circled the garden a couple of times before settling on a lemon tree and folding their wings.

They were soon followed by a posse of men, thirty or so strong, young and old, who parked their cars, Fords, Citroëns, Renaults, Peugeots, and Seats, as well as mopeds, on the road outside our gates. They wore hunting jackets with zippered pouches, peaked caps, and old flying helmets and they looked like Sicilian bandits. Shotguns lay on the backseats of some of the cars. I watched mesmerized from our driveway.

As they approached the open gates on foot the birds rose again, wheeling and free falling high in the sky, feathers bright in the afternoon sun.

The "bandits" stopped in their tracks, some making notes, others aiming field glasses at the birds.

The two-car Alicante train piped its way through the thick citrus groves at the foot of our broad-browed mountain, Montgo, half a mile away. An aircraft chalked a line across the sky.

Watched by Jones and the two cats, the birds swooped and settled again, this time on a grapefruit tree. A collective sigh issued from the visitors as they swarmed through the gates and took up positions behind the house.

I approached one of them who had the presence of a leader, a Sicilian Godfather, squat and strong with wary eyes in a seamed face, and asked him what was going on.

He put one finger to his lips.

He was telling *me* to be quiet on *my* property. I took a step forward.

At that moment Diane, who had been taking a siesta, emerged from the house and coolly appraised the visitors.

"I don't know who they are," I said, "or what they're doing here but they've got a nerve."

"Shush." She put her finger to her lips, just as the Godfather had done. "It's all about sex."

"Sex?" Had the rough red reached some untrammeled region of her libido?

"I'll explain later."

The little train tooted again as it took off from the village station and the birds rose once more.

As they flew away the Godfather approached. "We're very grateful," he said. "Don't you know who I am?"

I shook my head.

He pointed at the dining hall. "I'm Tomás, your builder. You didn't recognize me in my flying helmet."

"If you're that grateful," I said, "perhaps you could start building again—it's been weeks."

But he was gone, heading for a green Dodge, a status symbol in the post-Franco era, followed by the rest of the pack.

Sex?

Pilar, the owner of one of the village groceries, young and pretty with a fringe of black hair, had apparently told Diane about the sort of spectacle we had just witnessed: it was an early stage in a Spanish-style pigeon race.

"But they weren't pigeons," I said. "They looked more like parrots."

"Pigeons with wings painted in the colors of their owners," Diane explained.

She went into the kitchen to make tea and I followed. Apparently the gaudy cock birds all pursued one dowdy hen. One by one they dropped out, vanquished by superior wing power or, occasionally, by beak and claw—feathers spotted by blood sometimes spun to the ground—until only a single suitor remained.

Its owner was declared the winner and picked up the prize; in a prestigious race it could be a new car or an apartment at a beach resort. And millions of pesetas changed hands in bets.

A fast and amorous pigeon was expensive, said Diane, heady with insider knowledge. One breeder bought a potential champion for five thousand dollars and it was killed the same day by a sparrow hawk.

We had chosen accidentally to live in the heart of pigeon-racing country, which was why, by unwritten law, we were expected to allow *aficionados* onto our property.

Tomás arrived at dawn the following day. One of his two pigeons had won yesterday's race, he told us, but the other was missing. He accepted a cup of coffee and splashed brandy from a hip flask into it.

"Thank you again," he said, "for allowing us onto your property." He slugged his coffee with a second shot of brandy. "Work will start again on your dining hall later today."

And it did. But I doubted whether it would have done so if he had seen the handful of blood-stained feathers at the end of the garden. Nor would he have been impressed by the single painted feather protruding from Jones's jaws.

The Night Spiderwoman
Fell in My Lap

As night fell, the vacant lot near the balding football field in the village was empty except for two dogs twitching in fleabitten dreams and a courting couple sighing in each other's arms.

By the following morning it was covered by a tent as dew-wet as a mushroom at dawn.

The circus had arrived bringing with it threadbare glamour—and two mysteries—on its coattails. I had never enjoyed circuses, but the excitement generated in the village was infectious.

Traveling circuses visited some Spanish towns twice a year, their appearance heralded by exotic strangers. Leathery impresarios with dyed hair and gold teeth; fan-snapping wives carrying their years with aplomb; young dudes assessing the local talent; girls with flashing eyes and hoops in their ears. And at night the cough of lions could be heard.

This circus didn't have quite so much impact, no big cats, only the moth-eaten domestic pets that accompanied it. But posters advertising Superman and the Amazing Spiderwoman and other daunting acts did appear on walls alongside faded posters from long-forgotten elections. Tickets promising half-price admission were distributed in bars and a van toured the countryside, loudspeakers blaring.

One mystery began to unfold when Jaime, the jockey-size barman at the Paraiso, announced that he had served a beer to a customer claiming to be Superman.

At lunchtime Pilar, the pertly pretty owner of a cramped little grocery, revealed that she had sold *chorizo*, cheese, and a packet of chewing gum to a clown in her store.

Sightings multiplied. A cashier at the bank claimed he had cashed a traveler's check for the juggler; a seamstress had sewed sequins onto the costume of the knife-thrower's partner; the pharmacist had served the strongman with an iron tonic.

If all these appearances were genuine, even if the players weren't dressed for their parts, the streets should have been strutting with characters from Marvel comics. But they weren't.

This mystery was soon solved: it was a small family circus and its members performed a variety of acts.

The clown was both the strong man and Superman; his plump wife was Spiderwoman, a rodeo rider from the "Wild, Wild West" *and* clerk at the pay desk at the entrance to the tent.

The second mystery was more worrying—an outbreak of burglaries in the area. Gypsies were often blamed by the police for such crimes, more common since Franco died, taking his repressive rule with him to his grave and, well, circus people weren't that far removed from gypsies, were they?

The villagers didn't apportion blame, they merely relished the presence of the swaggering performers from the little tent as they watered their ponies on the waste land, flexed their muscles in the winter sunlight, and laundered their gaudy apparel in the public wash house beside women scrubbing and wringing Bible-black skirts.

The village girls haunted the two young men, as sleek as panthers with Romany faces, like fans doting on pop stars, while men of all ages gazed wistfully at Superman and Spiderwoman's daughter-in-law, who wore a molting leopard-skin coat and looked like Gina Lollibrigida.

I met her in a bar where she was drinking chocolate milk and eating a slice of potato tortilla. She beckoned me over to her table and said: "You're not from around here, huh?" She spoke with an Italian accent. "You're a writer?"

"How did you know?" I sipped my cup of black coffee.

"You're watching all the time. Making the notes up here." She tapped her black, upswept curls with one chipped shell-pink fingernail. "Why don't you write a story about our circus? Our movie-star lives. Two caravans, one-horse towns, breaking my ass twice a night to please peasants hoping I fall off the high wire . . . Not so high in my case." She smiled, revealing lipstick on one of her front teeth. "You should travel with us."

"Maybe I will one day," I said. "Why do you stay if you hate it so much?"

She explained with one word, as though it summed up all the torment in the world. "Family." She nibbled the last crumb of tortilla. "My husband's mama and papa . . . I leave, they die. Maybe you write a story about us and sell it to Hollywood. *Little Big Top?*" She looked at me hopefully. "You write a part for me?"

"What do you do?"

"I spin from a rope tied to a collar round my neck," she said. "I walk on the wire. I go around and around on a wheel while my hus-

band throws knives at me. If we fight before the show, then, poof."
She put one hand to her heart. "At half-time I sell sodas and popcorn. I look out for you. I give you free popcorn."

"You've got yourself a deal," I said. "One pack of free popcorn
and one day I'll write a book about you."

"And one day the pigs will fly. I suppose you think we are thieves
too." She finished her chocolate milk and swept out of the bar onto
the street.

Later I heard from Emilio that there had been three more robberies. Cash from a house in a grove of grapefruit trees, paintings
from the attic of a mansion, and jewelry from a newlywed couple's
cottage.

Could the circus people be responsible? I doubted it: the fact
that the burglaries coincided with their arrival was too obvious. I
decided to try to help them.

That afternoon two young *Guardia Civil*, a far cry from the Civil
War stereotypes who had stopped beside us in the orange groves,
arrived in the village in a small green-and-white car. Debonair and
friendly, wearing olive-green uniforms and peaked caps, they
inspected the circus and its two caravans, talked tersely into hand-
sets, and frowned wisely.

The *Guardia* were responsible for law enforcement outside cities
and towns and as Spain was the second largest European country
after France they controlled a considerable patch.

The officers called at our house two hours after their arrival.

One of them, freckled with crew-cut hair, saluted and said: "We
understand you are the owner of a spinning wheel."

True—I had bought an antique weaver's spinning wheel, small
and made of wood, its wheel controlled by a single foot pedal, in an
antique shop in Denia. I thought it would add a touch of class redolent of the past to the dining hall.

The other *Guardia*, slimmer with shiny black hair, said: "A spinning wheel is among the items reported stolen in the past few days."

"Not my spinning wheel," I said. "I bought it."

"Who from?"

I gave him the name of the shop and he wrote in his notebook.

"Does this mean I'm a suspect?"

The crew-cut *Guardia* shrugged. "Do you know where the owner of the shop got the spinning wheel?"

"No," I said. "And I don't know where the shopkeeper got these when I bought them," pointing at my shoes.

"*Tranquilo, señor.*"

"I know, you're only doing your job . . ." I said.

"You have been interviewed by the police before?"

"Only for rape and murder."

The slim *Guardia* smiled. "Careful, *señor*, we might take you seriously. Do you mind if we take the spinning wheel and check it out? We will return it, of course, if it's . . . clean. Is that how you say it in English?" He smiled again.

My father, a bank official, had warned me: "Beware of smiling policemen and con men who shake your hand."

"Take what you like," I told him. "Take the dog if you want."

Jones barked.

Fury at the injustice of the implied accusation possessed me, but I had to admit the *Guardia* had what seemed to be a genuine lead. Supposing the spinning wheel had been stolen? I would be detained, interrogated, brought before a judge, and probably released on bail. The delay before my court appearance could take as long as six months followed by a hefty fine if I couldn't clear myself. Imprisonment if I had a previous record (no fear of that) or if I was convicted of the other break-ins. Not so different from procedures in the United States or Britain except for the cavalier attitude here to delay.

Watched inscrutably by Ethel, followed by Jones still yapping—Emilio and Ángel had vanished—the *Guardia* poked around for a while and asked to see my papers.

Three factors saved me—Diane was shopping in Denia—from closer scrutiny. One, the dining hall. They looked at the deep pile of powdered cement, gazed at the mirror-bright toecaps of their shoes, and turned away.

Two, the revelation that I was a writer.

One of them stared at my chaotic desk—books on the Trans-Siberian, last night's empty whisky glass, and this morning's tea mug.

"You write here?" the slim *Guardia* asked.

I nodded.

"What sort of books?"

"I'm working on a thriller."

They continued to stare at the desk in disbelief. Did acts of derring-do really emanate from such disarray?

"What does your wife do?" Crew-cut asked.

"She paints." I pointed through the window at her easel on the terrace. "She also writes."

"Here?" He prodded the desktop.

"Sometimes."

"Romances?"

"Not quite." Diane had started working for a glossy English-language magazine in Spain, *Lookout,* and had just written an article about our friend Beryl Kranz, the American painter of nudes, entitled "Bosoms, Bottoms, and Beryl."

At this point Hoppity came tapping into the room on his wooden leg. That was the clincher. The two *Guardia* took one look at him and decided to make a strategic withdrawal from such a madhouse. Before they could leave, in the interests of the circus people I gave them the benefit of my days as a crime reporter, my instincts sharpened perhaps by my own excursion into thriller writing, before they left.

The robberies, I told them, all had the hallmarks of inside jobs. The thieves all seemed to have gone unerringly to the locations in each of the houses where the loot had been kept. No one in the circus could have had that knowledge. Burglars often cultivated maids or handymen who innocently divulged the whereabouts of valuables. Perhaps all three victims had the same employee . . .

They nodded indulgently, the way police patronize meddling private eyes in TV series, and departed in their neat green-and-white car, taking the spinning wheel with them. I felt like grabbing it from them, but that would have guaranteed a night in the slammer.

Meanwhile, theories about the identities of the thieves had begun to sweep through the village as joyously as floodwater.

In the Bar Paraiso, an old man who was paid to stop snails roaming from a stall in a market—he merely detained them when they made a protracted run for it—sipped cornot, the locally distilled moonshine, poured from an unlabeled bottle, and whispered: "Superman," adding, "but keep that to yourself," those fateful words that make a town crier of every one.

The suspect favored behind conspiratorial billows of suds in the wash house, we were told, was the traveling grocer. The knife-grinder also had his accusers. And, of course, we foreigners were high on everyone's lists.

I consulted Emilio. He smashed one fist against a studded door—he was rumored to drive home nails unimpaired by a hammer—and said enigmatically: "Necessity makes a thief of every man."

I sought out Ángel, although I should have known better, and asked him what he thought.

He put down his trowel and scratched his head through the hole in his straw fedora. "There are strangers in the village," he said.

"How do you know?"

"I have seen them."

"You mean apart from the circus people?"

"They are from the north."

Unsure whether this incriminated or absolved them, I asked him how he arrived at this conclusion.

"I have heard them speak."

"What were they talking about?"

"Money," Ángel said. "Or lack of it."

"You think they are the thieves?"

"They know who they are," he said, completing a masterly digression on the obscure.

That day, a few hours before the circus was due to open, there was another robbery. A house just outside the village, owned by a young bachelor who worked in a bank in Denia, was broken into and traveler's checks and a pair of loudspeakers were stolen.

Later that day as we took our seats in the tent, we noticed villagers glancing at the loudspeakers high in the canvas, but they were so battered, the music issuing from them so cracked, that surely no one would have bothered to steal them.

"Such terrible speakers need to be replaced." said Ángel, who was sitting next to me, Diane, and Jonathan. "Maybe—"

But any dark suspicions he may have harbored about them were cut short by the arrival of the ringmaster, wearing black boots, a jacket of hunting pink, and a top hat, whose bark commanded the audience's attention. Children's fingers relaxed their grip on the licorice roots they were chewing, women's hands lay motionless in bags of popcorn.

The first act was a rodeo rider—the proprietor's wife from the "Wild, Wild West," who was said to have taught movie stars to ride horses.

We waited expectantly, the smell of wild herbs that grew on the vacant lot which had been crushed underfoot strong in our nostrils; layers of cigarette smoke lodged in the glare of the spotlights.

Finally a gray pony emerged and trotted prettily round the ring pursued by a plump equestrienne in buckskin who jumped on and off a couple of times, finally standing unsteadily on the saddle. As pony and rider disappeared through the exit we heard a fleshy thump. She didn't look like a thief to me.

The audience applauded enthusiastically and Jonathan spat out the husk of a sunflower seed he had been nibbling. So too, I noticed, did Diane.

Next a clown. White cheeked and red nosed, a clown to be sure, as he poured a bucket of water inside his baggy trousers but, I now knew, Superman in disguise.

He was followed by the tightrope walker, a beautiful shiny-haired girl carrying a cane and wearing fishnet tights, breasts straining at a black bodice. The girl I had met over a glass of chocolate milk.

Ángel's wife, petite and pretty with lustrous dark eyes, dug her husband in the ribs as he gaped at her.

Then the strongman (the clown), taxing his retiring muscles as he bent a few nails and, with a sharp cry of pain, snapping a brick with the edge of his hand.

During the intermission a girl wearing a blond wig sold sodas and popcorn. Gina Lollibrigida again. She threw me a packet of popcorn, refusing to take any money. "What was all that about?" Diane demanded.

"Payment for services to be rendered," I said.

The second half began with an act in which the girl, a collar round her neck, rotated from a rope attached to the roof of the tent. Soon her husband would be throwing knives at her; I hoped they hadn't had a fight.

When she had finished spinning, one of the young bloods in the village shouted: "Where's Spiderwoman?" and a girl demanded: "Where's Superman?"

The lights went out. Girls giggled nervously. When the lights came on again there was Spiderwoman, alias the rodeo rider, standing on a nylon rope web stretched between two beams at the top of the tent.

She wore a gray bodystocking, inked webbing stretched by the generous contours of her body into confusing patterns.

With a shrill scream she launched herself down from her web into space, skimming dangerously low over our heads.

Behind us she kicked herself off from a metal tent support and swept back again across the sawdust in the direction of her web, falling short by a foot or so. By now she was in danger of hanging ignominiously from the rope suspended above the ring.

Not this arachnid. She created momentum like a child on a swing and made it back to our territory, dropping into the space between Ángel and myself. There she unbuckled her rope and fell into my lap. A not entirely pleasurable experience because she was a lot of woman.

Disentangling herself, she stood up and raised two fists above her head, a gesture that sent the threads of her web on her bodystocking into spasms.

This was followed by the knife throwing—no prior fight, apparently—some juggling, and an act in which the proprietor's son sawed his sister in half in a coffin.

It had been rumored that Superman would dive from a high platform into a tank of water. And suddenly there he was, trespassing above the ring on Spiderwoman's web, resplendent in cape and blue tights that sagged alarmingly at the crotch.

Had no one told him there was no tank of water in the ring?

The silence in the tent thickened. Jonathan clapped one hand to his mouth and, not too convincingly, I tried to reassure him.

Then Superman launched himself into space on Spiderwoman's rope. He landed in front of us and chased Spiderwoman, coyly waiting for him, out of the tent with a lumbering gait. A fitting climax, it seemed to me.

While Diane drove Jonathan home, I went to one of the two shabby caravans to find Gina—I didn't care if her name was Mavis, she was Gina to me—and thanked her for the popcorn.

She was sitting in front of a mirror lit by a single bulb. Her husband, Chimo, the proprietor's son who had just sawed his sister in half, sat in a canvas director's chair.

I asked her if the *Guardia* suspected any members of the circus of the robberies.

"Of course," Chimo replied for her. He wore a pale blue T-shirt and muscles danced on his brown arms as he linked his hands behind his neck. "They always suspect us. We're traveling people, always guilty. You a betting man? I'll make a bet with you. The thief is a foreigner, one of your kind."

I bristled, the Irish in me. "Why the hell do you say that?"

"Because he's a slob," Gina said. "He hates everyone." She glanced at his throwing knives slotted into a mahogany case lined with green baize.

"I don't hate everyone," Chimo said. "Just you sometimes," nodding at Gina. "And foreigners who come to my country and take us for idiots. Think they can rob us blind."

I tried to control myself. "As a matter of fact I love Spain and all the Spaniards I've met so far. With the possible exception of you." He selected a knife from the box and tested the blade with his thumb. "I want to be accepted here but with people like you around I'm not so sure." He drew a spot of blood on his thumb. "And by the way," I added, "I've told the *Guardia* how they may be able to prove the robberies were nothing to do with the circus."

I struck a one thousand-peseta bet with him that the thief wasn't a foreigner. I took his address in a small town in Andalusia and told Gina that when I came to write a book about a small circus I would bear her in mind.

I frowned. "You're Italian, aren't you? What are you doing in a Spanish circus?"

"I met Chimo," she said almost spitting, "when he was on vacation in Italy. Napoli, where all the crooks come from. He felt at home there . . ."

The circus left the following day.

⁂

Chimo was right: the thief was a foreigner. A Dutchman. He was caught red-handed with the loot from the robberies in a house in a village five miles away in the hills.

The two young *Guardia* called again at our house and gave me back my spinning wheel. So it hadn't been stolen. "We want to thank you," Crew-cut said. "We took your advice and traced the girl who cleaned the houses where the robberies took place. She comes from the village where the Dutchman lived . . . He had been asking her questions about the contents of the places where she worked."

They saluted and departed, heels of their polished shoes tapping crisply on the driveway.

I sent Chimo a one thousand-peseta bill, harboring only one regret about the whole affair. I wished that instead of Spiderwoman her daughter-in-law had fallen in my lap.

SEVEN

Quake in the Kitchen

By March, work on the dining hall was progressing slowly but majestically. The cinder-block walls stood ten feet high. The hearth was big enough to accommodate a blazing tree stump. The inglenook, or chimney corner, was furnished with a stone bench covered with terra-cotta tiles. The wing of a small castle was rising before our eyes.

In the garden Ángel's vegetables were burgeoning. Lettuce tied with raffia to keep their hearts crisp; rows of beans heavy with pods; turnips, swedes, and parsnips visibly swelling just above the surface of the ground; tomato, eggplant, and pepper seedlings sprouting.

Diane and I were long-term city dwellers

but now, watched over by Ángel, we raked and hoed and watered late into the bat-flitting dusk. Ángel even allowed me to sow radish seed; within a fortnight we were eating pink and peppery roots.

The purple bracts (not flowers, Ángel told me) of bougainvillea framed the arches of the covered terrace; jasmine scented the twilight; the blossom of wattle (not mimosa, Ángel said) hung from trees near the pool in powdery yellow tresses. Delicate green leaves were unfurling on our two grapevines that only last month had looked as dead as driftwood; tiny green grapefruit and oranges crowded the citrus trees.

We were melding with the life of the region, and we were pleased to see this was especially so with Jonathan.

His name had been put forward for one of Denia's *fallas*, the eight or so carnival groups whose activities, although not markedly religious, reached a climax at the time of San José (St. Joseph) in March, when towering papiér-mâché statues of politicians, statesmen, local dignitaries, tourists, and anyone worthy of ridicule— they were made by specialized craftsmen in towns all over the region and took a year to build—were put to the torch in the darkened streets. He had put the carnival ghosts and skeletons of that first day at school behind him and become an ardent supporter of the Valencia city football team.

Our lives seemed to be proceeding as fluidly as the passing of the seasons, the friendly curiosity of the villagers dispatching our doubts until we heard a subterranean disturbance in the garden. A rumbling growl accompanied by a fetid waft of gas from Hades that reached the kitchen.

Maybe it was an earthquake. There had been a mini-tremor a few years earlier and stories persisted that Montgo, our olive-green-and-gray guardian mountain, had once been volcanic—it was featured in a 1968 movie, *Krakatoa, East of Java,* about the eruption there in the 1880s.

Ambrosio, who was working in the pump room, hurried into

the dining hall to advise us because, as he was the one who dug craters and sank pipes for swimming pools, he was an authority on underground phenomena. Ángel followed him—the disturbance *had* occurred in his domain. Emilio, being an authority on all topics, joined them.

The three builders who had reported for work that morning and their foreman, a chain smoker with a mat of gray hair sprouting from the top of his shirt, were already there. They seemed to be unmoved by the noise and the smell but Emilio yelled for calm just the same. Ángel went out and patroled the limits of the dining hall; Ambrosio lapsed into deep thought, occasionally sniffing the sulfurous air.

The ground beneath us trembled, the faintest of movements but ominous just the same.

The foreman pointed at the floor with his thumb and spoke in broad Valenciano.

I turned to Emilio. "What did he say?"

"He said that when they laid the foundations they may have struck a fault."

"Maybe Montgo has reawakened," said Ángel, who had returned from the garden.

I suspected that the sewer pipes were at the root of the disturbances, but Emilio would entertain no such mundane explanation. "There could be a major tremor," he said, "right under the dining hall. Here where we're standing. It could bring down the walls!"

Emilio's dramatics got to me. I imagined the walls cracking, falling in slow motion, dragging the rest of the house with them.

I consulted Ángel, hoping for some soothing message from the clouds. "The problem," he said, fingering a pink birthmark on one pale cheek, "is underground." Far away from the jurisdiction of the heavens, I supposed.

Stunned by such a blindingly obvious deduction, everyone else fell silent.

As dusk fell, the men, who had resumed work, departed leaving

Diane, Jonathan, myself and the animals to face the night with whatever lurked underground.

When we woke the next morning, a gray wig of cloud lay on Montgo, often a prelude to rain that could last two or three days. If it was relentless enough, it transformed roads into canals and flooded the low-lying streets of Denia, occasionally sweeping cars into the harbor to join the small fishing fleet and the modest yachts moored outside the Club Nautico.

If the heavens really opened maybe the rain would drown the restless spirits beneath our house.

One of the workmen arrived at eight A.M., collected tools from the garage, and threw them into the back of a van.

I asked where he was going and he said: "We won't be able to work there," waving one hand toward the dining hall. "Not in the rain without a roof."

"Then build a roof."

He laughed uncertainly and drove away. More inside work in Denia probably. Somewhere there existed an owner of a new house who prayed for rain as devoutly as I prayed for fine weather.

The first fat drops fell a few minutes later. Ambrosio arrived on a moped to tell me he couldn't clean the pool yet because this was red rain, from the Sahara, which left a residue from the desert and he would only have to clean it all over again.

Emilio covered the lengths of wood he had been amassing with a tarpaulin—his proposed minstrel gallery had become a certainty, as though I had missed a committee meeting in which a final decision had been rubber-stamped.

Ángel, gazing at the cloud over Montgo, said the rain would probably be so intense that it could strip the fruit from the trees and cripple the plants in the vegetable patch.

"You said we needed rain," I reminded him.

"Not red rain," he said ominously.

Red rain sounded Biblical. An exotic upgrade on the minor

vicissitudes we had recently experienced. No water for two days, because workmen mending a road had bulldozed the supply pipe— we washed with water from the pool and drank bottled water.

No electricity, because lightning had blown out a power station.

Mold on our bedroom ceiling and a noise like a skirl of Scottish bagpipes when we turned on the taps in the bathroom.

I phoned half a dozen plumbers to get the noise fixed. Each time a woman said: "He'll call you when he gets home from work," a formula apparently agreed upon by a committee of plumbers' womenfolk. None of them ever called me.

Finally I made contact with an actual plumber who ill-advisedly picked up the phone himself. With a sigh he agreed to investigate the source of our piped lament and turned up half an hour later, a short and bird-bright artisan carrying a dusty leather tool bag.

He listened to the skirl of the pipes so appreciatively that I thought he was going to conduct them with a spanner. He replaced the spanner in the bag, said: "It's an airlock, I'll be back," and hurried away. When I called his number two days later, a woman said: "He'll call you when he gets back from work." We never saw him again.

The mold grew on the wall above the bed, which had been repaired since I had broken it. And it grew luxuriously, as swiftly as mustard and cress, green in its infancy, black as it matured.

I scuffed it with steel wool, saturated it with bleach, painted over it, and replaced broken bricks on the outside wall, but it was resilient, this fungus, and whatever I did, it returned with renewed vigor.

Then one evening the first mosquito of the year flew in through the window and I sprayed the bedroom with insecticide. The following morning the mold looked decidedly off color; within two days it had disintegrated into powder that I removed with a duster.

As the first drops of supposedly red rain fell, Jesús arrived with a canister of gas, arranged himself comfortably in the living room, and accepted a cup of camomile tea—he was a hypochondriac and believed it settled his stomach.

Emilio sat opposite him and made a few unfavorable observations about the new attitudes that had followed the death of Franco, a liberated attitude to sex, freedom of speech, and leniency in dealing with crime among them. The conventional argument against these reforms was the crime and prurience they had spawned; the argument in favor of them was the reinstatement of man's birthright to say and do what he believed to be right without being locked up for treason.

"Junkies? They would have been given an overdose in Franco's day." With one finger Emilio sawed at the cleft in his chin where a thicket of bristles grew. "Rapists? They would have been castrated."

"Emilio is right," Jesús said, deliberately intimidating him with outrageous assent. "Enemies of the State? There weren't any—they were all garroted." He leaned back in his chair, lean and sleek and provocative.

"But wasn't it a crime simply to speak your mind?" Diane asked.

"It depended what was on your mind." Emilio gave the plastic table a thump. "What drove our enemies all over the world crazy was that under Franco we had peace. Socialists everywhere hated us for that. But when Franco died . . ." He opened his fist as though it were full of spiders.

"Your family did flee from Franco," Jesús observed.

"So? I was born in America. I can't speak for my parents."

"Of course you can't." Jesús rolled a cigarette and lit it with an old flint lighter.

Rain drummed on the roof but thankfully there had been no more underground eruptions, although I detected faint traces of brimstone in the air. I felt as if this was a waiting time, that Emilio and Jesús sensed that unplumbed forces were about to be released and were relieving their tension with words.

"Yes, Franco was a good man for the country," Jesús said. "Spain needs a strong leader. Only today a widow put a gas container outside her gate for me to change. It was stolen before I got there. That wouldn't have happened in Franco's day." He smoked serenely.

Emilio punched the palm of one hand with his fist. "Of course it wouldn't have happened in Franco's day. In Franco's day she wouldn't have been able to afford gas."

"But she would have lived in peace."

"If she hadn't starved. Haven't you heard of the Years of Hunger after the Civil War? And what about the camps?"

"What camps?" Ángel asked innocently.

"The camps where anyone who spoke out against Franco was left to rot."

Jesús, canny advocate, stood up, pinched out his cigarette, and made for the door. If there had been a jury present he would have winked at its members.

Emilio retired to the garage.

Diane said: "I'm confused. When that spat started Emilio was pro Franco."

"And when he finished he was anti. Compromise . . . Politicians could learn a lot from both of them."

We were interrupted by an underground growl from the direction of the kitchen.

We went outside. The rain hadn't persevered—what had fallen wasn't even red—and the dripping clouds were lined with sunlight.

Emilio was kneeling in the driveway, one hand cupped to his ear. I couldn't hear anything but he seemed to be receiving Stygian intelligence.

"What is it, Emilio?"

"It could be the faults . . ."

I knelt beside him. The earth shook, the unmistakable smell of sewage filled my nostrils. To hell with Emilio and his half-baked suppositions.

"It's the sewer," I shouted. "There's a blocked pipe down there. Call a specialist."

He looked at me reprovingly. "I already have," he said.

The specialist, Paco, was a hairpin of a man with a raffish white mustache. He arrived on a bicycle.

According to Emilio, he had once worked in a bank. Finance and sewage were certainly disparate, but bank clerks often led dual careers. I frequently had to wait in my bank in Denia while the cashier attended to his deck-chair franchise; a clerk in charge of foreign exchange ran a boarding kennel.

The specialist, wearing jeans and a scuffed leather jacket, parked his bicycle in the garage and, waving aside introductions, walked to the site of the septic tank with the sure step of a water diviner obeying a sprig of hazel.

He laid a gauge with a quivering needle on the ground, nodding with melancholy satisfaction as the needle went into convulsions.

"Is it serious?" Diane asked.

He favored her with one of those tight smiles that experts bestow on laymen and held up one hand. Then he knelt, one ear to the ground, at various locations in the garden. Finally, he shook his head fatalistically, combing his mustache with the tips of his fingers.

"Well?"

He addressed Emilio in Valenciano.

"He says," Emilio translated, "that you have more than one septic tank, possibly two."

"That's good?" I asked.

"Not when the pipe between them is blocked."

"Then tell him to unblock it."

"It's not as easy as that—he doesn't know where the pipe and the other tank are because it doesn't have a lid. He says it will cost money . . ."

"How much money?" The vague estimate sounded ominous.

"That depends . . ."

"For heaven's sake," said Diane irritably, "he's not looking for the source of the Nile."

"Do you want him to go ahead?" Emilio demanded. "He's a very busy man. There are a lot of old pipes in this neighborhood." No. 1 septic tank coughed and its heavy iron lid moved. "He is the best," Emilio added.

"Okay, tell him to get on with it," I said quickly, because I had no option.

The specialist knelt again, grasped the metal handle on top of the lid, and pulled. It came out like a cork and he peered into the heaving abyss.

He replaced it and went to his bicycle. Returning with an *azada*, he followed what I presumed he thought was the underground route of the pipe leading to the second tank on the other side of the house. There he crossed the lawn to a bed of petunias and began to dig in it. Luckily Ángel, who had taken his wife to the hospital for a checkup, wasn't present to witness the desecration.

An hour later he was standing knee deep in a hole.

Diane brought him a bottle of beer and he conferred with Emilio.

"What does he say?" I asked.

"He says the pipe isn't there."

"I can see that. What does he intend to do?"

"Dig somewhere else."

The specialist began to hack rhythmically at rain-softened earth beneath the cypress hedge.

Half an hour later he stopped and summoned Emilio again.

"What does he say this time?"

"It isn't there either."

"He's going to dig somewhere else?"

Emilio nodded and while the specialist debated where to excavate I wandered around the garden, seeking inspiration. Foolishly I hadn't made any arrangement about payment and it was beginning to look as if I would have to ask for a bank overdraft to settle the bill.

I was standing between the two almond saplings, already bearing a few nuts covered with green velvet skin, when the ground stirred beneath my feet.

I poked it with a twig. The twig sank inches deep in mud. Reasoning vaguely that I might be able to release a pocket of gas trapped in the earth, I fetched a steel stake from the garage and hammered it home.

The specialist was deep in his third hole when a full-blooded eruption shook the ground between the two saplings. This was followed by a surge of sludge that tossed aside the stake.

The specialist nodded sagely and conferred with Emilio.

"What's he saying?" I demanded

"He says his work is done."

"*His* work? *My* work. All he did was dig two and a half holes."

"He says it was the holes that did the trick. Narrowed down the site of the blockage to where you sunk the stake. The stake pierced the pipe and relieved the pressure. But it will have to be repaired. He says you took advantage of his skills."

"Bullshit!" I said. "I found the blockage. The earth actually moved under my feet. After that there was nothing to it, just like pricking a balloon. Tell him I'll pay him for his time, not his skill."

Emilio told him; at least I think he told him, because he spoke in Valenciano.

The specialist penciled a sprawl of figures in a notebook, tore out a page, and handed it to Emilio. Obviously he wanted no physical contact with a perfidious foreigner.

"Tell him I'll pay him half what he's asking," I said. "When he's filled in his holes." Which was fair: I had located the blockage and I would get someone else to repair the pipe I had pierced.

Emilio spoke to the specialist again, then turned back to me. "He says a surgeon doesn't have to sew wounds."

"But a butcher has to clean up his mess," Diane said. Although emotional, she was more level-headed than I was when she thought someone was trying to outsmart us. She didn't destroy the opposition, she withered it.

Emilio spoke to the specialist, who shrugged and resignedly began to fill the holes.

Relief surged through me. I had won a practical and moral victory.

When he had finished, I settled the bill at 50 percent of the asking price and went for a stroll with Diane.

※

We walked to the village a few minutes away, passing a Judas tree with diamonds of rainwater clasped in its pink blossoms. Crossed the dangerous intersection where impacted glass lay as much a fixture as permafrost in Siberia, passed the pharmacy with its illuminated green cross outside, and turned into the main street.

It was early afternoon and the windows of the houses were shuttered. Children waiting for the yellow school bus played marbles among the puddles on the sidewalks. A group of teenagers clustered around the window of a small shop—closed like others until four-thirty or five—peering at a list of wedding presents that a couple about to get married wanted. Laughter spilled out from the bars onto the somnolent street.

We went to a functional new bar-café where young people met in the evenings and ordered coffee and chocolate éclairs oozing with frothy cream.

When we got home, clouds were gathering again on the horizon and Ángel was harvesting broad beans in his stockade.

I told him that while he'd been at the hospital with his wife, Emilio had called in a specialist to cure the underground eruptions. I had found the site of the blocked pipe but he had tried to claim the glory.

Ángel handed me a plastic bag filled with beans. "Paco always does."

"Always? What do you mean, always?"

"It's just a question of time," Ángel said. "He digs a few holes and waits for the pipes to clear themselves. They always do even though it takes time." His English was improving much faster than my Spanish.

"Why didn't you tell me?"

"I didn't know Emilio was going to call him. Did Emilio recommend him?"

"He didn't bother, he just phoned him." Suspicions about Emilio's loose interpretation of integrity surfaced again. "Why?"

"Paco is Emilio's uncle," Ángel said.

"You guessed the problem was in the pipes?"

Ángel nodded.

"So why didn't you tell me?"

"Because they are underground." He had the good grace to avert his eyes and continue picking beans.

"Of course," I said. "How stupid of me."

It rained hard that night. Red rain.

EIGHT

Scheming and Shopping

We felt guilty, almost as if we were committing adultery. Normally we shopped at Pilar's in the village, but on several occasions we defected to the indoor food market in Denia.

Worse, like furtive bed-hoppers, we discovered ways to justify our transgressions, and even implicated Jonathan.

It wasn't that Pilar's store was inadequate. You could have stocked up for a nuclear fallout in her cramped emporium that smelled of washing powder, dried fish, and ripe fruit.

Pickled onions bobbed like corks in a huge jar of vinegar. Strings of yellow candles hung from the wall linked by a common wick that had to be cut when they were bought. Dusty bottles of herbal aperitifs from the Mediterranean island of Ibiza stood shoulder to shoulder with bottles of cheap wine, *corriente*. Manchego cheeses from the heartland of Spain sweated beside cuts of smoked ham, which Pilar shaved into transparent tongues with a circular slicer with a wicked blade. Long *chorizo* sausages hung from hooks like dead snakes; they could be sliced and eaten cold as *tapas* or tossed into a stew, or skinned to extract the filling to make a spread called *sobrasada*. Fresh fruits and vegetables nestled in a rack in one corner.

Forage and you could stock up with rat poison, after-shave, balls of string, pumice stones, beach shoes, rainbow-colored bars of soap, sulfuric acid, aspirin, razor blades, or licorice roots to chew— almost anything hawked by a salesman on whom Pilar took pity because he was a father of eight and had tragic eyes, or a frail grand- father who should have been resting on a bench under the acacia trees at the end of the street trawling the past.

To her customers Pilar, who was in her thirties, rosy-cheeked and petite, was victualler, arbiter, and financier.

While parochial argument—the pros and cons of installing traf- fic lights at the murderous crossroads, the use of Valenciano on road signs, noise abatement in the bars (pretty much a lost cause)—raged around her, she adjudicated, measured sugar into twists of brown paper, netted pickled eggs floating in liquid as murky as pond water, weighed an artichoke or a turnip—purchases were often meager— and scribbled debts in a notebook with the stub of an indelible pen- cil, wetting the mauve point with a cat lick of her tongue.

Her customers were a mixed bag. Grandmothers in black, young wives in curlers and bathrobes rationing their pesetas, swarthy gypsy women with wads of money stuffed down their blouses.

The gypsies, about twenty of them, lived nearby beneath tarpau- lin and plastic covers on a smoking rubbish dump. They shopped ambitiously and were collected by a patriarch in a battered Mer- cedes. Where their money came from I had no idea, only that if your

home was a mountain of combustible garbage then you were entitled to a few of life's trimmings. They spoke conventional Spanish
peppered with a few pungent words of their own.

Gypsies, many of them far removed from any Romany bloodline,
had a rough ride in many parts of Spain. The purveyors of flamenco,
which originated in Andalusia in the eighteenth century, were well
respected, but outside that hand-clapping, guitar-strumming, heel-
tapping brotherhood they were often treated with contempt.

Foreigners at Pilar's were sparse, but a retired British Army
brigadier and his wife shopped there. They were as fragile as moths
and as tough as turtles, legacies of wars in which they had learned
self-sufficiency. They patroled Pilar's counters as a unit, clutching
onto each other, and departed balanced with laden baskets, driving
away in a small white car with imperious aplomb.

Some customers came just to talk, resuming conversations they
had begun in the wash house, others handed Pilar shopping lists
while they called at the butcher's, where two women chopped up
chickens with savage application, or the *pasteleria* to buy cakes for
birthdays, saints' days, weddings, first communions, and fiestas, or
the sepulchral tobacconists, or the drapers that also sold glassware
and toys.

Diane was enlisted by Pilar to help her pass judgment on food.
Pilar, married to a salesman, was busily and brightly independent,
occasionally summoning her parents or her sister-in-law to cope
with a Saturday morning scrum of customers, brushing at her black
fringe of hair with impatient fingers, but she valued Diane's cosmopolitan tastes.

I watched one day from our car parked outside—I was con-
scripted only as carrier and driver—while they sampled a consign-
ment of fruit; the delivery man, fiery cheeked and impatient, fumed
while they sniffed and squeezed and nibbled.

When they shook their heads, he savagely struck an item from
his invoice. When they nodded, he penciled an extravagant tick. I

went into the shop when Diane, in the absence of Pilar, who had taken a tray of bananas into the storage room, was tasting what appeared to be a tomato and arguing with the delivery man.

"Here, try this," She thrust a shiny red fruit into my hand. I nibbled. It was so bitter that it contracted my cheeks. "He's trying to tell me there's nothing wrong with it."

"There isn't."

She glared at me. "A tomato like that could shrivel your tongue." Maybe not such a bad idea, her tone suggested.

"Except that it isn't a tomato."

"Listen, I might not be Julia Child, but I do know a tomato when I see one."

"It's a *caqui,*" I said. "As bitter as alum when it's delivered to a shop. But it ripens almost immediately and becomes as sweet as honey."

The delivery man who seemed to be getting the drift of our conversation raised his pencil expectantly and glanced at me gratefully.

Diane grinned. "Okay, as *caquis* go it's not too bad."

The deliveryman scrawled a triumphant tick on his invoice. His place was taken by another wholesaler, and Diane and Pilar moved onto *chorizo* and its skinnier cousin, *fuet*, Manchego cheese, and dried fish.

Occasionally Pilar delivered our groceries to our house by van, and she and Diane debated romances, marriages, births, and deaths in the village over infusions of mint tea. The friendship was only casual but it made our defections seem even more treacherous.

But the boisterous call of the market in the center of Denia was irresistible. Housed in a cavernous hall built in 1955, the clamor of transactions between vendors and customers trapped beneath lofty rafters, the hundred or so stalls were as competitive as a stock exchange, as rowdy as a tobacco auction.

One March morning when clouds sagged over Montgo and lightning blinked out to sea, we slunk through its portals as stealthily as smugglers.

Jonathan, now a fully fledged member of a *falla,* a neighborhood carnival group in Denia, was taking part in warmup processions for the spring fiesta, and we convinced ourselves that we had driven into town just to watch him.

And for a while we did as he marched around the town in a procession with his friend Arturo, the son of a Spaniard, Miguel Senti, and his English wife, Jenny. The streets smelled of spring flowers and the sea and, just occasionally, sewers. Both boys wore traditional dress—kerchief, white shirt, brocade waistcoat, culottes, rope-soled shoes laced ankle high, and shawls of many colors over their shoulders. The elaborate and decorative costume had caused me some misgivings but, as the men wearing it all looked more masculine than any football hooligan, I buried my doubts. Jonathan was integrating, that was what mattered.

As he paraded with the rest of the group's fifty or so *falleros* of both sexes down the main street, the Marques de Campo—an avenue of shops and banks and bars shaded by plane trees leading from a square furnished with a puny fountain to the harbor—we made our way through the market past butchers' stalls to the fish counters where brine-fingered women eyed prospective customers across heaps of a Mediterranean flatfish called *lenguardo,* red mullet, squid and baby octopus, prawns, and live lobsters with roving pincers. We bought a white-fleshed *lenguardo* and some succulent prawns.

Then we wandered down the center aisle, past piles of artichokes, sweet potatoes, oranges, lemons, and green apples; past nuts, prunes, garlic cloves, and sunflower seeds, blue-veined cheeses, brown farmyard eggs, dried cod, and jars of olives, buying only when we spotted items not stocked by Pilar.

Two florists' stalls faced each other at the hub of the market. They sold evergreen plants, carnations, and daisies with petals dyed in exotic colors, which were purchased by the armful by husbands with guilty faces.

There we met an electrician from the village and his wife buying a rubber plant. We winked conspiratorially. *Just visiting. Don't tell Pilar.*

Three bars and a grocery selling cheese and ham and olive oil, adorned with a mural of Joseph holding Jesus, were grouped around the florists. We stopped for coffee at the Viciano, where the owner, Antonio, bespectacled and nimble, toothpick protruding from his mouth, presided. Caterer and comic, he served tortillas, potato salad, sizzling slices of pork, and coffee from a machine that howled like a jet taking off; joked with customers that they owed a thousand pesetas instead of a hundred; held onto the banknotes when he gave change and, like a juggler, caught bottles he snatched from the shelves as they fell.

Two canaries sang sadly in a cage hanging on the wall while life teemed around them. A policeman, blues stretched across his paunch, stopped for a brandy and a *cortado,* a small coffee. A pretty, red-haired woman, crippled in a road accident, sold lottery tickets from her wheelchair.

A hairdresser with a blue rinse from the village stopped to speak to Diane. "I didn't expect to find *you* here," she said, as though she had caught us in a sex shop.

Diane told her we had driven into the *big* town (population about twenty-five thousand compared with one thousand in the village) to bring Jonathan to the preliminaries of the carnival. The hairdresser ran her fingertips through her soft curls. "Of course—you can't get everything at Pilar's."

We wondered who would catch us next. Lowering our heads, we sipped our coffee.

Shopkeepers, bank clerks, and road sweepers traded insults, punched and hugged each other, tossed back nips of eye-watering brandy, and threw coins from their change into a can on the wall for Antonio's staff. The prospects of the Valencia, Hercules (Alicante), and Denia football teams were hotly debated, as were those of Real Madrid and Barcelona.

The customers also cracked jokes of exuberant vulgarity, reviled well-dressed visitors from Madrid for their toffee-nosed arrogance and irresponsible driving; discussed the storm gathering over the sea, because, although the British have the reputation for being unsurpassed bores when it comes to talking about the weather, the Spanish have the edge, pretending to swoon in the heat and drown in the rain. In fact, they are all as addicted to meteorological reports as the men are to football and the women to TV soap operas.

Only the arrival of a baby in a pram halted the badinage. Bruisers with fists like hams uncurled their fingers; hecklers, oaths shriveling on their tongues, cooed like doves; comedians swallowed blue jokes and blew kisses.

From the bar we strolled to the street market outside the hall, passing a stall selling brown-and-white Roman snails. Here you could buy herbs reputed to cure most known maladies. Shop selectively and you could loosen or tighten your bowels, dissipate gas, cleanse your blood, sharpen your eyesight, oil your joints, rekindle your libido.

I bought a couple of packets of herbs. While I was paying the stall holder, who looked as though he suffered from all the complaints he professed to heal, I felt a tap on my shoulder.

I turned. "*Hola*, Pilar," Diane said. "Fancy meeting *you* here."

Though Pilar never referred to our defection again, retribution for that day was not far off.

For lunch Diane tried her hand at *paella,* the Spanish rice dish that originated in the province of Valencia where, in spring and summer, workers, watched by white storks and egrets, toiled like coolies in coastal paddy fields of short-grain rice. *Paella*—originally the name of the pan in which the dish was prepared—came in many guises and could contain quail, rabbit, chicken, pork, almonds, prawns, sausage, clams, lima beans, pea pods, and snails. A Spanish food guru, Antonio de Vega, described *paella* as "a gastronomic miracle." I hoped Diane could sustain that wondrous description.

At least she had saffron. The yellow spice, at two thousand dollars a pound possibly the most precious in the world, was harvested from purple pastures of crocuses elsewhere in Spain and was an epicurean indulgence in this region. Cheat with turmeric or Mexican marigolds and picky guests turned up their noses. Luckily only a pinch of saffron, the dried stigma of the crocus, was needed.

I lit a fire in the barbecue with orange and almond twigs—Ángel once caught me burning oleander and told me that it was poisonous and its smoke could decimate the village—added charcoal, and went indoors to mix a pitcher of sangria with a bottle of red wine, a couple of tablespoons of Grand Marnier, sugar, slices of orange, and soda water, and poured a glass of *horchata,* a milky drink flavored with tiger nuts, for Jonathan.

I sensed that, as she cooked chicken broth and rice, saffron, onion, olive oil, rabbit, and other ingredients, Diane was behaving furtively. But, at the time, I was too hungry to care.

Finally she placed the pan on the table on the terrace. Jones drooled and we began to eat. Diane, I discovered, had even managed the alchemy of *socarrat,* the crisp layer of rice beneath the softer grains.

"Delicious," I said, putting down my spoon. "Especially the savory bits. What were they?"

She gazed at her plate and nibbled a grain of rice. "Snails," she said eventually.

Silence broken only by the call of the little train burrowing through the orange groves. Diane was well aware of my paranoia about edible snails: this was premeditated sadism.

I pointed at a Roman gastropod heading for a bed of nasturtiums. "That sort of snail?"

She nodded. "I bought them in the market this morning while you were at the herb stall. You just said they were delicious—I'm glad you enjoyed them."

That evening I had an attack of the digestive affliction that has many names, most commonly the runs.

I blamed the snails.

"Then why haven't I been affected?" Diane demanded. "Why hasn't Jonathan?" She followed me from the bathroom into the bedroom and picked up one of the bags of herbs I had bought in the street market that morning. "What are these for?"

"The tightening of," I told her. I had made an infusion of them as soon as we got home.

She read the label and shook her head. "These," she said, "are for the loosening of."

Well, if that packet was for loosening the other was for tightening. I went into the kitchen and made myself another infusion.

In Denia the twin climaxes of the carnival, known by the same Valencian word as the participating neighborhood groups, the *fallas,* approached. First the judging of the papier-mâché groups of statues, as bright as berries and as vulgar as saucy postcards, looming roof high in the streets, then the night when, primed inside with gasoline and fireworks, they were put to the torch.

The statues, built all over the combined region of Valencia and Alicante provinces, two hundred or so miles long, forty miles wide in places, took a year to make, cost millions of pesetas, and were burned, according to some authorities, in memory of carpenters in the Middle Ages who, in the spring, set fire to the detritus of winter. The big burn, the *crema,* took place on March 19, the saint's day of the most illustrious carpenter of them all, Joseph. It was the busiest night in the fire brigades' calendar.

For the two mornings leading up to the final day, I drove Jonathan at dawn into Denia to join a team of adults and children from his *falla,* Port Rotes, at the harbor end of the main street. They roamed the neighborhood, hurling small fireworks that exploded on impact at walls and balconies. I went with them. Cats ran squawking from doorways, and women in dressing gowns tossed buckets of water from their balconies onto us.

At two P.M. strings of firecrackers, *mascletas*, tied between posts and trees, exploded with a venomous roar that rattled the eardrums.

Tourists stared uncomprehendingly at the papier-mâché groups labeled in Valenciano, each lampooning different targets—politicians, councilors, movie stars, financiers, fraudsters, local characters, and the tourists themselves. In Franco's day the *fallas* were one of the few mediums in which protesters could criticize the regime without being tossed into prison. Jonathan, picking up Valenciano effortlessly, loved them all even if he didn't understand the innuendo.

But which of the statues would win? Losers always claimed that the rich neighborhoods, which could afford to pay fortunes to sculptors, triumphed, but this year there were high hopes for Port Rotes, even though its finer points were lost on me.

Flags fluttered over the ramparts of the ruined castle high on its spur. Processions of male *falleros* and female *falleras*—girls with combs in their polished hair, gold and silver threading their bright, full-skirted gowns—shimmied through the terraced streets of houses, apartments, and whitewashed cottages in the old part of the town. Tipsy bandsmen who accompanied the processions took their thumping music with them into heaving bars. Miles of *churros,* ropes of pastry cooked in oil and dunked in oceans of hot chocolate, were devoured at street stalls.

With Jonathan, blond hair tucked in his kerchief, I inspected the *falla,* erected by Port Rotes, which he had joined at the invitation of parents of school friends—his Spanish was as fluent as a four-year-old's is in any language, and he had adapted to classes in the kindergarten as readily as any other child. He gave the impression, to me at least, that he was in charge, translating captions in Valenciano, identifying lampooned dignitaries, and greeting Port Rotes stalwarts as though they were equals. Like all the other entries the statuary was made by out-of-town specialists and assembled by members of the *falla*. Papier-mâché caricatures of politicians and fishermen, clerks wearing pince-nez, red-kneed tourists, and wantons with breasts like blancmanges . . . thirty or so outrageous figures in one, gathered around a principal statue fifty feet high.

But Port Rotes never had a chance to shine, because that evening an errant firework set their *falla* ablaze long before its time. Diane and I watched helplessly as politicians melted, fishermen sank without trace, breasts drooped, pince-nez slid from ferret noses . . . Such was the heat of the fire that windows of apartments cracked and the lettering on the Bar Mediterraneo opposite the harbor across the street from the *falla* dribbled to the ground like molten sealing wax.

No one seemed to be unduly worried. The president of the Port Rotes *falla*, a robust young man, wiped the sweat from his face with his kerchief and announced: "Tomorrow we will have a truly Valencian *falla*."

And sure enough the other *falleros* and *falleras* worked all night—Jonathan was asleep in the car before we got home—and built a replica of a Valencian cottage with a typical pointed thatch, balanced on the charred bones of the original structure.

Some optimists thought the judges would find it in their hearts to make a special award, but adjudication was strict and Port Rotes came last.

Before the climactic act of arson on March 19 the replica of the cottage also caught fire, giving rise to speculation that there was an arsonist with a grudge against Port Rotes in town. The fire brigade arrived too late. By the time they had unraveled their hoses the *falleros* and *falleras* were cooking sausages in the embers of the cottage, Jonathan munching away in their midst.

I tried to commiserate with him but he stared at me incredulously. "It's the floats in the summer fiesta that really count. Would you like something to eat?"

He handed me a burned sausage.

N I N E

Long Live Death

etween them, two men knew most of the secrets of the village. One was the priest, the other the debt collector. The priest because miscreants poured out their sins to him in the confessional, the debt collector because he made it his business to pry into other people's lives.

The priest, Father Ignacio, middle-aged, balding, and plump, who wore a darned soutane and big boots, sometimes walked with his shoulders slumped as though he was bowed with the sins of mankind. Then a child would greet him, blow out a balloon of bubble gum, and dance away, or a couple of newlyweds would thank him for making them man and wife, and a smile would light his plump face and his big boots would take wing. He had come to the village five years ago from a dull town in La Mancha, the arid plateau in the center of Spain, but he was as near to God as any prelate in the Vatican.

Pepe, the debt collector, wasn't bowed: he was bent. But as spry as an Edwardian dandy. Rowing himself along with a silver-topped cane, a rose in his buttonhole, he confronted debtors with calculating courtesy.

He was employed by a debt-collecting agency in Alicante more than an hour's drive to the south, but he operated in small towns and villages. He lived inland near the town of Alcoy in a small, self-contained house that had about it an independent, debt-free air.

Pepe called at our house ten days before Easter. The scarlet flowers of the hibiscus bushes had opened for the first time in the spring sunshine. The carefree knife-grinder (known as Peter Pan because he announced his arrival with a flourish of notes on a flute), was in the driveway sharpening our kitchen knives; swallows perched on the telegraph wires like notes of music.

He appeared on the rear terrace, told Jones to sit—Jones uncharacteristically obeyed—and asked me: "Is Bernardo here?"

Bernardo was one of Emilio's part-time workers,—a protégé from Almería, 150 miles or so south of Alicante. Work had stopped yet again on the dining hall—progress virtually unchanged since the stoppage for rain—because the roofer was attending his grandmother's funeral on the Mediterranean island of Majorca, and Emilio who, as a craftsman, wouldn't stoop to menial work, had brought Bernardo to the house to do odd jobs.

In his mid-fifties, Bernardo wore rope-soled shoes tied at the ankles, blue dungarees, and the vague smile of a boozer lost in fermented visions. He was a wastrel, but he acted like a man with a secret and that gave him an air of mystery. This reputation hinged flimsily on his reticence about his past but it was sufficient to give him charisma.

I liked him because, during my years as a journalist, I had discovered that a peck of delinquency is sometimes more worthy than a pitcher of piety, and I speculated why he had become what he was. Through some congenital weakness beyond the vision of those who sit in judgment, perhaps. All that anyone knew about him was that he had been a traveling salesman of some sort before unspecified disaster had struck. Chatting with him one day while he cleaned and oiled Emilio's chisels, I sensed I was in the presence of a decent man. And close to discovering the origins of his plight. Then Emilio arrived at the house, dissipating the rapport.

What Bernardo's secret was gave rise to much speculation in the village. It reached its peak at the beginning of *Semana Santa,* Holy Week, when, like a punch-drunk boxer training for a comeback fight, he prepared for his regular annual disappearance, renouncing liquor, and exercising to prepare himself for the vigors of seasonal martyrdom.

Where he went no one knew. What was known was that when he returned his eyes were slitted with fatigue, his knees crusted with dried blood visible through rents in his Sunday-suit trousers. Obviously he had been participating in an act of contrition. For some heinous act in his youth or, perhaps, the sins of his fathers.

There was no shortage of such sinful acts in the 1936–39 Spanish Civil War when reputedly half a million died—it was still a disputed figure. Brother killed brother; Republicans slaughtered priests; Nationalists, in particular the Spanish Foreign Legion, whose motto was *Long Live Death*, butchered anyone who got in their way. Our region had been largely in the hands of Republicans. They were said to have herded supporters of Franco to their deaths over steep cliffs near Denia; later, when Franco's Nationalists triumphed, they allegedly marched Republicans over the same precipices.

Shame had long since been stashed away with medals and guns and uniforms in cellars and attics, in quicklime and in the Confessional, but it had never been totally expunged, as the old men in their berets resting on the benches beneath the acacia trees would doubtless confirm. Maybe the septuagenarian drooling over his grandchildren had gunned down clerics who'd been corraled in a bullring.

In our peaceful village it was sobering to reflect that inbred slaughter might occur again, as it almost did in 1981, when a *Guardia Civil* officer took over the *Cortes*, the Parliament in Madrid, at gunpoint and tanks came out on the streets of Valencia only sixty miles north of our new home. Whom would I have supported if King Juan Carlos hadn't appealed for calm and aborted the uprising? The Right or, like the International Brigade in 1936, the Left? Would the villagers have strung me up, a meddling foreigner, from the nearest orange tree? We recent invaders, British, German, and Dutch settlers, were not welcomed by everyone.

"Who wants Bernardo?" I asked Pepe. I had met the debt collector once before as he sat alone and ostracized in a bar and I wondered now if he could be the missing link in the story of Bernardo's decline.

"Tell him Pepe's here."

I didn't think that would have much impact: shout Pepe, Pedro, Paco, or Pablo in any square and half a dozen claimants would leap to their feet.

"Any other name?"

"Just Pepe—he knows me."

Bernardo was sweeping dust and debris from the floor of the dining hall. Like the village street cleaner, he used a palm frond. Unlike the street cleaner who used his dexterously, he moved as though in a trance, occasionally swigging from a bottle of cheap red wine.

I told him Pepe was here. He stood transfixed as the color drained from his face. I thought he was going to faint. He moaned and dropped the bottle. It smashed on the cement floor, not yet tiled, and wine spread as bright as blood.

"Tell him I'm not here." Wine dribbled from his mouth, coursing through the unshaven bristles on his chin.

"But you are here," Pepe said. He stood in the gap where the dividing wall of the original dining room, by the rear terrace, knocked down to allow open-plan access to the new dining hall, had been. "How are you?"

Bernardo didn't look too good. His hands shook, one bloodshot eye twitched. "What do you want?" he finally asked.

"I've brought you a message."

"A message?"

"*Señor* Garcia sends his regards."

"*Hostia!*" Bernardo shouted and, dropping the palm frond, ran through the doorless portal of the dining hall, kick-started his moped, and rode away, narrowly missing Diane, who had just arrived in the little secondhand Citroën she had just bought.

"What's wrong with Bernardo?" she asked as she walked through the same entrance.

"He's just met Pepe." I pointed at him. "Pepe's a debt collector."

"I'll make coffee for the three of us." I didn't particularly want to entertain him, but these days Diane viewed anyone with an unusual occupation as potential material for her magazine.

We drank our coffee on the terrace with madeleines baked in Denia, while Pepe explained in English how he extracted money from debtors, a job more conventionally undertaken by bruisers with jackets tight across bulging shoulders.

"I haunt them," he said, lighting a black-leafed Celtas cigarette.

"Haunt?" Diane, a natural interrogator whose green eyes would make a mute garrulous, regarded him quizzically.

"*Si, señora*. Wherever they go, I go. To church, grocery, restaurant, bank. To a club—" the euphemism, as we had discovered, for a brothel on the main road between Valencia and Alicante.

"How can that help?"

"When they emerge from their homes, I am there to greet them. When they return, I bid them goodnight."

"That's all?" Diane asked incredulously.

"I also bring them greetings from the man they owe money to. The man who has called the agency that employs me and pays me a percentage. '*Señor* X sends his regards,' I say, and they begin to sweat."

"And they pay up?"

"Oh, they pay all right. Would you"—addressing me—"want me at your side every moment of the day?" He coughed, his words emerging in wraps of smoke.

I didn't really want him at my side at any moment of the day. But *every* moment . . . I imagined him at mealtimes, during working hours, at intimate moments, blowing lungfuls of smoke at me.

"Are you haunting Bernardo?" I demanded.

"Why do you ask? Do *you* owe money?" His laugh was as dry as the rustling of parchment.

Diane said: "I can't believe Bernardo owes much money." Like me, she had developed a perverse affection for the reprobate. Perhaps she also imagined him in his youth when the future beckoned as brightly as a guiding star. And, like me, suspected that Pepe had resurrected some long-ago shame.

"I didn't say he did and I never reveal the name of a debtor," Pepe said reprovingly.

"But you make it pretty obvious," I said. Maybe enforcers who broke legs, not spirits, were preferable to Pepe.

Bernardo returned after his precipitous departure from the house and I asked him if he was making his annual Holy Week pilgrimage. He nodded sheepishly. Tentatively, I asked him why, in case Pepe's visit had jolted some escape valve in his conscience, but he merely offered me a crooked smile, murmured: "Don't worry about Pepe," and got on with his work.

On the morning after Palm Sunday, Bernardo came into the Bar Paraiso while I was drinking a *café solo*. He was obviously about to depart. He was shaved, sober, wearing a dark suit a couple of sizes too small for him, rents in the trousers from last year's odyssey now darned, and he was carrying a cardboard suitcase tied with string. With his black, unkempt hair freshly shorn and his cheeks pale where bristles had proliferated, he looked like a prisoner just released after a long stretch in the slammer.

I beckoned to him, but he shook his head. He asked for a glass of water, drank it, and headed in the direction of the railroad station. I wanted to accompany him, but I thought he would have been embarrassed.

I noticed Pepe outside the bar leaning on his cane, a yellow rose in the lapel of his tight-waisted jacket, peering after Bernardo's retreating figure. There was an air of menace about him that suggested more than mere debt collecting. Maybe he knew Bernardo's secret. Dormant journalistic instincts stirred and I felt that, for Bernardo's sake, I had to follow this through.

Diane and I decided to go away with Jonathan for Easter so, in the furtherance of my new mission, and without sharing it with Diane—we both believed in occasional private initiatives—I booked a room in a hotel at Bernardo's birthplace, Almería. On the coast, surrounded by near desert, it was also the location where Sergio Leone had filmed his spaghetti westerns.

We spent Good Friday morning on the old film set, now a tourist attraction, and watched two gun-slinging actors shoot it out in a last chance saloon. Later we went to church; in the evening, still walking tall like Clint Eastwood in *A Fistful of Dollars*, I took Diane and Jonathan to watch a Holy Week procession.

The leading penitents wore crimson, blue, or white silk robes and pointed conical hoods, eyes glittering behind slits. (The Ku Klux Klan were said to have copied their hoods from participants in Seville parades, who in turn had copied theirs from heretics condemned by the Inquisition.) Then floats carried by sweating pall-bearers swayed past, one with a figure of the Virgin Mary, cheeks touched with rouge, aloft, the other with Christ at the Crucifixion.

After the floats came more penitents, barefoot with chains around their ankles, carrying heavy crosses through the streets of Almería just as Jesus had once carried his in Jerusalem. Unlike those up front who were members of a religious confraternity, these were private sinners seeking atonement. Occasionally they half-heartedly lashed their backs over their shoulders with thongs.

Diane spotted him first. "Look!" She pointed.

Sure enough there was Bernardo, walking with his cross, knees like raw meat through the tears in his trousers. I was shocked but not surprised.

"How did they get like that?" I asked.

A prosperous-looking Spaniard in a black suit overheard me. "Some penitents who don't have robes perform their own rituals and *walk* part of the way on their knees. Your friend must have sinned a lot—he isn't even wearing pads."

I waved at Bernardo and detected a flicker of recognition in his eyes. Then he bowed his head, retreating into his personal torment.

Whatever that was. Was a woman somewhere accusing him of a terrible deception? Had he been responsible for a death? He was too young for the Civil War. I wondered if Father Ignacio knew. If he did he would never tell. No, my only possible source of enlightenment was Bernardo himself. Maybe I would be able to help him purge his torment—and persuade Pepe to haunt someone more resilient. I wasn't sure why I was so concerned about the village drunk. Maybe it was because I had seen so many of the rich and privileged get away with murder.

After the procession I told Diane I would see her back in the hotel and followed Bernardo to the flophouse where he was staying. I invited him, still wearing his torn trousers and a blue shirt, to a noisy café, where he devoured *merluza* (hake) and soggy chips, washed down with a bottle of mineral water.

I would understand, I said, if he wanted to keep the reason for his penitence to himself but if he wanted to share . . .

He sipped the mineral water and for a moment I saw him as he might have been before he had anesthetized himself with cheap wine: perhaps an office equipment salesman who had finally earned himself his own corner desk.

"Why," he asked, "do you want to dig up the past?"

"Because I'm a born inquisitor."

He smiled. "At least you're honest. And so am I—the truth is I didn't go that far on my knees." He spoke better English than he had in the house.

He ordered a flan, the quivering caramel custard dessert, and talked as though he had been stockpiling his guilt.

"Years ago I was a gambler. The lottery, poker, pelota . . . I ran up such frightening debts that my wife committed suicide rather than face the shame. This year a loan shark found me in the village and commissioned Pepe to retrieve the money I still owe." He stared at me across the table, his ravaged face angled to one side. "Now are you happy?"

"Not happy. But if I have helped . . ." I hoped that by extracting the confession, I had staunched his guilt, but I acknowledged to myself I had also been motivated by incurable nosiness.

"Talking to you was better than drinking two bottles of red wine," he said.

Surely the ultimate compliment from Bernardo.

When Bernardo appeared at our house a week later to sweep the dining hall once again, a specter from Spain's past was sitting on the terrace dunking a madeleine in his coffee.

With his black beret, baggy trousers, and rheumy eyes, Don

Eloy Morál Ortega, a far more cosmopolitan cleric than our Father Ignacio, looked like an onion seller. But forty years ago he had worn the black-and-silver uniform of the German SS and had a photograph of himself, wearing a peaked cap at an arrogant angle, to prove it.

He had been a chaplain to the Blue Division, the SS unit mustered by the Spanish dictator Francisco Franco as a gesture of thanks to Hitler for supporting his cause in the Civil War. Don Eloy had served with the division in Russia in World War II and later become Franco's personal chaplain.

Diane, hunting for material for *Lookout* magazine, had discovered that although he was in his eighties, he still conducted services in a chapel in Las Rotas, a wealthy residential area of Denia on a rocky stretch of coast close to the cliffs where Republicans and Nationalists had supposedly dispatched each other during the Civil War.

Bernardo, back on the sauce, came onto the terrace, saw the priest, took a hurried swig from his bottle, and fled: obviously one nemesis, Pepe, was sufficient unto the day.

Diane fed Don Eloy, from Burgos, a cathedral city in the north of Spain, another madeleine, switched on her cassette recorder, and started her interview. "How can a man of the cloth identify with Fascism?" He took off his beret, laid it beside his copy of the right-wing newspaper *ABC*, and told her.

"Our cause was to uphold Catholicism against Communism. There had been many atrocities by the Republicans. Churches burned, priests killed, innocents murdered indiscriminately—businessmen, Catholics, supporters of the Right—"

"But surely," Diane interrupted, "Franco's Nationalists also committed atrocities?"

The priest's fragile voice strengthened. "Vengeance is part of war. If your husband, wife, or child is killed, the hate will not go away until you avenge them."

The interview progressed at a lively pace until, toward the end, one key question remained. Had Franco during his last confession in the presence of Don Eloy admitted to crimes against mankind?

The frail little cleric refused to elaborate. But he did relay a few words from the dying dictator. "Tell me Don Eloy, to die . . . is it necessary to suffer so much?" Franco had asked.

"It is God's will."

"*Sí, sí*, it is in *His* hands."

Emilio appeared on the terrace. "Has anyone seen Bernardo?"

Diane said he had vanished when he saw Don Eloy. "Why?"

"Jesús just stopped by outside the gate," he said. "Someone's killed himself in the village."

Jaime, the barman at the Bar Paraiso, told me that Alfonso, a staid businessman whom I had known casually, had been found hanging from a rafter in his garage, a chair apparently kicked away from beneath the noose.

Conjecture about the suffering that had driven him to take his life was rife but no one ever put forward a reasonable explanation. Maybe there wasn't one, merely an aspect of despair outside the understanding of those of us who valued life. If anyone did know of a more substantial reason then it was Father Ignacio, but he shared such knowledge only with God. Personally I doubted whether there was one: as a reporter I had covered many suicides, and often the motive was an inability to cope with the savage swings of the human condition.

Certainly, Alfonso's death, although an isolated tragedy, was yet another illustration of the violent mood swings within Spain. An obvious tendency when you thought about it. Iberians, Celts, Phoenicians, Greeks, Romans, Vandals, Goths, Moors . . . all their legacies cut off and trapped in the great sack of land that embraced Portugal, knotted at the neck by the Pyrenees.

Two days later Alfonso was slotted into a cavity in the wall of the cemetery; if there was any protocol about not interring suicides in consecrated ground it was waived.

That evening in the village women in black were once more sitting in stiff-backed chairs outside their doorways, stitching table-cloths and weaving straw lampshades.

And Bernardo was asleep among the weeds and tomato plants in the yard beneath his attic, a smile on his face as tiny green lizards darted across his wine-stunned limbs.

Father Ignacio came into the bar a few days later and smiled conspiratorially at Pepe. You have debts to collect, the smile said, and I have sins to absolve. Neither of us will ever be out of a job.

A man with a creased neck scooped coins from the slot machine and, with measured application, put them back one by one.

The machine spewed more coins. He dropped them into his jacket pocket and headed for the bar to pay his bill.

I left the table where I had been scanning two of the regional daily newspapers, *Las Provincias* and *Información*, and approached Pepe, who looked as though he was getting ready to chase someone.

I sat at the table and asked: "Are you still 'haunting' Bernardo?" and when he guardedly said he might be, I asked him: "Did you know that Bernardo's debts drove his wife to suicide?"

Pepe shrugged. "The circumstances of debts are not my concern: all that matters to me is repayment of the money owed."

I handed him a page from my notebook on which I had written: *If you don't leave Bernardo alone I will haunt you to your grave.* Sometimes the written word was more effective than the spoken.

At the same moment the man with the creased neck started to leave. Stuffing the sheet of paper into a pocket, Pepe just made it to the door in front of him.

I read Pepe's lips. "*Señor X* sends his regards."

The debtor lowered his head and hurried down the street followed by Pepe rowing himself along with his cane.

Pepe would probably haunt him at *almuerzo*, the morning snack, at lunch, at *merienda,* the afternoon snack, and maybe at a 'club' where his spectral presence would be singularly unnerving. Doubtless the debtor would ultimately pay up.

I finished my coffee and got up to leave. Somehow I doubted whether Pepe would continue haunting Bernardo—a spook wouldn't want a specter at his own graveside.

"Señor!" Jaime, the diminutive barman, left the coffee machine. "Pepe forgot to pay his bill."

I settled Pepe's debt and said: "Next time you see him tell him *Señor* Derek sends his regards."

T E N

Pursued by a Poet
in the City of Light

The funeral that had taken our roofer, Vicente, to the Mediterranean island of Majorca had been anticipated prematurely: his grandmother was still alive and unwilling to be buried. Rather than waste the fare, he had decided to stay to await developments. As there were several centenarians on the group of islands, the Balearics, and his grandmother was a mere eighty-five, his decision did not bode well for the dining hall roof.

While we waited for Vicente to return, we decided to take a look at the frontiers of what we had decided was our homeland. The cities of Valencia to the north and Alicante to the south. To the east the Mediterranean coast, known as the Costa Blanca and, fifty to 150 miles out to sea, like an armada poised to invade, the Balearic Islands—Majorca, Menorca, Formentera, and Ibiza, the latter linked to Denia by a rusty white ferry. A haze of sierras and plains, sometimes blurred by rain, unfolded inland, so we gave up on them, consigning the rest of Spain to the "other side of the hills."

First Diane and I investigated "this side" of the hills, their flanks covered with pine, prickly oak, and gorse, finding villages where V-necks of ocean were just visible in the distance, painted pigeons wheeled in blue skies, and the air was redolent of jasmine and goats, stopping at bars with patios where they cooked *paellas* on fires laid with twigs of rosemary and served hunks of bread and *alioli* and small earthenware pitchers of red wine as raw as moonshine.

Inhabitants were sparse in the streets, but behind the brass-studded doors and bars and crouching shops, life was as vigorous as it was in any street market, fading only when the afternoon *siesta* stilled the wagging tongues.

Heavy with food and wine, we ambled along shepherds' trails and dried-up riverbeds that still drained floodwater, strewn with boulders and clotted with pink and white oleander blossoms, before driving back to our house, where swallows skinny-dipped in the pool and bracts of bougainvillea had blown into mauve drifts on the terrace.

Then Diane's father died from a heart attack in Montreal. We decided that I would stay in Spain to keep an eye on the builders and complete some paperwork connected with the house while she flew with Jonathan to Canada.

I thought I might have to drive to Valencia, one of the outposts of our homeland, for the paperwork.

We had already been there to buy makeshift furniture. Wandered around its baroque facades; attended the outdoor meeting of the Water Tribunal, convened every Thursday at noon since 1350, where members in black smocks passed judgment on market gardeners' disputes over water rights; knelt in the fourteenth-century cathedral with its museum, often claimed to be the home of the Holy Grail, Christ's chalice at the Last Supper. But I was summoned instead to a lawyer's office in another outpost, Alicante, and traveled there with an uninvited companion, a dotty poet.

Like most poets he was poor. He wandered the streets of Denia—no one seemed to know where he had come from—and sold his poems for a few pesetas to panting suitors, sighing girls, and cheating husbands. Once when I had been detained in a bar and was late for lunch, I bought one of his sonnets in Valenciano and gave it to Diane. She read it, tore it into small pieces, shouted "Bastard!" and strode out of the house. I never found out why.

On a drowsy May afternoon I packed a bag and made my way to the railroad station, not much bigger than a bus shelter. And there was the poet, small and middle-aged, sparse hair uncombed, wet-eyed gaze vague.

He stood at one end of the platform waiting for the train, ambitiously called the Costa Blanca Express—it took two hours and nine minutes to traverse fifty-six miles, thirty-seven stations and halts, from Denia to Alicante. A swallowtail butterfly fluttered along the track. He noticed it and scribbled energetically in a red notebook.

Five minutes until the train was due.

I read a notice on a concrete pillar: THIS STATION IS A REQUEST STOP. THE TRAIN WILL NOT STOP AT THIS STATION UNLESS YOU SIGNAL THE DRIVER TO STOP FROM THE PLATFORM.

In fact it arrived seven minutes late at five-fifty-five.

As one, the poet and I stuck out our hands, balancing like two comics trying to end their vaudeville act on a note of artistic harmony.

The two coaches stopped, hissing and throbbing. We boarded one of them, sitting opposite each other surrounded by schoolchildren eating sunflower seeds.

"*Sí, señor?*" The young conductor, crisply dressed in blue trousers and shirt, stood beside me, keeping an eye on the children in case they dropped the striped black-and-white husks of the seeds on the floor.

I bought a ticket to Alicante.

The little train burrowed south through the citrus groves, skirting Montgo, granite gray on the side facing our house, sienna on this, the other side, never far from the coast.

First stop Gata de Gorgos, a small town that conducted its business on the N332 highway, its private life in squeezed streets and somnolent squares. That business was selling cane and wicker furniture, some of it made in China, in scores of cramped shops.

A young German couple boarded accompanied by a wicker donkey. The husband was massively built with thighs like hams protruding from khaki shorts and an innocent, sun-reddened face; his wife was Pekinese pretty, and bored-looking.

He patted the donkey, blew her a kiss, and began to take photographs through the open window with a 35mm camera.

The train passed over an arched bridge across a gorge, the sort that saboteurs dream about. The husband clicked away. He photographed scrub, sheep, and the inside of a tunnel. Anything pictorially stimulating eluded him, worthwhile shots materializing as he changed the film, disappearing around a curve as he took aim.

We were in guerrilla-style country now: rust-colored precipices holed like Gruyère cheese with caves. Cold air breathed through the windows as we dived through tunnels.

The poet licked his pencil and wrote industriously, glancing at me as though we were in telepathic communication.

The German photographed a cement quarry. As he did so, his wife caught my gaze and raised her eyebrows. What lies ahead? the eyebrows asked. Long winter nights showing slides to neighbors? Pictures of prickly oak, sheep, and quarries? Heaps of photo albums to show our grandchildren? Have I done the right thing marrying this man? the eyebrows asked.

The train plunged into another tunnel and emerged at the town of Teulada, where it waited for a small boy running toward it across a field of knee-high vines.

To the left I saw the sea at Calpe and, rearing up from it like a miniature Gibraltar, an isthmus named Ifach.

The German finally sat down, pointed at the wicker donkey, and said to me: "Such industry is good. Local products I like."

I debated whether to tell him the donkey might have been made in Shanghai. No—I suspected a lot of disappointment lay ahead of him.

He, his wife, and the donkey alighted at Altea, a coastal hill town clustered around a church with a blue dome like a glazed pincushion. On the platform he took a picture of me through the window. His wife raised her eyebrows and then they were gone.

They were replaced by an American family who took over one corner of the carriage. Two freckled girls, a plump mother and a handsome father with graying hair who looked like an Italian film star. They sat enveloped together in an aura of unity.

The hotels and apartment blocks of Benidorm halfway to Alicante crowded the skyline on the Mediterranean side of the track. Wherever you met a Spaniard here he would say: "You should have seen it thirty years ago," just as residents in other parts of the world peer at torrential rain and say: "You should have been here last week. Boy, was it ever hot . . ."

What the Spaniards meant was that two decades ago Benidorm was a fishing village and now look at it. It had become the Elysium of pensioners who had worked hard all their lives, an affordable seaside resort plucked from rainswept northern shores and deposited in the sunshine, sauce bottles still on the café tables.

The poor man's Miami Beach, it hugged the coast for about a mile. Planeloads of Brits were the strike force, but there were plenty of support groups from other European countries, among them retired Spaniards from the north who meekly followed shepherding couriers all day but in the evenings hurled themselves around their hotel dance floors like whirling dervishes.

The train swung to the right, shook off Benidorm, and bolted across clay-colored scrub.

At Villajoyosa it waited for an oncoming train to pass it on a stretch of double track. Beyond the station, houses painted in pastel colors swept down to the sea. The stationmaster, wearing a red cap and brandishing a flag, waved us on; we cantered through wild hills waiting for Sioux or Apache to appear on their crests and approached the beaches outside Alicante.

Some grand villas now, one with Grecian columns. Then a gully occupied by a herd of goats, holiday chalets giving way to a scimitar of pale sand deserted except for a plump woman in a bikini performing daunting exercises beside the waves.

The engine gave a final hoot and came to a halt in the beautiful, blood-stained city of Alicante, the City of Light, according to the Romans.

The poet tore a page from his notebook, thrust it in my hand, and made off along the platform. I asked an elegant, middle-aged Spaniard who was leaving the train what the words written in Valenciano meant. He read them and glanced at me strangely. "They say 'All life is bullshit,' " he said, and hurried away.

In the bar of the station, as neat as a breast-pocket handkerchief, I read about Alicante in an antique Baedeker I had bought.

Behind the bar a muscular Spaniard with a bandaged hand served beer, strawberry flan, and tortillas—solid potato-based omelets that bore no relation to their Mexican cousins—and cut slices of paper-thin Serrano ham. In the tiny kitchen a pretty girl with a pale face chopped anemic steaks.

Alicante, I read, sipping a beer, had been involved in many wars. The War of Spanish Succession, the Peninsular War . . .

In the kitchen the pale girl took a vicious swipe at a steak, getting her thumb out of the way just in time.

I ordered a slice of strawberry flan and consulted a more recent book about Alicante's role in the Civil War. The dashing young leader of the fascist Falange, José Antonio Primo de Rivera, had been executed by firing squad here; in 1939 Republican refugees trying to flee by boat from Franco's troops had committed suicide when they realized there was no escape.

The girl aimed a blow at a chop, the barman winced and fingered his bandaged hand: I ate the last strawberry in my slice of flan.

I walked along the promenade, café to the right, beach to the left. A junkie and a scruffy dog lay asleep under a palm tree.

Opposite the harbor, where yachts lay at rest in the luminous sunlight for which Alicante was famous, I entered the Paseo de la Explanada, Alicante's tiara, a pedestrian walkabout unsurpassed in elegance anywhere in Spain, an avenue paved with swirls of red, cream, and black marble, hedged with indolent palms.

Aging Spanish dudes sat on benches like Mafia godfathers clinching deals, mottled hands wagging, prodding, fisting.

A prayer of nuns in gray drifted around the bandstand where the municipal band played during fiestas and on weekends. Girls with shiny hair and young men, truculently self-conscious, traded smiles in rehearsal for the evening *paseo,* the twilight parade that was the prelude to serious courtship. Pigeons pouted beside flowerbeds filled with pansies. A small girl dropped an ice cream cornet and squashed it with her foot, as though she were finishing off a wounded beetle. Through the palms I glimpsed elegant terraces beneath the walls of Santa Barbara castle.

After I had seen the lawyer about the house, I adjourned to a bar for *tapas:* prawns in pink armor, mussels, salted tuna, meatballs, beans in thick sauce, snails, *empanadillas,* squid and clams and slices of Manchego cheese in oil.

In one corner stood a collection of antique radios and wind-up phonographs. On the bar among the *tapas* an ancient cash register. On the wall signed photographs of Manolete, the bullfighter, whose melancholy eyes seemed to accept his fate on the horns of a bull as inevitable; another matador beside him, the swashbuckling El Cordobés. There too were Salvador Dalí and Ernest Hemingway.

The owner of the bar, Pepe Gallego, a silver-haired man of commanding height, light on his feet, with sun spots on his temples, fiddled aimlessly with the knobs of an old wireless, its vocal chords wasted long ago.

"Tomorrow," he said, "I will tell you about Hemingway and Dalí."

"Why not today?"

"Because I have to think." He tapped his sun spots with his finger and ordered a Scotch for himself and a finger of chilled sherry for me.

"I may not be here tomorrow."

"Then you will miss revelations."

I strolled to the old quarter to explore. By day it was a hungover labyrinth. Bar girls wearing slippers sat on doorsteps, talking about their children and their wayward pimps.

Here, a few hours earlier, adventure and sexual promise, lit by the stars, lubricated by drugs and alcohol, had spilled onto the thin streets. Here disease had been sown, marriages broken, wallets lifted.

A small bandit with a walnut face and hair dyed the color of plum juice leaped from a doorway and grabbed my shoulderbag.

"I want it," he said.

"You can't have it."

"I have a knife."

He pulled and I pulled.

"I must have it," he said.

"Sorry."

He gave the shoulder strap another tug but the Taiwan plastic was made of stern stuff.

Finally he let go and, tears gathering in his eyes, said: "I must have money."

"For a fix?"

"No fix."

I gave him one hundred pesetas and comforted myself that instead of drugs he might buy a shot of plum-colored dye.

I woke the following morning in a hostel overlooking a square where young men with motorcycles cradled their crash helmets like babies while they chatted to girls in jeans, undecided whether to stay another day and night in this patrician city, largely ignored by tourists hell-bent on reaching the beaches of Benidorm, or whether to catch the next train home.

I had breakfast, freshly squeezed orange juice, a cup of hot chocolate, and toast smeared with grated tomato at a boulevard café beneath the palm trees in the Paseo de la Explanada, its marble floor still wet from its early morning rinse.

Smoky clouds hurried in from the sea. The sunlight had a silvery luster to it. A gypsy urchin in a torn frock stuck out her small and grubby hand and I gave her the change from my breakfast, one hundred pesetas or so. She stared at the coins incredulously before dancing away.

I debated whether to stay. The problem was that Diane and I believed that sharing was everything, and here I was alone on a marble avenue designed to be shared.

I went back to the hotel, half packed my bag, and stared out of the bedroom window still undecided. There on a bench in the square below was the poet, scribbling in his red notebook, a fairly alarming spectacle because it raised the possibility that he had been following me.

I had no doubt that whatever he was writing was intended for me. (I learned later that he saw the two of us as a literary duet and I had to enlist Emilio to disillusion him.)

But he served his purpose: he convinced me I should go home and share the City of Light (and the rest of Spain) with Diane and Jonathan some other time, certainly not now with a stalker who thought life was bullshit.

I finished packing, paid the bill, left the hostel by the rear exit, and caught a taxi to the railroad station.

As the little train gathered speed, hooting impatiently, the poet appeared on the platform waving his notebook. I waved back and relaxed among another gaggle of schoolchildren nibbling sunflower seeds.

ELEVEN

Honeymooners and Hoofers

Diane was only just coming to terms with the premature death of her father, an extrovert French Canadian whom she had adored, and I decided that a therapeutic visit to one of the Mediterranean island outposts of our new "homeland" would be timely while Jonathan stayed for a couple of days with his friend Arturo.

I chose Majorca and bought tickets for a three-day break there. What the travel agent didn't tell me was that the package deal was primarily for honeymoon couples.

And there they were at Valencia airport canoodling and nibbling each other's ears, a convention of lovebirds assembled by Cupid and an enterprising tour operator.

As the jet flew over the 110 miles of sparkling sea between mainland Spain and Majorca, cooing stewardesses served fizzy white wine. The twenty-five or so couples touched glasses and swore undying devotion and we did the same.

I was disturbed, though, by the couple sitting beside us, Federico and Cristina. He was as blond and as routinely handsome as a California tennis coach, she was a pale wallflower from a village near Valencia. How they had met I couldn't imagine, only that I wouldn't bet on their finishing the obstacle course of marriage, or the honeymoon for that matter.

The couple on the other side of the aisle appeared to be better prospects for the good name of matrimony. He had the look of a man of the fields, face wind-whipped and sun-dried; she looked amiably prepared for the hardships and togetherness that lay ahead. Throughout the fifty-minute flight they stared into each other's eyes, whispered, and sipped wine from the same glass.

From the airport at Palma, the capital of Majorca, its bay clustered with resorts as thick as barnacles, we were driven in a minibus to various hotels.

Both Federico and Cristina and the couple from across the aisle, Juan and Marisa, were in the same hotel as we were on the waterfront.

While Diane was getting ready to go out to a show—part of the package—I went down to the pristine white bar and ordered a Scotch. Federico came down a couple of minutes later and ordered a large brandy.

I greeted him: we had after all shared air space.

He nodded and stared into his glass like a busted financier during the Wall Street Crash.

I persevered. "Are you coming to the show?"

"Maybe." He ran his fingers through his hair. He was wearing a white suit and an open-neck cream shirt and looked ready for aprés tennis action rather than a night of bliss with his bride.

Cristina joined him. She wore a blue short-sleeve dress and sat demurely beside him. He bought her a mineral water. They didn't speak. Diane had nicknamed them the Unlikely Couple, Juan and Marisa the Likely Couple.

The Likely Couple came into the bar. He ordered a couple of Cokes and they sat together at a table gazing at the yachts in the harbor, nuzzling and whispering.

Diane joined us and we all piled into the minibus. The driver picked up couples from the other hotels and took off on a tour of Palma, a sophisticated city with a looming Gothic cathedral, as black as storm clouds in the evening sky.

The show was staged in a club with raised seats at the rear like a small movie house. Drinks were served, the lights were doused, and spotlights picked out the two principals.

I was unprepared for what followed. So were the other couples. Maybe I should have guessed—it *was* staged for honeymooners—but I thought some of the Puritanism from the Franco era, when even bikinis were banned on beaches, still lingered.

Not in the view of the show's impresario it didn't. Without preliminaries the couple, a lithe young man with oiled, blue-black hair and his partner, an older, buxom brunette, stripped off their robes, lay naked on a pile of cushions and began to perform simulated sex.

The effect this had on the honeymooners must have been traumatic. Many of the girls who came from villages where morals were still as strict as health farm menus were probably virgins. And their bridegrooms' experience was most likely limited to furtive one-night stands—sexual activity in some rural areas was still discouraged outside marriage.

Whatever their experience, it must have seemed to them that true love could be consummated with a few yelps and shouts and no physical contact. A disheartening prospect for the night ahead.

I gave it a couple of minutes before indulging in an act of such histrionic prudishness that I surprised myself. I stood up, announced grandly, "I don't think we need to put up with any more of this," and led the way out.

The two stars of the cabaret lay back on their cushions panting. The other couples followed Diane and myself into the foyer.

The club owner protested but relented when I told him that if he didn't let everyone leave without paying for their drinks I would report him to the police for staging a lewd act.

Couples dispersed pensively.

The following morning I rented a baby Seat and we toured the island with its mountains in the northwest splashed with scarlet poppies and yellow wattle, its beaches on the east coast where tourism was growing as abundantly as the poppies, and the plains and valleys of the interior ripe with almond, apricot, orange, and lemon orchards.

Wherever we stopped, the Unlikely Couple, Federico and Cristina, materialized like pictures in pop-up children's books: at Validemosa where in 1838–39, Chopin stayed with his lover, the trouser-wearing authoress George Sand; in the village of Deja, home of the English poet Robert Graves until his death in 1985.

Federico greeted me gruffly when, that was, he condescended to acknowledge me at all. His bride stared at us sadly, whispering a few words in Valenciano. I feared the worst: her expectations of married love had been sent packing by the remote control coupling in the Palma club. Or maybe their visitations indicated some more complex trauma.

The minibus picked us up at the hotel after lunch on the third and last day of the vacation.

Federico was beaming, the smile of the accomplished lover who has scored yet again. The head of his bride, hand tucked under his arm, was bowed but at an angle of fulfilled supplication.

Federico winked at me, an unnerving experience.

Next into the minibus were the Likely Couple, Juan and Marisa.

He was staring ahead of him like an automaton, she was dabbing her eyes with a tissue.

My journalistic instincts got the better of me at the airport. I approached Federico in the check-in line.

"What happened?" I asked him.

"At first I was scared," he said in hesitant English. "Cristina is the daughter of the mayor in the village where she lives. A lady! What am I? A waiter! I worried the honeymoon wouldn't work out . . ."

I stared at him in astonishment. "*You* had a complex?"

"Like I say, I was worried."

"So what changed everything?"

"You did," he said. And before I could express incredulity: "You and your wife, you seemed so happy together. You know, sharing . . . So we followed you. And I pointed at you and said to Christina, 'See, that is what we will be like in the years to come.' And finally last night she said she love me and, well . . . everything was all right." He shook my hand.

There were flaws in his reasoning—I wasn't a waiter and Diane wasn't a mayor's daughter—but I was pleased to hear that, unwittingly, we had acted as marriage guidance counselors.

"Tell me one thing," I said, "and I will leave here a happy man. You do play tennis, don't you?" I had been so wrong about him that having always seen him as a tennis coach, wanted to salvage some pride.

He frowned. "Never in my life, *señor*. But I do play pool. I give you a game? We play for money. Say five hundred pesetas?"

I left them and made my way to the end of the line where the Likely Couple were standing apart like an estranged husband and wife outside a divorce court.

"I'm sorry to bother you—" I began.

Marisa interrupted. "Don't be sorry. Never be sorry in the presence of this man. He is a pig!"

"But what—"

"He was married before," she said. "That's what."

"So was I. But Diane and I are very happy now."

"But you told your wife you had been married before. This man"—jabbing her thumb toward Juan—"didn't tell me until last night. It is over, everything is over."

Her husband stared at his big countryman's hands, rubbing the thumb and forefinger of one of them together as though he was sowing seed.

I also took Diane to a couple of coastal towns between Alicante and Valencia, including Jávea in the south. In fact it comprised three towns—the old neighborhood, its terrace houses, wearing wrought-iron grilles like jewelry, gathered around a fortified Gothic church, the small port beside a beach where waves left hissing messages on the shingle, and the Arenal beach, a stretch of sand separated from the street by cafés and gift shops perfumed by melting ice cream and tanning oil.

We went to Gandia on the way north to Valencia, to the original town complete with ducal palace where a branch of the Borgia dynasty once lived, Pedro Luis, brother of the bad and beautiful Lucretia among them. And to its sandy beach two and a half miles away, laundered daily by the municipal valet service and guarded by sentinel apartment blocks.

We also made a second visit to Benidorm between Javea and Alicante, a sprawl of beachside skyscrapers colonized by the British.

We booked into a flaky hotel where a palm court ensemble played Strauss waltzes while middle-aged women knitted contentedly and their husbands read the British tabloids.

If we wanted to see more life, a girl at reception told us in fractured English, we should go to a hotel specializing in Spanish package deals. "Wow, you should see them old guys, and grannies from the north," she said. "They're something else." She flapped one hand and returned to the shawl she was crocheting.

We took an evening stroll along the seafront beside a flat beach lined with palm trees. Mature couples, British, German, Dutch, Scandinavian, and Spanish sauntered arm in arm, reminding me of the vacations of my childhood when orchestras played Gilbert and Sullivan in the bandstands and the air smelled of petunias and night-scented stock.

Diane and I ate fish and chips drenched in vinegar and dusted with salt in paper bags wrapped in newspaper. Behind us high-rise apartment blocks stretched toward the coast road.

We had a beer in one of the scores of pubs and went looking for grandpa and granny action. Music led us to it—*Rock Around the Clock!*

The dance floor in the hotel was heaving with bodies jiving to the beat of a piano played by a woman who looked like Shelley Winters. The youngest dancer was fifty-five or so.

As we entered, the floor cleared for one couple. A retired coal miner by the look of him, from Asturias, the cider-drinking region in the north of Spain, broad-shouldered and bow-legged with a jolly, seamed face. She was fiftyish, gray-haired and bouncy, wearing a short skirt and sneakers.

They started well enough. She twirled and spun and the spectators clapped as the steps became more ambitious. Too ambitious. She suddenly emerged from between his legs, skidded on a discarded slice of lemon and, arms outstretched, ran toward me like a wife greeting her soldier husband after a long war.

I steadied her then held up one arm. She pirouetted beneath my hand and returned to her husband, who was standing on the dance floor, head lowered, looking for her as though an illusionist had spirited her away.

The spectators, assuming they had witnessed a set piece, applauded wildly.

Diane and I moved on to an area of bars and discos where

younger vacationers besported themselves until dawn and beyond. Rival gusts of music billowed onto the street; bouncers stood beside touts beckoning passersby into dark depths where the first drink was always free. The touts were not forthcoming about the price of the second.

Outside one such establishment a bouncer was attacking two crew-cut teenagers with a baseball bat. He was a very small bouncer but his bat was big enough and he was flailing it with such energy that everyone on the sidewalk was threatened.

I caught the bat on a backward swing and asked him why he was attacking the two teenagers.

"They insulted my mother," he said, adding: "I am from Cuba," as if that explained everything.

As we neared our hotel we saw some British youths wearing boots leaping along the rooftops of a line of parked cars. They ran away as a police car skidded to a halt, siren wailing—into the arms of riot police who had anticipated their escape route. The police whacked them halfheartedly with batons, bundled them into a truck, and drove them to the police station, small fry in a routine night's haul.

Palm fronds rustled in a nocturnal breeze . . . waves murmured on the beach . . . the stars glimmered. Back at the hotel I fell instantly asleep and dreamed that jiving to the beat of Bill Haley and the Comets, I emulated the coal miner and threw Diane across the floor.

Breakfast. Pitchers of orange cordial, a buffet with fried eggs, bacon, sausages, tomatoes, and baked beans on offer; toast, butter, and plum jam; urns of scalding tea, and sachets of instant coffee, sugar, and sweeteners.

I have a weakness for hotel breakfasts and helped myself to everything from the buffet. Diane took one egg and a slice of bacon.

We were joined at the plastic-topped table by a middle-aged American couple from the Midwest. He owned an agricultural machinery factory and they were spending the first three months of his retirement touring Europe. They had visited Britain and France, with Italy and Greece lying in wait, but so far Spain got their vote.

"The people are so friendly," said Mary, small and quick with blue-rinse watch-spring curls.

"Great golf," said her husband, Charlie, lanky with a wise face, not much hair, and cornflower-blue eyes.

"Charlie's playing golf this morning," Mary said. "I'm doing aerobics on the beach. Do you play golf?" she asked me, and when I shook my head: "So why don't you both join me on the beach?"

Ever the party pooper, I shook my head.

Diane regarded me suspiciously. "So what are you doing?" she asked.

"I'm going dancing," I said. "You have a workout."

I checked out the two of them on the beach, dutifully following the commands of a blond Amazonian in a red track suit—Diane seemed to be one grunt behind pensioners twice her age—bought a newspaper, and headed for a seafront café that staged ballroom dancing from ten A.M. onward.

I didn't intend to dance, just to make notes for a possible magazine feature. From the café I could see families with children staking claims on the beach beneath umbrellas with lethal spikes. A few women were topless, white breasts aimed at the sun.

I ordered a coffee and watched an elderly couple fox-trotting to the accompaniment of an electric organ played by a bored musician with extravagant sideburns. They looked hypnotically absorbed with each other, transported back to the soft-shoe rhythms of their youth.

The organist started to play a tango, "Jealousy" "Would you like to dance?" I looked up from my newspaper. A tall dark-haired woman in her forties with an arched back, wearing a blue polka-dot dress, smiled at me nervously.

"I'm sorry—"

"Please." She leaned forward and whispered: "It's a bet." I gathered from her accent that she was from Birmingham in the Midlands of England.

"What sort of a bet?" I asked.

"That I wouldn't have the nerve to ask you and even if I did you'd refuse. You won't, will you?"

"How much did you bet?" I had never been much of a dancer—I was always apprehensive about going backward—but I did enjoy the occasional wager.

"A hundred pesetas," she said. "Not much, I know, but—"

"Why me?"—fishing for a compliment.

"Well, you are the only man sitting by himself."

She held out a slim hand heavy with rings and madness overtook me. I had never been able to master a basic quickstep let alone a tango, but the age of chivalry was not dead. I stood and followed her onto the floor.

She immediately took command. Strutting, gliding, tossing her head imperiously. She was a born-again Ginger Rogers, accompanied by a scruffy apology for Fred Astaire wearing jeans, a faded blue shirt, and tennis shoes that squeaked on the floor.

All went well enough until I found myself being propelled *backward*.

Panic overcame me and I tensed my muscles to try and control the momentum. It was like trying to plunge a manual gearshift from reverse directly into first. Pain stabbed my back.

Luckily the dance ended at that moment. My partner shouted: *"Olé!"* and strode back to her table to collect her winnings from two men with white hair and mahogany tans.

I limped back to my coffee and newspaper. The organist gave me a pitying, be-your-age look, slotted a Glenn Miller cassette into a play-deck, and headed for the bar.

When I got back to the hotel, Diane was hobbling across the foyer to the elevator, one hand pressed to the small of her back.

I reached her in a few faltering strides like a marathon runner about to collapse as he reenters a stadium. "What happened to you?" I asked.

"Those damned exercises," she said. "When I touched my toes a pain shot up my back like a blowtorch. And do you know what that butch bitch in charge of us said?"

"Don't be a wimp?"

"How do you know that?"

"It's what I would have said."

We helped each other into the elevator watched sympathetically by pensioners as fit as lifeguards.

We drove home that afternoon, to Jonathan, Jones, and the two cats, and in the evening Diane and I walked painfully to the end of the garden and listened to night settling. A nightingale singing, the chirrup of cicadas, the whisper of bats' wings . . .

Misadventures apart, the exploration of our territory had, I felt, been an unqualified success. We had flown to the island of Majorca and observed tourism squeezing its beauty. We had driven to the resorts of Gandia, where apartment blocks rose like a towering sea wall, and to Jávea, so British that it might have been an extension of imperial India.

But paradoxically it was Benidorm that had the most profound effect on us. It had not merely reaffirmed our belief that resort life wasn't our style: it had reminded us that outside our citrus groves there were other Spains, gracious and raucous, steel-bladed and sentimental, raw-tongued or eloquently muted.

A snatch of *cante jondo,* the tragic refrains of flamenco, issuing from a bar had reminded us that at Guadix, overlooking Granada, gypsies still lived in caves, some as neat at duplexes, others as primitive as foxes' lairs. The exuberant pensioners from the north had brought with them images of both alpine hardship dictated by the

health of a few head of livestock and the piston thud of heavy industry in cities such as Bilbao.

None of this was the stuff of brochure Spain.

The diversity of Benidorm's temporary Spanish immigrants—
pensioners often stayed the whole winter at knock-down tariffs—
also stirred the contradictory bones of Spain's blood-stained history.

Despite all the wars sparked by insurgents, territorial squabbles,
and royal succession, Jews and Arabs had lived amicably together for
three centuries—until the Christians finally conquered the Moors,
and in 1492 expelled the Jews or forced them during the Inquisition
to convert to Christianity. Perhaps it would benefit today's peace-
makers in the Middle East to study those three-hundred years of
medieval camaraderie.

Becalmed among the orange and lemon trees behind the Costa
Blanca, it was easy to forget that we lived in a still turbulent land,
and we resolved that evening to journey further afield again.

TWELVE

The Caliph and
the Napkin Man

The heat took its first swipe at the village at
the beginning of June. The ears of donkeys
hauling carts drooped; schools went onto half
days; the fans of the old women in the church
flapped as frantically as the wings of trapped birds.

A van delivered ice. The fishmonger made
his rounds every week in his van, announcing his
arrival with blasts on his horn. Gypsies sold red-
mouthed, black-toothed watermelons as big as
beach balls.

On roadsides the yellow spires of mi-
gnonette and mauve viper's bugloss wilted and
died. At night glowworms switched on their
lights on drystone walls.

Such was the heat that the sight of a Moor

striding along the main street, manifestly cross, swiping at flies with a sword, didn't astonish me. Maybe he was a mirage.

He turned into the Bar Paraiso with a flounce of his silky red-and-white robe. As I followed him, the roar of the coffee machine subsided and the minute hand of the wall clock slipped backward: stay there long enough and it would be yesterday.

The Moor, it soon became apparent, wasn't illusory. He ordered a Dyk whisky, Spain's answer to Scotch, tossed it back, and addressed a handful of regular customers. "What are you staring at?"

The voice was familiar. So was the truculent figure wearing the turban and exotic finery.

"Emilio," I said, "what the hell are you doing?"

Rehearsing, it transpired, for the Moors and Christians, a fiesta in which locals dressed as Moors from North Africa, who flourished in Spain for seven hundred years, and Christians, who finally vanquished them in the fifteenth century, marched down Denia's main street and staged a mock battle.

The fiestas were held elsewhere—the most ambitious in Alcoy, fifty miles away—with processions of combatants, Christians in armor and chain mail, and swaggering Moors, accompanied by the drumbeat and cymbal crash of marching bands.

There was a deafening battle with swords and muskets until finally the keys of the castle were handed over to the Christians. Recently in a nearby town, so I was told, the Moorish leaders shouted: "Come and get them." The battle took a realistic turn and members of both armies ended up in the hospital.

Although the Moors had lost their holdings more than five hundred years ago, their presence was still tangible in the region, not on the majestic scale of the Alhambra in Granada, but in the fallen fruit of history. You could see stone walls built to contain cultivated terraces on steep hillsides, alleys that had once led to the souk, and young men with hawkish faces who looked as though they should have been riding Arab stallions through the Atlas mountains in North Africa.

It was all much more evocative than the legacies of the Iberians, Phoenicians, Greeks, Romans, and Visigoths who had all sojourned in Spain, probably because the Moorish presence was more recent.

Emilio told me he had always wanted to take the part of a Christian: predictably perverse because most participants wanted to be Moors, not because they felt any allegiance to them, simply because the passage of time had infused them with a roguish quality, probably spurious.

"Why?" I asked.

Emilio gripped his plastic sword. "Because they won."

Only that week he had tried to defect to the Christians, he said, but they wouldn't have him. Which, I suppose, accounted for his bad temper.

He ordered another whisky and lit a flaking cigar. "You like a bet, *Señor* Derek?"

"If the odds are right."

"Then be here next week at eleven in the morning—I've organized an arm-wrestling contest."

A challenge, I decided, that would have to be approached warily if Emilio was in charge. I respected him these days, but he was unpredictable just the same.

He picked up his sword and strode out of the bar. On the wall the hands of the clock retreated another minute.

We had now been living in Spain for six months, and most of the excuses for not improving our Spanish had evaporated. We enrolled for classes at an institute in Denia. Diane was relatively fluent, but I had always struggled, grateful to those Spaniards who spoke a little English or those, like Emilio, who spoke a great deal.

One Monday morning we drove into town in Diane's little secondhand Citroën, primrose yellow and liberally dented, for our first
lesson. We took the back lanes passing through citrus groves, first
oranges then tangerines and mandarins.

Once when Denia had been the center of the raisin trade, this
corner of Spain had been planted with far more grapevines. British
traders had besported themselves in the town's brothels and casinos
while the grapes dried, but at the turn of this century a disease, phylloxera, had killed the vines and the British had departed, not bother-
ing to return when some of the vineyards were replanted.

Ahead of us on a spur stood the remains of Denia castle, mostly
towering walls with little inside them. The site of the Temple of
Diana supposedly lay close to the town walls and a golden statue of
the Roman goddess was said to be buried nearby. Once, so it was
rumored, the body of a Roman centurion had been excavated, but
he had taken one look at the results of evolution and disintegrated.

We passed a matronly cyclist, a fisherman swinging a dried
octopus by its tentacles, and a carpet seller with a glossy quiff of hair
sitting on a rug beside his van drinking his morning bottle of beer.

Diane stopped to let a flock of sheep and goats get past. They
approached us warily, then made a dash for it on either side of the
Citroën while the young shepherd smiled gently as his two dogs did
his work for him.

We passed a yellow-walled mansion, its turrets crowned with
what looked like garbage can lids. Then we were on the outskirts of
Denia.

Diane parked the Citroën and we walked through a tunnel
under the castle, emerging into sunlight so bright after the dripping
gloom that it made our eyes ache.

The director of the English Institute where Spanish was taught
to foreigners and English to Spaniards was a dashing, curly-haired
teacher named Julio, who had been a pilot in the Spanish Air Force.

Diane was assigned to an advanced class. I was relegated to a roomful of duds, mostly that breed of foreigners who insist that although they can't speak Spanish they can read it.

Certainly the inability to pick up the language was the most common cause of frustration among expats. I was lucky—I had Diane.

I was placed between a swaggering gray-haired German named Klaus who, during World War II, had been a tank commander on the Russian front—he walked with a Soviet-inflicted limp and gleamed with gold chains, identity tags, and rings—and Sonje, a glamorous Dutch artist who manifestly loathed him.

Julio greeted us cheerily in the classroom and a woman in the back row told him that he spoke too quickly, the familiar misconception about any foreigner who speaks his own language at conversational speed.

Sonje returned his greeting with a few well chosen and, I suspected, well rehearsed phrases; Klaus responded crisply as though ordering the destruction of a Soviet tank. They glared at each other across the no-man's-land where I was sitting.

Julio asked all of us for our names and we gave them one by one. An Englishman with tufted eyebrows from a village near Jávea embellished his with unnecessary credentials and a fluency that suggested that by attending such a lowly class, he intended to show off.

The British and Americans were adequate students of Spanish. Italians, French, Portuguese, and Dutch were the best among the Europeans.

The secret of learning fluent Spanish was to mix with Spaniards. Better still to take a Spanish lover—but most foreign residents were of an age where all their faculties would have to be concentrated on performance rather than linguistic foreplay.

Sonje supplied her name with a smile and a wink. Klaus rose unsteadily to his feet: if he forgot his game leg and cracked his heels together, I feared he might fall into my lap. I braced myself but he stayed upright.

Julio addressed us in Spanish informing us that he was our teacher and we were his pupils and it was Monday and the sun was shining.

Outside the classroom, which was above a bookshop, the summer day beckoned. Coquettish laughter in the street, mopeds coughing, the beat of pigeons' wings in the air . . .

A hand gripped my thigh. I glanced down. It belonged to Sonje, not the tank commander.

"That man is a fool," she hissed.

"Which man?" I asked.

"The German sitting beside you."

"Why is he a fool?"

"The way he holds himself," she whispered mysteriously.

"Silencio!" Julio glared at us.

He asked Sonje what day it was and what the weather was like and she told him it was Monday and the sun was shining.

Tufted Eyebrows guffawed. Klaus nudged me and whispered: "She has a terrible accent, that woman beside you."

"Yours is good?"

"*Ja*, is very *gut*."

Julio asked him what day it would be tomorrow and what he thought the weather would be like.

Klaus told him fluently enough, but he sounded as though he were giving the command to attack Stalingrad.

Sonje, who was displaying the foothills of a tanned bosom, gripped my thigh again and said: "He has a terrible accent."

Toward the end of the lesson hostilities between Germany and Holland heated up.

Sonje laughed immoderately at any mistake perpetrated by Klaus; he invoked *Gott* whenever she made an error. At each outburst the Englishman raised his eyebrows a centimeter higher. After a while he directed his weary scorn at me; when I confused *cervesas* (beers) with *servicios* (toilets), I heard him confide to another student that I was "letting England down."

The situation did not improve during the next couple of classes. My thigh remained under attack and when I escaped to a chair by the wall Klaus and Sonje took up positions behind and in front of me.

Julio was a good teacher, but I was learning more Dutch and German expletives than Spanish.

So I quit. After a particularly harrowing session in the buffer zone between Klaus and Sonje, I crossed the street to a café to meet Diane for coffee.

I was sitting by myself at a table surrounded by middle-aged women eating sticky pastries when the Englishman with the tufted eyebrows came in and, standing in the doorway, surveyed the scene like a captain on the bridge of a battleship. I tried to hide behind a newspaper but he spotted me and sat at my table.

"Hear you've abandoned ship," he said, after he had ordered a black coffee and a brandy. "Mind if I give you a word of advice?" Whether I minded or not he gave it. "Don't give up too easily, it creates a bad impression."

"Not British?"

He nodded, smiling tightly. He drank his brandy in one gulp and sipped his coffee conspiratorially. "We've got to set an example." He tightened his cravat and finger-combed the waves of graying hair above his ears.

"Who to?" I asked. "The natives?"

"I'm only trying to be helpful." He twiddled one of the brass buttons on his blazer like a radio ham tuning an old-fashioned wireless. "Your attitude leaves a lot to be desired. Were you in the army?"

"Air force," I told him.

"Ah, navy man myself. You were a pilot?"

"Sorry."

"You look pretty fit," he said grudgingly.

"Gardening," I said, thinking of Ángel laboring in the compound.

"Play any sport?"

"Not any more," I said. "Do I get the job?"

"What job?" His eyebrows twitched.

"I got the impression I was being interviewed for one."

He ignored me. "I thought we might show the flag next week. I hear they're staging a contest in your village. Spot of arm wrestling. We can show them we Brits are made of stern stuff."

"Arm wrestling Spaniards?" I remembered Emilio's invitation. The Englishman looked trim enough with a golfer's tan and an upright back, but he wouldn't be a match for Emilio's bulging muscles.

"No, you and me," Tufted Eyebrows said. "That way at least one Brit wins."

I looked at him in astonishment. "What about my attitude? I thought it left a lot to be desired."

"Could do it the world of good. You know, British sportsmanship, that sort of thing." He eyed me cannily. "Thought we might have a bet on the side. Say fifty pounds?"

"You're on," I said. I had never really included serious gambling among my assorted vices, but now I was ready to splurge because I realized there was more at stake here than mere antiquated patriotism: we were going to battle over attitudes to settling in a foreign land. His banner was isolationism, mine was integration. I suspected that he was more proficient than he was admitting. "Make it a hundred pounds," I added.

"Done." He stood up and shook my hand; his grip was surprisingly strong.

"How did it go today?" I asked Diane when she came into the café.

"Terrific."

"Terrific?" How could irregular verbs be terrific?

"I'm changing classes."

"Promotion?"

"Not exactly—Julio has asked me to teach English to a class of children."

"*Mein Gott,*" I said.

I didn't tell Diane about the arm wrestling, which meant I didn't have to tell her about the wager either. She would have been supportive, but some initiatives are private and personal. I spent the next few days arm wrestling walls and squeezing a small rubber ball, which I had been told strengthened the muscles of the forearm. Diane caught me once in a trial of strength with the wall of the garage and looked at me as though I had been drinking.

I was haunted by the strength of Tufted Eyebrows' grip when we shook hands over the café table—a Rambo-Rocky squeeze that suggested iron-pumper's biceps lurking beneath his blazer.

By the time the day of the arm-wrestling dawned my right forearm was drained of strength and a pain shot through my wrist when I knuckled my fist. I searched for Emilio to seek tactical advice, but he had taken a week off to rehearse for the Moors and Christians and spent most of his time in Denia drinking, smoking the big flaking cigars that were an obligatory accessory for Moors, and swatting flies with his sword.

When I got to the Bar Paraiso for the contest at eleven A.M. Emilio was sitting at the counter next to Jesús, the gas delivery man. His black, silver-threaded hair was oiled and plastered flat, his craggy face wore its usual expression of resolute honesty confused by glimmers of cunning.

The first bout, he said, would be between two relative strangers.

He pointed at a table behind the crowd thronging the bar. Tufted Eyebrows was sitting next to a legendary visitor to Denia, the Napkin Man.

A Catalan, he materialized in the village every month or so, burly and jolly with a head of gray curls and stubby fingers with which he fashioned ballet dancers from white paper napkins.

Children gathered round his table as he tore and twisted the paper into tutus. With a sweet smile he distributed his creations, one for each outstretched hand.

He also brought with him scarlet napkins; with these he made carnations for any girl who took his fancy, and many a paper blossom probably rekindled sunlit memories in chilly homes far away from Spain.

I stared at Emilio. "Why those two?"

"Why not? Everyone's welcome." Emilio lowered his voice to a stentorian whisper. "And the Napkin Man is the favorite."

The bets were laid with Jaime the pint-sized barman, who recorded them in a notebook. Spaniards were compulsive gamblers—the national Christmas lottery, *El Gordo* (the Fat One), was the biggest in the world in terms of money invested—and wage packets were lost at poker, fortunes made on forecasting results of matches on the football pools.

In an illegal casino in a nearby town, one gambler was reputed to have lost his house in a game of poker; another was said to have lost his wife, although rumor had it that he had thrown the game and offered his condolences to the winner.

I turned to Jesús. "You think the Napkin Man will win?"

"I agree with Emilio." The carpenter clenched his fists. "What do you think, *Señor* Derek?"

Remembering Tufted Eyebrows' handshake, I massaged my right hand. "It won't be as easy as you think."

"Then bet on the Englishman," Emilio said. "Can you guess who he wants to wrestle if he wins?"

"I know who he wants to wrestle," I said. "Me!" The original scenario had been a single bout between the two of us but he must have decided on a double whammy.

I opted to go with the smart money. Diane had given me one thousand pesetas to buy strawberries and cream so I put it on the Napkin Man at 2-1.

The crowd drifted toward the table where the Napkin Man and Tufted Eyebrows were sitting. The Napkin Man made a ballerina from a white serviette, placed her on the table, and watched her pirouette in the breeze from the ceiling fan.

An old mongrel came in from the heat and collapsed on the floor. Jaime left the hissing coffee machine and pushed his way to the front of the twenty or so spectators, all men.

Eyebrows rolled up the sleeves of his white shirt. Muscles rippled on his forearms. He spotted me and raised an eyebrow. An acknowledgment that we were showing the flag?

He and the Napkin Man planted their elbows on the table and, insides of their forearms almost touching, locked hands. Each bout was the best of three falls in which one contestant, keeping his elbow on the table, had to flatten his opponent's arm.

Eyebrows said: "Ready?" The Napkin Man smiled and nodded. Their arms strained against each other. The bar became quiet, probably for the first time in its history. Veins stood out on the Englishman's temples. His arm started to bend backward. The Napkin Man, wearing a thick checked shirt despite the heat, winked at a friend in the crowd. Inexorably Eyebrows's arm continued its descent until his knuckle touched the top of the table.

A collective sigh from the crowd: the smart money looked safe. The hands of the wall clock slipped back a second, the ballerina the Napkin Man had made fluttered toward the edge of the table.

One down, two to go.

Beer, cornot, and brandy flowed; Eyebrows ordered a Scotch and soda, and Jaime poured him a generous measure of whisky. The Napkin Man asked for an absinthe—illegal in France and elsewhere because one of the ingredients, wormwood, was said to rot the brain—that was distilled in a nearby village. A plump German girl staying in the village sat at the bar and ordered a Coke; he caught her eye and started work on a red carnation.

Eyebrows gulped his whisky and soda. "Ready?" he asked his opponent.

The Napkin Man said he was and put down the embryonic carnation. The German girl raised her glass to him.

Hands locked again. The Englishman's arm bent backward and I prepared to collect my winnings.

Suddenly his arm convulsed like a dying fish. The Napkin Man's arm jerked backward and Eyebrows flattened it on the table.

One each, one to go. Maybe Eyebrows was a hustler. I hoped not. An English con man visiting the village would damage the national image and impair our efforts to integrate.

The eyebrows *spoke* to me again. I didn't know what they said— "That taught the foreign devils a lesson," perhaps—but I felt my own eyebrows, powered by some imitative force, trying to reply.

The Napkin Man finished his glass of brain rot, smiled at the German girl, and fashioned a few more petals of red carnation.

Eyebrows asked the Napkin Man if he was ready for the third and last trial of strength. The Napkin Man said he was—a mere formality, his tone implied.

Knuckles white, tendons corded, the two arms bent first one way, then the other. Sweat trickled down the contestants' faces. The silence thickened.

From the direction of the crossroads came the crash of breaking glass. At the same moment the Napkin Man's arm collapsed. The collective sigh this time was plaintive, but they were gamblers all and they accepted such disappointments as loss items in the weekly budget. My loss was more tangible: strawberries and cream.

I noticed Jaime hand Emilio money.

"I thought you backed the Napkin Man," I said.

"No *Señor* Derek. I only said he was the favorite."

"You could have warned me that he wasn't going to try very hard."

"I didn't know he wasn't," Emilio said. "But I did know the Englishman was. His sort never give up."

"So who are you going to back in my bout?"

"No one," Emilio said. "We are friends, you and me."

I turned to the Napkin Man. "You didn't try, did you?"

He shook his head, gray curls bobbing. "To begin with I did. Then I thought, 'There's too much struggle in this world,' and I relaxed."

He handed me the ballerina and walked out of the bar with the German girl, paper carnation nestling above one of her ears.

I took his place at the table and faced Eyebrows, who was drinking his second whisky and soda. He looked disconcertingly composed.

"Good man," he said.

"Showing the flag," I said.

We clasped hands, his eyebrows rose, and we commenced battle, he the champion of expat insularity, I the exponent (or so I liked to think) of respect for our hosts' customs. As soon as I exerted pressure his arm slumped back and his knuckles hit the tabletop.

I accepted a beer from Emilio and we took up our positions again. Eyebrows's grip was firmer this time, muscles moving on his jawline as he clenched and unclenched his teeth.

I applied pressure but his arm was as obdurate as the garage wall. I felt the strength draining from my own.

The old dog hauled itself to its feet and rested its whiskery head on my knee.

I made a last push. Nothing. He tightened his grip and thrust forward, staring at me with his ice-blue eyes. I didn't give up but my arm did.

One each, one to go.

I finished my beer. I was sweating like a leaking water cart.

Emilio materialized behind me. "I've made a bet," he said.

"Who did you put your money on?"

"The man who's going to win." He was beginning to sound like Ángel.

I massaged my wrist and forearm, put my elbow on the table, and asked my opponent if he was ready. We faced each other again and locked hands. Silence except for the whining of the old dog.

Together we exerted pressure. Pain shot up my arm. Then unwittingly my opponent came to my assistance. I remembered his words in the café opposite the English Institute. "Your attitude leaves a lot to be desired."

Adrenaline flowed. I felt a surge of power in my arm as potent as an electric shock. His arm bent back an inch or so, the veins on his wrists bulged. His arm retreated another inch, then recovered.

Attitude be damned! I gave a last push. The fight went out of his arm and he bowed his head in defeat.

"Well fought," I said. I mopped the sweat from my face with a handkerchief. "By the way, you owe me a hundred pounds."

"Is a check all right?"

"Of course. An Englishman's word . . ."

He scrawled a check and with a final twitch of his eyebrows walked out of the bar into the sunshine. His check cleared but I never saw him again.

I noticed that Emilio wasn't collecting any money from Jaime and said to him: "I thought you were backing the best man."

"You let me down, *Señor* Derek," he said. "You won."

When I got home Diane asked me why I hadn't brought the strawberries and cream. "I brought you this instead," I said, and handed her the paper ballerina. And later, the check for a hundred pounds.

THIRTEEN

Ordeal by Fire
and Fur

July. And the countryside gasped for water. It hadn't rained for weeks; serpents of heat lay coiled in hollows in the vineyards; the hills turned desert brown; figs withered and, despite the water that surged in irrigation channels, oranges shriveled and dropped before their time. Wells ran dry, diviners carrying metal rods or hazel twigs, both sensitive to subterranean water in the hands of those with a mysterious affinity to H_2O, trudged the fields in search of sites where wells could be sunk.

The local council published notices forbidding householders to hose their gardens or top up their swimming pools. Water from the mains supply tasted salty, so we filled plastic bottles from an emergency tank provided by the council in the village.

Arrangements were made to pipe sweet water to Denia from Pego, a small town fifteen miles away, but bad feeling between the two towns had run high for years and the pipeline was sabotaged by militants who didn't see why they should bring succor to an old enemy. Brawls broke out between the two factions and the *Guardia Civil* were summoned—but not before the relief pipe had been wrecked.

Underground water dried up, weakening the strata of subsoil, so drastically in an orange grove a mile from our house that a crater opened up and a house fell into it. Would our dining hall, still without a roof, finish up as a basement?

Every morning we looked hopefully for clouds but all we could see was a haze of latent heat. Jones lay flattened on the floor tiles, only moving if a bitch in heat passed by. Hoppity clumped lethargically around on his wooden leg; Ethel ate, slept, and blinked.

The lack of water didn't affect our garden too drastically. The red and yellow lilies shed their blossoms prematurely and the springy Bermuda turf became more like a trampoline than a lawn, but the fruit trees and Ángel's vegetables were unaffected. Ángel, pale aesthetic features solemn with reverence for the forces of nature, said they were being sustained by an underground river.

The owner of a cottage near our house didn't fare so well. Plump and worried, a few strands of hair plastered from ear to ear, Ernesto was a fanatical gardener and, although he furtively watered his flowers and vegetables at night, they were dying.

We were awoken one morning by a thump that shook our bed and sent lemons thudding onto the driveway.

We dressed and walked down the street to investigate. A crowd had gathered outside Ernesto's detached, whitewashed cottage. In the middle of the lawn stood a drill twice the height of the cottage—a rusting metal pole supported by struts, powered by a generator, and operated by its owner, a phlegmatic water prospector with rust-colored hair.

"Drill" was a misnomer, because gravity rather than rotation seemed to be its propellant. As we arrived the shaft hit the ground and again the earth trembled.

Ernesto told me the "drill" would strike water in three days to enable him to sink a well. Spectators were already making bets about the time the strike would be made.

The owner of the cottage next to Ernesto, an orange grower with malicious eyes, as complacent as Ernesto was harassed, said three months was a more realistic wager.

The generator picked up power and the thumping fell into a regular rhythm, continuing through *siesta*, stopping at dusk.

On the third day, when it was expected that water would be struck, a dozen villagers reassembled outside the cottage. Midday was the most popular bet. The shaft rose and fell. Midday passed. So did *siesta* and dusk.

One week. Two. Three. Villagers advised Ernesto to throw in his hand, but a streak of obstinancy provoked by the knowing smile of the orange grower had entered his soul. The shaft continued to rise and fall, a pulse that was scarcely noticed anymore.

Ernesto's dilemma crystalized one of the dangers that had always plagued this region, more so since the Moors first planted citrus fruit and rice. Water was its lifeblood, and its people lived in constant fear that one day its arteries would dry up.

When a drought threatened the crops, another enemy arrived on its coattails: fire. Every summer, flames ignited by the sun's rays through a piece of glass, by a campfire, a cigarette butt, or an arsonist's burning brand, swept down pine-clad slopes on the hills beyond the citrus groves, leaving behind charred humps of land as stark as slag heaps.

This year the first local warning that fire had once again stalked drought was a stem of smoke behind Montgo.

I didn't take a lot of notice—I was busy at my typewriter describing permafrost in Siberia. Diane was in Denia teaching English at the Institute and Ángel was tending a mysterious plant he had sown in a replica of an amphora, a tall earthenware jar used by the Romans and Greeks for storing oil. The plant looked like a datura, a bush bearing bell-like blossoms, usually white, which Ángel warned me were poisonous. But there was a difference: instead of hanging like a carillon of bells these flowers pointed skyward. Local botanists were baffled. Where had Ángel obtained the seeds? they asked. He didn't know, because although he "borrowed" cuttings and seeds from other gardens where he worked, nothing like this was growing in any of them.

In fact our garden was a breeding ground of enigmas. Oranges *and* lemons grew on the same tree. Two white egrets settled here. They were wading birds who required shallow water, and even the shallow end of the swimming pool would have been too deep for them.

I asked Ángel why he thought the datura-like blooms were upside down.

"Maybe I planted the seeds the wrong way up," he replied.

It was the only joke I ever heard him make.

The next fire warning was a change in the color of the sunlight from gold to bronze. Smoke had begun to obscure the sun's rays, but I failed to react because I was still writing about a blizzard in Novosibirsk and, in any case, I hadn't lived here long enough to appreciate the danger.

Diane arrived home as a fire-fighting helicopter clattered overhead, disappearing behind Montgo. The stem of smoke had thickened into a trunk and from a distance the mountain looked like the volcano it had once simulated in the Krakatoa movie. Supposing a spark set fire to our house . . .

We went up to the roof terrace. In the distance orange fire-fighting aircraft were skimming the surface of the sea, scooping water into cavernous tanks in their bellies and dumping it on the fire on the other side of Montgo. Fire engines, ambulances, and police cars brayed. Spurts of flame flickered in the high smoke like gunfire on a battleground.

I decided to see if I could help. Our village wasn't yet threatened, but the lemon grove that was for sale at the foot of the terraced wall below our garden was tinder dry, so I left Ángel on guard.

By the time I reached the lower levels of Montgo in Diane's Citroën, it was late afternoon and flames had spread to the slopes overlooking Denia.

Descending traffic clogged the roads, but climbing them in the Citroën was relatively easy. By five P.M. the flames had burned away the scrub on the mountain's broad summit and from the road I could see them leaping through the pines below.

Most of the houses in the foothills had been evacuated, but a middle-aged English couple with a menagerie of pets were still in residence in a house with a patio bordered by a white wall. They had spent most of their lives managing a tobacco farm in Africa in what was then Rhodesia, and we had met them in Pilar's store.

When I knocked, the door was opened by the wife, Jane, comfortably built and exuberant, who said: "Come in and have a gin and tonic."

Their house, now only half a mile away from the flames, was already sweltering in the heat. A mixed bag of dogs and cats barked and meowed on the patio. Sparks floated overhead like fireflies. The fire, fueled by resin in the pines, surged toward us. Jane's husband was hosing down the walls of the patio.

"Don't be bloody fools," I said, "you've got to get out and bring your zoo with you."

"The car's kaput," Jane said tipsily, "and we can't leave the animals. Are you sure you won't have a g and t? Just a little one?"

"I'll take the animals," I said. "You get your money and papers and some clothes and walk to our house—it's only a couple of miles away."

I grabbed a shaggy mongrel by its collar and dragged it barking and snarling to the Citroën.

"Well, really!" Jane splashed gin into her glass.

"I think he's right, dear," said her husband, a skinny sharp-boned colonial.

"Of course I'm right," I snapped.

I picked up two spitting cats and deposited them in the Citroën beside the mongrel as an aircraft dumped seawater, hissing, onto the advancing flames. A hose connected to a hydrant one hundred yards away thickened as water coursed through it toward the yellow-helmeted firemen fighting the fire. Just as the water spurted out a pine tree exploded, tossing burning embers into the air.

Jane said: "Be careful with Winston, he can't see very well." I picked up a bulldog with glazed eyes and put him beside the two cats.

Jane's husband collected a daschund and a yelping terrier of some sort.

By the time we had finished, the Citroën was stuffed with canine and feline life.

I phoned Diane and asked her what the situation was at home.

"Ángel says everything is under control," she told me. "There are clouds on the horizon. He reckons it will rain later this evening."

Jane, traveling bag in one hand, gin and tonic in the other, made her way unsteadily to the gate followed by her husband.

"About Winston—" she began.

"I know," I said, "his eyesight . . ."

"He's also incontinent."

I cleared the driving seat of living fur. A spaniel licked my face. I looked in the driving mirror but all I could see were my passengers. One of them was a cross-eyed Siamese cat.

I eased the Citroën into the downhill traffic and headed for home. By the time I got there Winston had proved beyond any shadow of doubt that he was indeed incontinent.

I left the car outside the gates, windows open a little so that the animals could breathe, and went to the end of the garden to check out the highly combustible lemon grove.

The burning was still about one and a half miles away but flakes of glowing ash were floating on the hot air. As I reached Ángel standing guard, garden hose in hand, one of them settled among the ravaged lemon trees.

The long grass, as dry as straw below the trees, caught fire immediately. I envisaged the flames leaping through the garden, scaling the bougainvillea on the terrace, and engulfing the house. And I hadn't insured it yet.

Ángel ran to the hose-pipe tap beside the swimming pool and turned it on. Water spurted from a leak halfway along its length. Ángel should have checked it. I would have to sack him.

The flames in the lemon grove were on the move, setting light to the unkempt trees.

Ángel mended the leak with insulating tape. But water then spouted from other leaks further down the hose.

I told Diane, who had joined us, to call the fire brigade, but I doubted whether they would come—they were too busy on Montgo and the last time Diane had reported that she could smell fire half a dozen fireman had rampaged through the house finding nothing more dangerous than an exposed wire in the oven ventilator.

The fire was now rampaging through the lemon trees. Ángel aimed the leaking hose at the flames but the puny jet didn't even reach the end of our garden where we had made our original ascent with Emilio.

Ángel pointed at the clouds looming on the horizon. "Don't worry, *Señor* Derek, they are full of rain."

I wasn't worrying: I was panicking. The flames were inching toward the cypress hedges on both sides of our garden. If they got to them, two prongs of fire would race toward the house.

A breeze sprang up, fanning the flames toward the hedges. Smoke rose from their dark and dusty depths. Tree rats who nested in them were making a run for it. Ángel aimed the hose at both hedges, but the water seemed only to thicken the smoke.

Suddenly tongues of flames flickered out of the smoke and began to race toward the house. Could the glorious vision Diane and I had shared be extinguished by a flake of burning ash?

I ran from one side of the garden to the other trying to douse the flames with buckets of water. But they gathered speed as though I were tossing gasoline on them. The house was doomed.

Diane ran down the garden from the house. "The fire brigade is on its way—I told them the whole village was threatened."

A fire engine drew up on the roadside next to the lemon grove. The firemen located a hydrant and aimed their hoses at the blazing trees. The water cannon hit them instantly, killing the flames.

The firemen trampled through the smoking ash and showered the two hedges.

As the last flames died, a swarm of dogs and cats, released from the Citroën by Jonathan, who had just arrived home after spending the afternoon in Denia with friends, charged down the garden.

The cats disappeared into the smoking hedge while the dogs, led by Jones, chased after them.

A fireman asked me: "Are all those yours?"

"Not exactly," I said. I started to explain but he wasn't listening.

Finally Jane and her husband arrived on foot, downed a couple of gins and tonic and rounded up their boisterous pets.

I checked through binoculars that their house was safe—firemen had contained the flames about half a mile away—and drove the menagerie home, making sure that Winston and his leaky bladder were on Jane's lap.

✳

Five minutes after I got back, the clouds opened up and, standing under an umbrella on the roof terrace, Diane and I watched torrential rain snuff out the last of the flames on Montgo. Ángel had driven off home so, mercifully, he couldn't gloat about the accuracy of his weather forecast.

Rainwater swept joyously through the orange groves, flooding the baked soil. Foolishly we drove into Denia with Jonathan to have a look at the inevitable floods; they were extensive—the lower levels of the town had become a little Venice, cars floating like gondolas.

When we drove back, the access road to the house was also flooded and the Jaguar stalled one hundred yards from home. We waded back in the dark and the three of us slept together in the big bed.

It was still raining the following morning, but by the afternoon it stopped. At four P.M. Ernesto struck water, six weeks, two days, and nine hours after he had begun to drill for it in his garden.

At first it was assumed that the bore hole was flooded by the rain, but an official from the water company confirmed that the water was subterranean.

The following day the same archaic drill was erected in the garden of the patronizing orange grower next door. It struck water within three days.

FOURTEEN

The Roofer Who
Couldn't Stand Heights

V icente the roofer arrived one July morning when the rain-soaked garden was
steaming in the sunshine. His grandmother had
regained her health—camomile tea had done
the trick, apparently—and because she looked
good for another few years he had caught the
ferry back from Majorca.

He was stout with a weather-beaten face,
unruly brown hair, and frightened eyes. He
mounted a ladder tentatively to assess the work
ahead of him.

I asked Emilio what was the matter with
him.

"He's afraid of heights," Emilio said.

"A roofer who's scared of heights?"

"He didn't want to be a roofer but he didn't have a choice, that's the way it is here. You do what your father did. That's why I'm a carpenter."

The ladder wobbled and the roofer stopped climbing.

Emilio shouted: "You're almost there."

"It's higher than usual," the roofer shouted back.

I stared at Emilio in amazement. "Supposing he worked in New York?"

"He usually puts roofs on one-storey bungalows," Emilio said.

"Is he related to you by any chance?"

"Distantly," Emilio said.

"Supposing he falls . . . Is he insured?"

"If he fell," Emilio said carefully, "you might have to pay some of his medical bills."

"You mean he isn't insured?"

"He won't fall. He might be scared but he's as steady as a mountain goat."

Vicente came down the ladder, went to his van, and began to mix cement. Roof tiles, treated with bird droppings to encourage mildew and make them look old, were piled beside him.

Life was complicated by Jonathan's activities with Port Rotes *falla* in Denia. It was the eve of the July fiesta and he was taking part in the competitive procession in which, with an imaginative float, Port Rotes hoped to recover some of the glory they had lost when their statue was burned up in March.

Twice a week I drove him into Denia to a warehouse where members of the *falla* were putting the finishing touches to the float. The theme was supposed to be a secret, but parents scouring attics for bowler hats, baggy trousers, and walking sticks were a giveaway.

I had just returned home with a borrowed stick when I heard a crash. I ran to the dining hall and stood ankle deep in rainwater. Above me I saw the horrified face of Vicente staring at me from atop the twenty-foot-high wall above the open fireplace.

"What happened?" I asked Emilio, who was assembling parts of the minstrel gallery on the terrace.

"He dropped a tile on the path," Emilio said.

"Is he all right?"

"He's an experienced roofer." A masterly evasion.

"How distant a relative is he, Emilio?"

"Not all that far."

"Supposing *he* had fallen onto the path?"

"He knows how to fall."

"You mean he's had a lot of experience of it?"

"He's never been seriously injured," Emilio said.

It was beginning to sound as if Vicente's mainstream profession was high-wire artist.

"But does he know how to lay tiles?"

"He is the best," Emilio said with dignity.

However accomplished he was, I didn't think he would be able to do his job properly if he was in the grip of vertiginous panic, so I climbed the ladder to see if I could inspire confidence.

It was now more than six months since work on the dining hall had begun, and the roof at least should have been in place. Having lived in Russia and Ireland, where the pace of life was just as leisurely, I had been prepared for procrastination in Spain. What I hadn't anticipated were some of its treacherous accomplices—unforeseen snow, ailing grandmothers in Majorca, a roofer who couldn't stand heights. Most of the time I envied this tolerant attitude to punctuality, perhaps because my working life had been dominated by deadlines, but occasionally frustration took hold of me. When it did, I was liable to succumb to foolhardy impulses. Joining Vicente on the walk was one of them. He was kneeling where he had been laying tiles on the framework of the roof. (The exposed wooden beams that were to give the interior baronial panache were, I learned later, purely decorative.)

His face was frozen with fear.

I had always believed I had a moderate head for heights but fear is infectious. I stared at the lake of rainwater below in the dining hall, felt dizzy, and had to sit on the wall beside Vicente, nonchalantly kicking my feet against the cinder blocks.

"It isn't really any different from being on top of a bungalow," I told him.

"It would be if I fell off." I tightened my own grip, one hand on either side of me on the wall.

"But you won't."

"How do you know I won't?"

"Because you're good at your job—it's just that you're a little higher than usual."

I suddenly appreciated the bravery of policemen who risked their lives on ledges of tall buildings to talk would-be suicides out of jumping.

"Who says I'm good at my job?" Vicente asked. "Emilio?"

"Well, aren't you?"

"I've fallen off a few bungalows," he said.

A sparrow perched on the wall and eyed us beadily.

"Maybe you should come down, then."

"No," he said, "I'll be all right—as long as I don't look down."

"But—"

"Please leave me. At least I know how to fall."

I realized that Spanish pride was at stake. This was as big a factor as losing face in China so, without displaying undue haste, I climbed down the ladder.

On the last rung I called out. "Are you sure you won't come down? No one will blame you." I certainly wouldn't, having shared his vertigo—the dining hall wasn't the Empire State Building but it was no bungalow either.

"Yes," he shouted back, "I'm sure." A scrap of wet cement dropped from the top of the wall and fell on the path beside me.

Vicente didn't return the following day and I feared that either he had lost his nerve or his grandmother in Majorca had taken a turn for the worse, but my misgivings gave way to preparations for the procession that evening.

Jonathan put on his bowler, baggy trousers, and stick-on mustache and posed beside the swimming pool while I took pictures with my antique camera.

Then I drove him with Diane to Denia where rival floats were lined up waiting to move off. Small Charlie Chaplins brandishing their walking sticks chased each other around the Port Rotes float, an ambitious creation with a Hollywood motif, complete with giant reels of film made with paper. Adults disguised as film stars from the past—Clark Gable as Rhett Butler, Vivien Leigh as Scarlett O'Hara in *Gone With the Wind* among them—stood aloof from the diminutive Chaplins. Clark Gable was having trouble with an errant mustache and his greasepaint was beginning to run.

Tractors stood ready to tow the floats in the evening sunlight. Spectators sat on folding chairs lining the main street beneath the plane trees. Hundreds of tourists thronging the sidewalks shouldered their way through crowds spilling from bars. Children threw streamers from apartment balconies, a silver balloon broke loose from a stall also selling bubble gum, licorice roots, and lengths of sugarcane and floated out to sea above the masts of the fishing fleet moored at the quayside.

At seven P.M. the procession, led by a chestnut horse ridden by an Andalusian horseman wearing a low-crowned Córdoba hat, set off, each of the floats, two hundred yards or so apart, accompanied by a band from a nearby town or village. At our partisan end of the main street no one doubted that the craftsmanship of the Port Rotes entry was the best. It was certainly the most original.

Children on the floats threw handfuls of sweets to the spectators. I waved at Jonathan; with his blond hair protruding from his bowler, he was an instantly recognizable Chaplin. He threw a toffee that hit me in the eye.

The floats passed us as sedately as galleons. Carousels, Olympian gods, totem poles and wigwams . . .

The judging took place further up the street. Would originality be recognized? Port Rotes had always been *avant-garde* in the themes of its floats, a trend not always appreciated in traditional Spain.

And it wasn't appreciated this evening: their float came second.

A triumph, Jonathan told me later as rockets burst in incandescent sprays in the night sky.

Wouldn't first have been better? I asked him. "Winning isn't everything," he said. "In any case it's the *fallas* in March that really matter."

Parental pride swelled inside me: I hoped he would always be just as obliquely philosophical.

Two days later Vicente the roofer, who claimed he had been suffering from a feverish cold, reappeared accompanied by Emilio. I sometimes wondered how Emilio's carpentry workshop survived when he was at my house, but he told me it was in good hands. Family presumably.

It was a hushed morning, dawn clouds pink, an eagle from an eyrie on Montgo making its way across the sky with lazy wing beats.

The lawn was covered with tiny spiders' webs beaded with dew that sparkled as the sun rose. A toad sat under a drainpipe where it had made its home. A fox hurried home.

I walked to the bakery in the village and came back with hot bread, which we ate spread with honey on the terrace while Vicente prepared for his ascent.

The preparations were so drawn out that by the time he took his first steps up the ladder, I had driven Jonathan to school and retired to my study and Diane had gone to Denia to teach her class. (One young troublemaker had asked her to find out why tomb, comb, and bomb were pronounced differently.)

I emerged from my office at eleven to make coffee. Emilio was sitting on a plastic chair on the terrace reading the local weekly newspaper *Canfali*. He said Vicente had already laid two dozen tiles.

From the direction of the crossroads came a metallic crash. Sirens wailed. Two Jehovah's Witnesses appeared at the gates, as neatly dressed as applicants at a job interview, retreating in good order when Jones curled his lip at them.

I talked with Ángel about the garden. He told me he had news. The tree bearing both oranges *and* lemons was originally a lemon tree that had been grafted with shoots from an orange tree; the two egrets had adapted to their new environment by standing on the steps of the swimming pool where they wouldn't drown. But he still couldn't explain why the blossoms of the plants in the amphora were upside down.

I returned to my study, content with the progress on the roof and Ángel's discomfiture at being defeated by mere flora—I hadn't sacked him after the episode with the hose but it had been close.

My concentration was broken at midday by a thump and a cry of pain.

I ran into the dining hall. Vicente lay on the floor in the dregs of the rainwater. Emilio knelt beside him.

I told him to call an ambulance while I carried out basic first aid procedures I had learned when I was a conscript in the air force years earlier. I covered him with a blanket and looked for obvious injuries such as fractures or hemorrhage. I couldn't find anything, but he seemed to be distressed. I asked him where the pain was, but he didn't reply.

Two medics stretchered him to the ambulance, and I accompanied him with Emilio to the hospital in Denia.

Still he didn't speak. Emilio did. "This will cost you, *Señor* Derek," he said, sympathetically.

From the ambulance he was taken to Emergency. Emilio and I waited in reception. It wasn't peak time for accidents and the only other occupants were an unshaven youth coughing horrendously and a woman with a black eye.

We were joined by a furtive young man with a long blond hair wearing a crumpled tropical suit who sat beside me and said: "Bad luck about that chap working for you." He spoke English with what could have been a Portuguese accent.

"How did you hear about it?" I asked him.

"It's a small town. Is he going to be all right?"

"I don't know," I said. "I'm not God." I picked up an old magazine and began to read it.

"He wasn't insured, was he." A statement rather than a question.

"None of your business," I said.

"But it is." He handed me a visiting card stating that he was an insurance broker. "I can do you a favor."

"You can," I said. "You can get lost."

"I can offer you a policy at very reasonable terms covering accidents to anyone working for you. Back-dated to yesterday!"

I glanced at his card. "What's your address?"

He ran his hand through his long hair. "Why do you want to know?"

"Because it will help when I denounce you to the police for attempted fraud."

Denunciations were one of the more Machiavellian legal processes in Spain: you could get away with all sorts of offenses until a neighbor or an enemy purporting to be a friend denounced you. Police who often looked shamefaced when they had to act on the information would never divulge the identity of the snitch.

He tried to grab the visiting card but I held onto it. "I'm only trying to help you," he said.

"Do you follow ambulances and hearses or does someone tip you off?"

At that moment Vicente emerged, as though he had risen from the dead. Walking upright, if a little unsteadily, he made his way toward us accompanied by a young doctor in a white housecoat.

"How is he?" I asked the doctor.

The doctor replied in English. "He's fine." He lowered his voice. "Frankly I couldn't find anything wrong with him but I told him he was a little concussed. A lot of patients appreciate that sort of thing—then they don't think they've been wasting my time."

I turned to issue a last threat to the insurance broker but he had disappeared. I heard an ambulance wail. Outside the clinic I saw him take off on a motorcycle in hot pursuit.

Vicente returned to work two days later a new man. He climbed the ladder with the agility of a monkey and began laying tiles as though he were dealing playing cards.

I consulted Emilio. What had brought about the transformation?

"All he needed was confidence," Emilio said. "He didn't know what it was like to fall from that height. Now he does, it wasn't too bad, and he's full of enthusiasm."

"You don't mean he liked falling?" I asked incredulously.

"He liked the attention he got."

A tile crashed onto the path. I looked up. The roofer grinned from his perch and raised a clenched fist in a gesture of triumph.

FIFTEEN

Running Water,
Running Bulls

If it hadn't been for Javier I wouldn't have run with the bulls.

He was the local plumber—a genuine craftsman, unlike the specialist summoned by officials of the water company who believed that because of his parochial knowledge, he would be able to locate the source of a leak in our driveway.

At first the leak had been nothing more than a damp patch, laced with silver snail trails, that lingered after the sun had burned away the dew.

By the end of July it had spread ominously from one end of the driveway to the middle and we could hear water trickling.

Ángel warned me that many old premises

had the same problem with underground metal pipes that had corroded. The leak, he said, was somewhere under the driveway in the
pipe feeding the house from the main supply under the road; if it was
located between the meter in the driveway and the house, I would
have to foot the repair bill.

"If it's on the other side of the meter closer to the road?"

"The water company pays," he said.

"It must be their responsibility," I said, pointing at the site of the
seepage, which seemed to be closer to the road than the house.

"Maybe."

"What do you mean maybe?"

"Maybe the leak isn't there. It could have spread under the
driveway until it found a weak spot."

"Where do you think it is?"

Ángel consulted the heavens but there wasn't a cloud in sight.
"One side or the other," he said.

I called the water company and within half an hour two workmen arrived in a van that had more dents than Diane's Citroën. I also
consulted them about the shuddering noise in the bathroom whenever the we turned on the taps, but they said that was an inside job.
Outside their jurisdiction.

One of them was squat with a bushy mustache, the other lean
with sandy hair, shoals of freckles, and a cough that came up from his
boots. One was Pedro, the other Pablo, but I never sorted out which
was which.

They surveyed the driveway for a few minutes, then went to the
van for their tools. Emilio drove up, surveyed the scene, and
departed for the village. He must have reported what was happening, because soon afterward half a dozen spectators arrived at the
gates, among them the specialist with the raffish mustache who had
tried to claim the glory for fixing our sewage congestion.

When Pedro and Pablo retired to the garage for their breakfast,
the spectators dispersed, all of them, that was, except the specialist,

who seemed to think the entrails of our garden were his responsibility. He stayed outside the gates stroking his mustache and offering advice. Pedro and Pablo turned their backs on him and went on eating their *bocadillos*.

Finally Pedro, or it may have been Pablo, selected a pickax, coughed exhaustively, and aimed a blow at what looked like the epicenter of the seepage, which was beginning to gain depth in the jigsaw of sand-colored paving stones. Stone chips flew and Jones, who had been mutely begging for scraps of *bocadillo*, retired to the terrace. The second workman aimed a swipe with another pickax and soon, oblivious to the gathering heat, they were working rhythmically together.

By lunch they had excavated a considerable cavity. Water oozed from the mud at the bottom of it.

They summoned Ángel.

"What did they say?" I asked him as they retired to the garage for a swig of water.

"They said the leak isn't there."

The words had a familiar and ominous ring. Could they be under the influence of the sewage specialist? As I glanced toward the gates he mounted his bicycle and jauntily pedaled away. Supposing the leak was on the stretch of driveway between the meter and the house? The destruction being wrought in the driveway would finally bankrupt me.

Vicente dropped a tile onto the path and, standing on a concrete beam like a latter-day Blondin, grinned and raised his thumbs.

"Where do Pedro and Pablo think the leak is?" I asked Ángel.

"They said it could be anywhere. The water *has* spread below the surface."

After *siesta* Pedro and Pablo returned and mounted an assault on the whole length of driveway with sledgehammers. When they left three hours later it looked like a section of the Somme battlefield, but they still hadn't located the leak. Despair overwhelmed me and I knew from the slump of Diane's shoulders that it had affected her as well.

"They're coming back tomorrow with an engineer," Ángel told me.

"It can't be all that hard to follow the flow of the water." Diane said.

"It's a lake under there," said Ángel, who was picking up a lot of English from us but little common sense—maybe we hadn't any to offer.

Why hadn't we bought a frame house in New England, an apartment in Paris, a chalet in Switzerland? A home where everything worked.

The swallows departed and bats took their place.

We went to the restaurant owned by the manic depressive who had left Diane to turn the steaks. He was in a bitter mood, tossing steaks onto the grill over the open fire as though he was throwing out garbage, sipping moonshine absinthe, and glowering at his customers from behind the bar. But we enjoyed the meal as we had enjoyed the one before.

When we got back to the house the cicadas were in full swing and the sky was crowded with stars. We saw one fall. I had read somewhere that it signified a birth. Or maybe it was death.

I took Jones for a walk beside the wall encompassing the grounds of the supposedly haunted mansion and its coach house on the other side of the road. Glowworms switched off their lights as we got close to them. An owl hooted in the swaying pines beside the coach house. I wouldn't have been surprised to see the coach take to the road—we had kept an eye open for it on Midsummer's Eve when, according to legend, it took off, but nothing had stirred.

My bleak mood was infectious: Jones whined and tugged me back to our house. Navigating the devastation in the driveway, I acknowledged that, if I had to foot the bill and if my novel wasn't written well enough to merit the rest of the staggered payments, I would have to admit defeat and abandon our vision in the sun. I gave us until the end of the year, another five months, to survive or succumb.

The engineer, a studious young man wearing a blazer, arrived at midday and reconnoitered the driveway carrying a meter with a flickering needle. He said there was water everywhere beneath the surface, got in his car, and drove away, evidently satisfied with his diagnosis.

Which was when Pablo, or it may have been Pedro, decided to call in Javier the local plumber because he might know the deployment of underground pipes in a property such as ours.

Javier was a perfectionist who boasted in detail about his triumphs over faucets and U-bends. Pale-faced and prematurely balding, he gazed at the driveway, which was now a quarter inch deep in water in places.

I asked him if he could he tell where the leak was. He seemed to find the question impertinent. "How do you expect me to know? I work *inside,* cisterns and ballcocks, that sort of thing," he said in English.

Did he know about the layout of the outside pipes? "Obviously from the main supply under the road to the house," he said. "But the pipe may have wandered if the original engineers struck rock. And then, of course, it would have branches to the kitchen, bathroom, annex, and swimming pool. All outside my control."

At that moment I heard a familiar shuddering through the open window of the bathroom. Presumably Diane had just turned on one of the taps.

Javier tightened his lips and shook his head.

"Is it serious?" I asked.

"The water isn't getting through to the bathroom properly." He pointed at the seepage in the driveway. "That could cause a lot of damage. Like an engine without oil."

He went into the bathroom, now vacant, and turned on a tap. The pipe below the basin went into a paroxysm before a trickle of water emerged.

"Just as I thought," he said.

"Isn't that because they"—indicating Pedro and Pablo leaning on their sledgehammers waiting for his verdict—"have turned off the water at the mains?"

"It will only get worse," he said, ignoring a layman's banality.

"Can you fix it?"

The question seemed to surprise him. "Not at the moment—it's fiesta in the village."

"You don't work during fiesta?"

"Nobody works during fiesta."

I should have remembered that at these carnival times a cavalier attitude to work was adopted. I once asked the foreman of the builders why one of his team had been absent for a week. He stared at me dumbfounded and said: "I thought you knew it was fiesta in his village."

"All week?"

"Half of it."

Javier interrupted my thoughts. "They're running the bulls tonight," he said.

At this time of the year bulls were run in small town and village fiestas all over the region. The idea was to sprint in front of the snorting cattle in a modest imitation of the running at the famous San Fermin fiesta in Pamplona in the north, where on a regular basis participants were gored. The "bulls" in our region were often heifers but they could administer bone-jarring blows and fatalities weren't unheard of.

"Are you running with them?" I asked Javier.

"I'm too old." With his fingers he massaged pinch marks from spectacles indelibly printed on the bridge of his nose. "How old do you think I am?"

"Thirty?"

"Forty-one. Forty-two on Wednesday." Today was Monday.

"You don't look it," I said.

"No? Then maybe I should run with the bulls. If I look ten years younger I might have the reactions of a thirty-year-old."

I clapped him on the shoulder. "That's the spirit."

"On one condition. That you run with me." He looked at me slyly.

"Done!" The madness that had made me dance the tango in Benidorm overcame me again. "On one condition—that you fix the noise in the bathroom."

We shook hands on it.

He lit a cigar and, trailing smoke, swept past Pedro and Pablo in the driveway. Behind him the pipe in the bathroom trumpeted.

Word had spread in the village that the *escritor,* the writer, was going to run with the bulls and that evening I was treated to a couple of glasses of wine in the Bar Paraiso.

Emilio gripped my hand. "Just what Churchill would have done. And Nelson and Thatcher."

Javier arrived, pale cheeks burning with excitement, and ordered a brandy.

It was the second running that day. During the first a bull, or a heifer, made a detour into a bar and stood behind a tourist, an Englishwoman, drinking tea at the counter. Feeling hot breath on her neck, suspecting perhaps an amorous waiter, she swung round and stared into a pair of brown taurine eyes. Unfazed, she gave their owner a lump of sugar and he wandered back into the street.

I finished my wine and went to inspect the livestock herded into a makeshift corral at the end of the street. They were a motheaten bunch that wouldn't have intimidated the most faint-hearted bullfighter if he had been blindfolded and hungover. But they were solidly built just the same, pawing the ground irritably as children made faces at them.

The route they took was lined on either side with timber barricades, slots left open at intervals to provide escape hatches for the runners. I noted their deployment carefully; some teenagers would leap over the barriers to dodge the lowered horns of the "bulls" but the years had taken some of the spring out of my heels.

Crowds were gathering and a uniformed brass band twenty-five-strong, disheveled after impromptu performances in various bars, wandered along the street past boarded-up doorways and windows playing the "Hymn of Valencia." It was a stirring tune, full of pomp and poignancy, and I found it moving, but brass bands always had that effect on me.

Ángel, sharply turned out in knife-creased pants and checked shirt, adoring wife on his arm, stopped me. Where was the *señora?* he asked.

"In Denia with Jonathan," I said. In fact Diane had told me she was going to see our Spanish lawyer to check my will, adding that widowhood would be preferable to living with a suicidal lunatic determined to get himself gored.

A small boy offered me a lick of a green Popsicle dripping with emerald tears and said: "We've never had a foreigner killed here before."

Javier joined me at the corral full of bluster. He offered me a swig of brandy from a silver flask; it burned holes in my stomach.

We chose a slot fifty yards from the corral. From there we could leap in front of the heifers when they were still a reasonable distance away and dive into the next escape hatch.

The band disappeared into a bar and the heifers, four of them, charged out of the corral.

Javier and I joined the young bloods—and a few older ones—who were running in front of the pounding hooves. Teenagers leaped over the barriers, old and experienced hands dived into the escape slots.

I had never been a fleet-footed runner and now it felt as though my sneakers were filled with liquid concrete. Behind me the "bulls" snorted, their hooves thudding as loudly as stampeding cattle. My heart thudded too. I glanced over my shoulder. The only other runner behind me was Javier. Where was the slot we had earmarked for our escape? I had passed it! The next one was another forty yards ahead.

I imagined horns ripping the artery on the inside of my thigh, the wound that caused most deaths in the bullring. I tripped and fell. A "bull" stopped and looked at me speculatively, its tongue hanging out. Because being licked to death didn't have quite the same charisma as being gored, I shouted at it. It stared at me reproachfully before galloping after its companions.

So I was now behind the herd. But where was Javier?

I noticed a knot of spectators near the slot where we had both intended to make our getaway and ran back to it. Two medics from the ambulance that stood by during the running were kneeling beside Javier's recumbent figure.

They put him on a stretcher and carried him to the ambulance. Was he badly wounded? I asked. They shrugged with somber eloquence. The ambulance drove away at speed, siren wailing. I felt sick with worry—and guilt because I had encouraged him to participate in the running.

I asked a spectator where he lived and collected his wife, dark-haired and gentle-faced, from her home and drove her to the hospital in Denia. Why had he done it? she kept asking. He had promised her he wouldn't.

I kept quiet. If I hadn't told him he looked younger than he was, he wouldn't have broken his promise . . .

"It's his birthday on Wednesday," she said, knuckles bone white on her clenched fists. "I've bought him a tie."

We waited at reception in the hospital where I had waited after Vicente the roofer had fallen from the wall of the dining hall. The same doctor who had examined Vicente came through the swing doors and beckoned Javier's wife.

She returned five minutes later. "First he met the bulls," she said. "Now he is meeting God."

But the meeting with the Almighty didn't last long. Apparently Javier had tripped but he had only struck his head on the curb. He was discharged from the hospital that night, suffering from concussion, the doctor's specialty.

The following day, my feelings confused by relief at Javier's recovery and annoyance at Pablo and Pedro's incompetence, I called a halt to the destruction of the driveway. There had to be an easier way of finding a leak.

I adjourned to the garage with Pedro and Pablo while they ate the identical breakfasts they brought with them—serrano ham *bocadillos*, bananas, and bottles of beer.

The sewage specialist stopped his bicycle outside the gates, threw up his hands, presumably horrified at the lack of progress, and pedaled away.

"*Cabron*," said Pablo or Pedro. Literally "goat" but open to other interpretations.

Diane summoned me into the house for poached eggs, marmalade, and toast and tea, relieved that she wasn't embarking on widowhood.

We listened to the roofer, the sound of water leaking, and the occasional rumbling from the bathroom.

Diane voiced our mutual feelings. "That vision we had . . . it's fading fast, isn't it." She eyed me over the steam from her mug of tea. "I met a Dutch real estate agent yesterday."

"You think we should sell the house?"

"What do you think?"

"It's admitting defeat," I said.

"Or being sensible for once in our lives."

"What about Jonathan?"

"I didn't say anything about leaving the area." She poured herself more tea. "This Dutch agent—"

"Knows of a place with stunning views?"

"It's a wreck," she said.

"Forget it."

"Going for a song. And, yes, it has got great views. And he says we could get a fortune for this place."

"Half a roof over the dining hall? The monster from the deep about to surface in the driveway?"

"He says he's got a client," Diane said.

I glanced at my watch. Ten A.M. "He should be in his office by now," I said. "I'll give him a call."

S I X T E E N

Mrs. Prodski in Paradise

The client, the English-speaking real estate agent said on the phone, couldn't view our house until the following day. When I asked: "Who is he?" the agent replied: "It's a she, a bit of a mystery but loaded."

"Nationality?"

"Bulgarian," the agent said.

"Why does she want to live here?"

"I told you, she's an enigma." Like so many Dutch away from their homeland, he spoke almost faultless English. "About the price . . ."

"What do you suggest?"

"I haven't inspected the property yet," he said. "Your wife said there were a few problems."

Diane had never been a master of understatement but she had outdone herself on this occasion. "You'd better come and have a look," I said. "And bring a pair of waders."

He arrived wearing black loafers with tassels and a cream, lightweight suit. A diminutive dandy with a tanned, poolside face.

He stared at the driveway with dismay. "Can't you get this fixed?"

"We're trying," I said. "Believe me, we're trying," stunned by such an asinine question. I had been listening, ear to the ground, endeavoring to follow the current under the paving stones, but so far my deductive powers had failed me.

He stood in the dining hall and looked up at the unfinished roof. Vicente the roofer waved at him, dropping a hammer that crashed to the floor.

"Your wife was right," he said. "There are problems. But my client is very anxious to find an old property in this area. Leave the price to me, I will sound her out. If you're not satisfied we can negotiate."

He inspected the house, noting its faults on a small and inadequate pad. "I have to prepare myself for any criticisms she might make," he explained.

"How are you going to explain the driveway?"

"That's a plus—you're having new pipes laid. There aren't many houses around here with new pipes."

"The roof?"

"By the time she moves in it will be . . . baronial. Is that a good description?"

"Couldn't have put it better myself," I said.

We sat opposite each other on plastic chairs on the terrace. I waited for Jones to stop sniffing his legs before asking about the ruin he was offering us.

"Not exactly a ruin," he said. "It has great potential. And stunning views." He held up one hand and chuckled. "I know what you're going to say—in real estate speak all views are stunning."

"I've been told it's cheaper to build a new house than renovate an old one."

"Your wife"—Diane was away teaching—"told me you were only interested in mature properties. Do you want to see it?"

"Why not? I've got nothing to lose."

While I was writing a note in the kitchen telling Diane where I had gone, Jones yelped. I guessed the agent had kicked him. On the way to his Mercedes parked on the roadside he stepped on a loose paving stone, which squirted muddy water up one leg of his cream suit.

"Are you sure that's a plus?" I asked him.

The ruin I discovered five minutes later about a mile away was a crumbling mansion with a long balcony supported by rusting metal pillars. Ten rooms on two floors contained by sturdy walls that looked as though they hadn't been occupied since the Civil War. It was probably about one hundred years old. On the first floor I found copies of the right-wing newspaper *ABC* dated 1939 and black-bordered invitation cards to a memorial service the same year. It wasn't connected to either the water or electricity mains but those, the agent said, could be installed cheaply.

"It also needs a new roof," I pointed out, wondering how Vicente would react to the dizzy heights of a two-storey building.

"Of course. But you will end up with a palace instead of—"

"What?"

"What you've got now."

I was beginning to dislike him. "Why isn't your client interested in this place?" I asked him.

"It's too big. And she wants to be closer to the village."

"Are you sure she's loaded?"

"As rich as Croesus," he said with the assurance of a professional who can smell money.

I climbed a rusty outside staircase and gazed across the citrus groves. On one side of the house I could see the sea a mile away, on the other the reassuring bulk of Montgo, its broad brow bathed in sunshine.

"How much does the owner want for it?" I asked with studied lack of interest.

"He hasn't decided yet. But he's very anxious to sell." The agent lowered his voice to a conspiratorial whisper. "Creditors are snapping at his heels."

Did he divulge such confidential details to all prospective purchasers? What had he told the Bulgarian woman about me? A deranged Englishman with an oversexed dog and a cat with a wooden leg?

He gave me a key to the mansion and that evening I showed it to Diane. She enthused, likening it to a grand old house in America's Deep South, envisaging herself in later life sitting on a rocking chair on the porch embroidering tablecloths—anything between total love and utter rejection had always been foreign territory to her. I liked the house too. And yet we had put so much of ourselves into the home we had first glimpsed in the moonlight . . .

We agonized late into the night.

"We could convert a ruin like that into a small hotel," Diane said ambitiously.

"I came here to fill pages, not stomachs," I said. "I'm not into real estate speculation." Anathema to me, in fact.

"But you do love the place, I can feel it."

"Do you see me as a southern gentleman riding through cotton fields?"

"Not really," she said.

We overslept the following morning, and when I finally got out of bed Vicente was already laying tiles with clattering abandon.

I put on a bathrobe, squeezed orange juice for the three of us, and went into the garden.

Montgo was etched sharply against a cloudless sky; the scent of jasmine was on the air. The green oranges were ripening, the blue trumpets of morning glory that had climbed the chain link around the vegetable garden, despite Ángel's efforts to exterminate them, were dimpled by a breeze coming from the distant hills. Jones trotted past on important business, Hoppity tried out a new wooden leg, Ethel washed herself.

I swam a couple of lengths of the pool and picked the last of the figs, green-skinned and pink-fleshed, for breakfast.

Could we possibly leave all this for a gaunt mansion without electricity or piped-in water where atrocities had probably been perpetrated during the Civil War, and bodies were perhaps buried under its flagstones?

I wandered round to the front of the house. From the top of the dining hall came a cry of triumph. Vicente raised both fists, swaying dangerously. "The last tile is laid," he shouted.

The telepathy that accompanies good marriages worked overtime at breakfast: we both now knew that neither of us wanted to leave the house, even with all its defects.

Diane, on her second, tongue-loosening mug of tea, said: "We don't have to sell, do we?"

I spread honey on a slice of toast. "We don't *have* to. But if we made a profit on the sale we could definitely stay in Spain."

"You mean as things stand we can't?"

"Not if we have to pay the demolition squad in the driveway, not if my book's a turkey. As a matter of fact I've given us to the end of the year to make or break."

"You have?" She looked crestfallen, then brightened. "Don't worry—the leak in the driveway will be on the other side of the meter so we won't have to pay and your book will be a bestseller, and we can take the house off the market."

At eleven I drove Jonathan into Denia to a private tutor who, during the summer vacation, was teaching him elementary math—a subject in which he could expect no help from his parents. When I got back to the house the Dutch real estate agent was there with his client, a beefy middle-aged woman in a miniskirt, with red hair combed into a sixties-style beehive. She laughed easily, seemingly at nothing, and spoke inventive English.

"I am charming to meet," she said, extending one hand, rings tight on dimpled fingers. "I shall like your house."

I said to the agent: "Could you excuse us a minute?" and led Diane to the kitchen where I asked her what was going on. "Why didn't you tell them we weren't selling?"

"I did sort of promise we would sell it through him when I first met him a couple of days ago."

"So what? We've changed our minds." Suspicions began to dawn. "You didn't sign anything did you?" A lot of agents asked vendors to sign forms giving them the exclusive right to sell a property. I had always doubted their legality.

She nodded. "I did sign something. He said it was a mere formality." She squeezed my arm. "It doesn't matter anyway, I've got a plan. What we do is this: we exaggerate all the disadvantages of the house. Do the opposite to what real estate agents do. That way she'll lose interest and we'll be off the hook. And he won't bring any more clients around if he knows we're going to badmouth it again."

"You mean tell her it's a dump?"

"Sort of. But be subtle. Watch my lips."

From the devastated driveway the agent led the client—her name was Prodski—into the dining hall, now roofed. She laughed, dredged up some obscure Bulgarian humor and said: "Vere are the bats?"

Playing into our hands.

"They come at night," Diane said.

"I loov bats," Mrs. Prodski said.

"We didn't think they'd stay," Diane said. "You know the fire smoked so badly when we first lit it we thought that would frighten them away."

"I loov woodsmoke." Mrs. Prodski breathed deeply. "Where I am coming from we smoke sturgeon fishes."

We went into the kitchen. "We're hoping they've fixed the electrical fault," Diane said. She was, I presumed, referring to the occasion when, smelling burning in the kitchen, she had called the fire brigade.

Mrs. Prodski said: "I worry not, my husband Serge will correct."

"It's a pity about the water," I said, taking my cue from Diane. "Sometimes it goes off for a whole day. Sometimes longer."

Mrs. Prodski laughed hugely. "Who drinks vater?" She wiped her eyes with a handkerchief embroidered with alpine flowers.

Her resistance to Diane's strategy was beginning to worry me.

On the way to the living room, out of her earshot, the agent grabbed my arm. "What the hell do you think you are playing at?" he demanded.

"Something you wouldn't understand," I told him. "It's called telling the truth."

Diane pointed at a cracked floor tile. "Sometimes that moves as though someone is trying to escape from a dungeon underneath."

Mrs. Prodski clapped her hands. "A tree that has not been properly gutted. Where I am born we had a cherry tree breaking into the eating room."

I led her to the bar made from an old wedding chest that I had installed in the original dining room where, when the weather wasn't good enough to dine outside, we ate while waiting for the new one to be finished. She pointed at the bottles behind it. "Wodka I loov. You have the Polish wodka?"

"Only Russian vodka, I'm afraid," I told her.

"That will do. No vater. That is spoiling it."

"Ice?"

More humor surfaced from the Balkans. When it had subsided she said: "Ice is vater, heavy vater."

I poured her a vodka. "That would not be enough for Serge." Not for her either because she picked up the bottle and topped up her glass. "With wodka you must be eating. You have the black bread?"

I appealed to Diane, who was pouring us each a beer, while the agent moodily sipped Bols gin. She found a sliced brown loaf and a jar of pickled gherkins.

When she had poured herself another vodka and noisily chewed a couple of gherkins Mrs. Prodski said: "And now the bedrooms I have to see." She winked.

In our bedroom Diane said: "A pity about the screech owls—they keep us awake."

"Ah, creatures of the nighttime," Mrs. Prodski said. "They are making me sleep."

She bounced on the bed. "With Serge I have to have the most powerful springs." She winked again.

"Even without him," Diane whispered to me.

As we headed for the terrace the agent tried to get into the act, which was undermining all the tenets of his profession. "It's a long way from the sea," he told Mrs. Prodski.

"I hate the sea," she said. "It has taken my father."

The agent smiled uncertainly. Then, believing that he was getting the hang of this sado-masochistic hype, told her the nearest town, Denia, was at least two miles away and there were no buses.

She punched him on the arm. "Vunderbar. Space! Let's have another snorting." She led us back to the bar.

Diane beckoned me into the kitchen. "She's acting as though she's the owner and we're the buyers."

"We'll have to change tactics," I said. "Damn the place with faint praise."

"Maybe. But I'll fire a couple more shots first."

We all went into the garden.

"We're hoping the snake won't come back," Diane said.

"For why?" Mrs. Prodski asked.

"I don't like snakes."

"Serge is getting them by the tails and jerking them like a whip so their backings break." She snapped her fingers.

"And the neighbors," Diane breathed.

Mrs. Prodski tugged her skirt, which was riding high on her nutcracker thighs. "What about them?"

"They make a lot of noise," Diane whispered. "Parties, that sort of thing." The neighbors were, in fact, quiet, amiable, and helpful.

"Orgies?"

"I don't really know about—"

"Serge and I are tolerable. We orgy sometimes."

I decided that it was time to change tactics. I gestured towards Montgo. "The view is beautiful but it gets a little boring."

"I am not liking your mountain." Mrs. Prodski shivered histrionically. "Mountains press upon me."

"The garden is adequate, nothing exciting," I told her.

"Serge likes to labor."

"And it's very quiet here."

"I like to hear living."

The agent, trying to adapt to this new strategy, asked Mrs. Prodski if she liked cats. When she shook her head vehemently he started to tell her there was a dearth of them in the neighborhood but Diane immediately reverted to her original tactics. "Litters of them. Look at her," pointing at Ethel. "She has kittens every time she looks at a tomcat. She goes with the house when we sell it," she added.

The little train hooted from the orange groves.

I pointed at it. "That will get you to Benidorm in one hour, if you like crowded beaches," I added, back to damning with faint praise.

"Trains are death," Mrs. Prodski said mysteriously.

The agent, now totally disorientated, played it safe. "Guaranteed sunshine all the year round," he said nodding toward the sun, which promptly disappeared behind a cloud.

"I loov rain."

"We get some, of course," he said.

"I loov it on my face. I open my mouth to it."

"It hasn't rained for three months," Diane said.

"You should be here in the spring," I said. "The wildflowers . . ." I was about to mention the rampant weeds as well but she interrupted. "I am only liking the flowers of the mountains,"

"But you don't like mountains."

Another joke bubbled. She stifled a laugh. "Serge fell off a mountain," she said.

"That was bad luck."

"He will not like your mountain."

The dialogue had now become so surrealist and confusing that I was becoming increasingly confident a deal would not be struck.

"Do you like oranges?" I asked her.

She stared at me incredulously. "Oranges are souring of the stomach."

"Grapefruit?"

"Grapefruit are the plague."

"We've got plenty of both," I said.

"Driving on the back roads can be pretty scary," Diane said. "They're too narrow, too dangerous."

"I am liking poum-poum driving. You know, ins and outs." She spun an imaginary steering wheel.

"For poum-poums you must find bigger roads." Diane turned to me and whispered, "Indianapolis?"

"I make my own poum-poums," Mrs. Prodski said with dignity. "Now I am thinking about another snorting."

As she poured herself a brimming glass of vodka I said: "I'm sorry the house isn't up to your expectations, Mrs. Prodski. But don't worry, you'll find somewhere else."

"Somewhere else?" She pretended to squeeze the last drops of vodka from the bottle. "I loov it here. If anything is going wrong Serge will correct."

"So how are you going to get us out of this mess?" I asked Diane as we ate lunch on the terrace. "Mrs. Prodski is very keen, according to your friend the agent."

"We did both agree we wanted to sell."

Jonathan finished his fresh fruit salad and said: "Sell what?"

"Go and pick some lemons," Diane said, "and I'll make lemonade."

"What exactly did that form you signed say?" I asked her when he had gone to the end of the garden.

"It gave him the exclusive right to sell our house."

"And that was all?"

"It was only one paragraph long." She spooned pineapple and nectarine.

The phone rang in the living room; I answered it. It was the real estate agent.

"I'm calling about Mrs. Prodski," he said.

"An extraordinary woman."

"Yes," he said wearily, "quite extraordinary."

"Does she want to make an offer for the house?"

"Oh, yes, she wants to make an offer all right," he said.

"But she doesn't even know the asking price."

"It's irrelevant."

"What do you mean, irrelevant?"

"She's offering to pay in her own currency," the agent said.

"Slotis? Something like that?"

"Levs."

"Not much of a demand for levs round here."

"Know what I think, Mr. Lambert? I think she is one of a breed.

We real estate agents meet a lot of them. Looking at other people's houses is their hobby. They have no intention of buying."

"But she *is* offering levs."

"Knowing you won't accept them. She's had a good morning out. A free ride. Lots of vodka."

"Wodka."

"But don't worry, I've got other clients."

I was sure he had. Buying and selling property was big business in the region and scams abounded. But the culprits were mostly foreigners who cheated other foreigners—selling houses they didn't own or properties on which money was owed or taking deposits and vanishing with the loot. The problem was that a curious naivete assailed many expatriates when they set foot in Spain: if they all observed the same procedures followed in their own countries they would put the property sharks out of business.

"I'll bring them around on one condition," the agent went on. "That you and your wife don't interfere."

"It doesn't matter," I said. "I'm taking the house off the market."

"But it's only been on it a day."

"I'm not selling."

"But your wife—" He sounded as if he was in shock.

"Signed an agreement, I know. All it does is give you the sole right to sell our house. But if we don't want to sell it's superfluous. And in any case, legally it's not worth the paper it's printed on."

"But—"

"Burn it," I said, and hung up.

I told Diane and she kissed me. We inspected the newly covered dining hall and wandered round the sunlit garden. Our vision was still on course.

"By the way," she said as we walked back into the house. "The fridge has iced up."

"Don't worry," I said. "I will correct."

Although we had navigated Mrs. Prodski and the Dutch real estate agent there were still dangerous waters ahead, in particular the leak somewhere between the road and the house. Donning the mantle of Agatha Christie's Hercule Poirot, I gave my "little gray cells" a good shake, stood in the driveway, and reviewed the evidence. The gray cells failed to respond.

I picked my way among the excavations, once again tried to follow the currents of water—they trickled prettily in all directions—and listened to the sounds of seepage. There was a clue somewhere there but it refused to stand up and take a bow.

Diane came out of the house on her way to the Citroën parked on the roadside next to the Jaguar—we could no longer maneuver either of them onto the ruins of the driveway.

"They're doing well." She pointed at a clump of marguerites in the flowerbed beside it. They were indeed: whereas most other plants had succumbed to the heat the white, daisy-like blossoms of the marguerites were proliferating.

My gray cells stirred. When Diane had gone I consulted Ángel, who was picking tomatoes in his prison yard, his face beneath his battered straw hat resolutely pale despite the fierce sunshine.

"When was the new driveway laid?" I asked him.

"A few months before you moved in," he said. He took a bite out of a large, overripe tomato.

"Was the previous one wider?"

"It wasn't narrower."

"So it was wider?"

"I suppose so," he conceded.

"So if a water pipe was laid under the old driveway it could now be under the flowerbed beside it?"

Like a witness in court perceiving a trap in every question,

Ángel warily admitted this might be so. I beckoned; he finished the tomato and followed me onto the driveway.

"Look." I pointed at the marguerites. "Doing well, aren't they?" Ángel admitted they were.

"Because they're being watered. Get your towel, dig there, and I think you'll find the leak because that's where the pipe was laid in the first place."

The denouement! Little gray cells in overdrive. Such a scene was usually set in the living room of an English country mansion but a shattered driveway next to a baronial dining hall would do just as well.

Ángel dug tentatively as though excavating an unexploded mine and finally uncovered a small jet of water escaping from a corroded pipe. It saturated the roots of the marguerites before heading for the substratum of the driveway.

But I wasn't yet finished. I went down on one knee and, like a golfer measuring up a putt, squinted across the driveway at the water meter. The leak was between the meter and the road so the water company would have to pay for the repairs and the destruction wrought by their employees.

At that moment Javier, the plumber who had been injured during the running of the bulls, arrived. He was, he said, on the road to recovery. "Concussion takes its time." He shook his head and winced.

I clapped him on the shoulder. "You were very brave," I said.

I led him to the bathroom. "Are you well enough to fix this?" I turned on one of the washbasin taps and the shuddering recommenced. "You promised . . ."

I didn't think the noise had anything to do with the leak in the driveway and I was sure Javier could fix it.

"I'm thinking of joining the Moors and Christians," he said. "As a Moor . . . I thought you might like to join with me."

"Not my style, Javier."

"All right, if you think I let you down during the running of the bulls . . ." He turned his back on the source of the shuddering.

"Aren't you going to fix it?"

"My head aches," he said.

"Okay, you win—I'll join the Moors and Christians with you. Next year."

Obviously a long and bruising relationship lay ahead of us.

He kicked the U-bend beneath the basin and the shuddering faltered. Spanish plumbing, I reflected, was pretty basic, but did that really matter so long as plumbers such as Javier understood its foibles?

The next time I turned one of the washbasin taps the water flowed without a murmur. Later that day Pablo and Pedro fixed the leak I had located and began to repair the shattered driveway.

I retired to the terrace and began to read an Agatha Christie paperback.

SEVENTEEN

Diane Grits Her Teeth

The heat welded August onto July. We had envisaged a leisurely month eating salads and drinking iced tea beside the pool and, after I had finished my writing stint for the day, driving into the hills in the cool of the evening to look for villages we hadn't yet discovered. We had reckoned without the roofing party.

The foreman of the building team that had constructed the dining hall told me it was a tradition, a get-together thrown after the last tile has been slotted above the rafters. The red and yellow Spanish flag is raised, all the irritations of gestation forgotten—or so he claimed optimistically.

Ángel and Emilio appointed themselves as

consultants. Both saw themselves as the ultimate authorities on roofing parties; both offered contradictory advice on almost everything
and sulked if their suggestions were disregarded.

The first minefield was the guest list. The only certainties were
the builders and their families and Vicente. After that selection
became invidious. Should we invite the mayor *and* Bernardo the
wastrel? Certainly we couldn't invite everyone we knew in the village—at least one hundred altogether.

Emilio submitted a list omitting Ángel. Ángel submitted a list
omitting Emilio. Both claimed the omissions were oversights. Both
of their lists were comprehensively different.

Finally we called on our limited reserves of diplomacy and
invited fifty, mostly tradespeople and casual friends we had met
at Pilar's and the Bar Paraiso. No mayor—we didn't really know
him; no Bernardo, who might binge and wreck the whole enter-
prise. Then we set about victualing; I ordered the booze, Diane
the food.

Paella, Diane decided, would be the hub around which the meal
would be constructed, after all it was said to have originated during
hard times as an economical stomach filler, and we couldn't afford a
seven-course banquet.

Both Ángel and Emilio, it transpired, were masters in the prepa-
ration of a *paella.* Ángel said the rice should be fried in *sofrito*—olive
oil, garlic, onions—before stock was added, the Alicante method.
Emilio said the stock should be added to the rice and they should be
fried together, Valencian style.

Ángel recommended the addition of meatballs. Emilio, pounding the kitchen table with a wooden meat tenderizer, denounced this
as sacrilege—chicken, pork, diced ham, lobster, shrimps, clams, and
mussels were the only true occupants of the *paella* pan. As far as I
was concerned anything was acceptable, except snails.

Diane didn't take any notice of either of them: she was doing the cooking: the party was her show and no one was going to mess around with her.

From the *pasteleria* in the village she ordered homemade *cocas*— open tarts filled with sardines, anchovies, onions, and tomatoes or peas, the forerunners of pizzas that the Spanish were said to have introduced into Naples centuries ago—tortillas, anise-flavored doughnuts, and custard-filled pastries.

From Pilar she ordered fresh pineapples, nectarines, muscatel grapes, and Manchego cheese. She herself would, she said, make *Gazpacho Andaluz,* cold tomato soup, also called liquid salad.

I ordered sparkling wine known as *cava*—the best barely distinguishable from champagne—red and white wine, brandy, and beer. When Emilio heard I intended to make sangria he said it was the best thirst quencher in Spain on a hot day. Ángel said it was rubbish concocted for tourists.

We rented a *paella* pan, brightly burnished and as big as a cartwheel, and I cut twigs from orange trees for the barbecue fire. Ángel and Emilio said they would help with the *paella,* a recipe for disaster as I should have realized.

Diane began preparations a week before the party and whenever possible I escaped to make the other arrangements—to hire a musician, a plump guitarist with black curls and cheeks as rosy as a Russian doll's, rent trestle tables and chairs, and buy cigars from the tobacconist in the village.

As well as cigars and cigarettes he sold postage stamps and glossy gossip magazines, creased by customers who came to read but not to buy.

A cracked bell above the door announced your arrival from the dazzling outdoors and from the depths of the cobwebbed gloom came reedy whispers.

Then he materialized, striped pajamas protruding from baggy

trousers, cardigan unevenly buttoned, searching his scalp for wisps of hair in case they had been stolen overnight.

Behind him, his wife was just discernible, clothed in Bible black, spoon poised above a bowl of soup, part of an old-fashioned tableau in a penny arcade waiting for a coin to drop.

If you bought a small bottle of beer, which he was licensed to sell, he became convivial, even more so if you bought him one as well. Once, after aiming the neck of the bottle into his mouth, he produced from under the counter a sepia photograph of himself, as a fierce young man with oiled hair and a bandolier heavy with bullets. He was dressed in one of the ragbag uniforms the Republicans wore during the Civil War and he looked as if he might have just killed someone.

Suddenly I saw him behind the counter, young and careless with his life, even more so with the lives of his enemies. I asked for a stamp for the United Kingdom and he grew old again, brooding darkly while his wife sipped broth. Finally he said: "How much is it?"

"Fifty pesetas," I said—enough to buy ten stamps but he could do with the money. His wife said: "And don't forget the two beers, you old goat." He regarded her affectionately through the muslin gloom. We have shared, you and I, the look said, and once you were a tigress.

I paid him; he tossed the coins into the open drawer of an antique cash register and a moth flew out. As I left he retreated through the gloom navigating phantom obstacles, sat beside his wife, and dunked a crust of bread in their shared bowl of broth.

I went back to his shop three days before the party to buy stamps—the tobacco and postage stamp concession handed down from family to family was one of the most prized possessions in Spain—but it was shut.

I learned later that he had died in his sleep. Nothing specific, the priest told me, just *los años,* the years. "I am waiting for his wife to join him," he said.

This she did a few days later, no doubt a tigress once again wherever they were now sharing a bowl of broth.

Friday, the day before the roofing party, Emilio and Ángel argued about everything; Emilio volubly, Ángel with lofty disdain.

The rented trestle tables that were to be put up in the dining hall—its walls still unplastered, its floor untiled—had been lost in transit from a warehouse in Denia. I phoned the rental company and the manager told me this was to be expected, because the driver of the delivery truck was from Cadiz in the south and hadn't yet memorized the local geography. I slammed down the phone, my fury fueled by the knowledge that instead of a gratifying bang, he heard only a click.

Rain was forecast.

Algae took over the swimming pool and it turned from blue to emerald green.

Hoppity's truncated leg began to fester.

Diane remembered belatedly that Friday was the day she had a weekly English-speaking slot as a DJ on a local radio station. The program for expats lasted only an hour in the morning but it would mean a significant interruption in arrangements for the party the following day.

For four days a week the father of Jonathan's friend Arturo, Miguel Senti, an irrepressible and genial son of Denia who, having worked in Manchester in the United Kingdom for several years, spoke fluent English, introduced the records. On Fridays his wife, Jenny, and Diane, took over. I recorded their show at home on the new music center we had just bought.

I was proud of Diane's initiative and urged our newfound expatriate friends to listen to the show. Spanish radio was very professional—good music and crisply pertinent chat shows—but it was refreshing to hear English on a local station instead of the BBC World Service and Voice of America on shortwave.

Diane usually rushed into the studio just as the show was going on the air and the sound of heavy breathing could be heard. Jenny, from Birmingham, a lady of great presence, would take over until the rate of respirations subsided.

Repartee of a fairly professional quality ensued although occasionally it became personal and domestic.

Jenny: "So what have you been up to, Diane?"

Diane: "Excuse me a moment, Jenny. Are you up yet, Jonathan?"

She meant "Are you out of bed?" but listeners must have wondered who Jonathan was and why a disc jockey had to ask him if he was up. Was he a pilot awaiting permission to take off?

Jenny, finding maternal worries infectious, sometimes followed up with queries such as: "Have you got your books together, Arturo?"

Listeners, unaware that she wanted to make sure her son was ready for school, must by now have been totally baffled. Did Jonathan's copilot need books to tell him how to get a Boeing 747 off the ground?

Requests for records were plentiful, but because the stock was limited they weren't always fulfilled. I regularly requested "Mack the Knife" and was rewarded once with a full-blooded rendering of "Land of Hope and Glory," the unofficial British national anthem, twice by Simon and Garfunkel with "The Sounds of Silence," a daunting title for any record show.

That morning I primed the music center and waited for the program, punctuated by commercials for local shops and services, to begin. Diane's contribution was preceded by the usual breathlessness.

Then she announced that she had received a request from a Dutch artist named Sonje. The German tank commander's adversary at my Spanish classes?

"She has asked for a song from World War Two for a gentleman named Klaus." So it was she.

"Roll Out the Barrel"? "Lili Marlene"?

A pause while, I assumed, a technical difficulty was sorted out. Then, loud and clear, "Land of Hope and Glory."

I brushed aside a ghostly hand from my thigh.

Saturday dawned hazily, banks of pink cloud on the horizon. Spiders' webs bearded with dew sparkled on the grass, small black-and-white birds, pied wagtails, strutted around the pool. The last star of the night was still pinned to the sky but fading fast.

The trestle tables arrived—they had been delivered by mistake to a neighbor's house. Ambrosio fixed the pool, adding crystals of copper sulfate to make it bluer and brighter. Hoppity's stump seemed to be healing again. Prospects for the party looked altogether brighter.

The only threats to its safe passage were the weather and the friction between Ángel and Emilio. And the unforeseen.

The guests were due at one P.M., early for the Spanish, but they have a flexible attitude to time. At ten-thirty the pastries and *cocas* were delivered, at ten-forty-five the drinks. I put the sparkling wine in the fridge, three bottles in the deep freeze, and drove Jonathan, who was once again spending the day with Arturo, into Denia.

When I got back, Ángel and Emilio were inside the covered barbecue complete with built-in bar, basin, and cupboard, preparing the ingredients for the *paella* for Diane to cook. Relations between the two of them seemed to be relatively calm.

Diane was in the kitchen in a state of controlled hysteria. The cold soup was warm even though it had been in the fridge . . . the pineapples seemed too soft, the bread stale . . . no one was going to turn up anyway.

I returned to the barbecue. Emilio was chopping meat while Ángel opened a plastic sachet of saffron. Neither spoke.

Clouds were gathering. A rain-smelling breeze ruffled the pool.

The portents were once again ominous: we had planned to serve prelunch drinks on the terrace so that guests could wander into the garden. If all of them were inside the house, tempers might fray, parochial hostilities surface.

I could hear Diane on the phone. "The first cancellation," she said, replacing the receiver, a note of grim told-you-so triumph in her voice.

"Let's have a drink," I said.

I opened the deep freeze to get a bottle of sparkling wine. All three bottles had burst, and their contents were frozen solid.

The first to arrive were the builders' foreman and his wife. He wore a births, deaths, and marriages suit, black and single-breasted, his chopped hair shone with oil, and the collar of his shirt had sawn a pink line on his neck. His dumpily pretty wife wore a floral dress and pearls. He asked for a beer, she asked for a soft drink. I stared at her blankly. I hadn't bought any. Mineral water would do, she said, but I hadn't got any of that either. Sangria? She recoiled in horror. I introduced her to Diane, leaped into the Jaguar and drove to Pilar's to stock up with Coke, Tri-Naranjus (a nonfizzy orange drink), and mineral water.

When I got back, Vicente the roofer had arrived with his girlfriend, a demure girl with long pale hair and glistening red lips. They sat on the terrace while Vicente elaborated to the foreman and his wife about the ease with which he had overcome his fear of heights.

"Four arrivals, forty-four more to go counting the cancellations," I said to Diane, who was dropping cubes of ice into the tureen of *gazpacho*.

She shook her head. "Tomás, the boss of the building company, and his wife canceled—he's gone to a pigeon race in Gandia, very apologetic. I doubt if anyone else will turn up. Not if they've got somewhere better to go."

Had I married a manic depressive?

From the direction of the barbecue I heard voices raised in anger. I strode across the lawn; rain had started to fall, the powdery sort that stalks English garden parties.

"What the hell's going on?" I demanded.

Ángel was wearing a chef's hat and a blue striped apron; Emilio had stripped down to shorts and undervest.

"That man," Emilio said, pointing at Ángel, "is an idiot."

"Why's that?"

"He's trying to ruin the *paella*. Look."

A plate of meatballs stood between Ángel and the *paella* pan.

"Diane's cooking the *paella*," I snapped. "You're just assistants. If the ingredients she has chosen aren't ready by one-thirty you're both fired."

Not the judgment of Solomon, but it left them both stunned. By the time I got back to the house the rain had thickened; all we needed was thunder and lightning.

Guests were arriving thick and fast now. The driveway, relaid with new paving stones, was crowded with cars, others were parked on the roadside.

Maria, Diane's slow-moving home help, was pouring champagne in tulip glasses—I had substituted a tape of the "Radetzky March" for a waltz to kick-start her—and distributing peanuts, slices of cold tortilla, and potato chips to guests who were drifting into insular groups dictated by profession, age, and means, most of them in the dining hall and living room.

The priest approached. "I haven't seen you in church lately, *Señor* Lambert."

"I've been very busy, Father."

"God is very busy too but he always finds time to listen to prayers." His plump face was damp with perspiration but a gray suit and clerical collar had transformed him from humble clergyman into ecclesiastical dude.

"I'll come tomorrow, I promise."

"Never make promises you can't keep."

"I'll be there, Father," I said.

He held out his glass and Maria replenished it. "Better than altar wine," he said appreciatively. "Do you always serve champagne before a meal?"

"Doesn't everyone?"

"Oh, no—in Spain it's served after a meal."

Glass in hand, I circulated, listening to incomprehensible Valenciano, taking my cue from the language of the hands. The women, freshly delivered from hairdressers, mostly wore lightweight suits, blouses, and necklaces, flapping their fans irritably when they were ignored by their menfolk. The men shed their jackets and lit cigarettes. No ashtrays! I found a couple in the back of our cabinets and supplemented them with saucers.

Diane, wearing an apron printed with tropical fruit, went out to the barbecue to cook the *paella*.

Rain drummed on the new roof of the dining hall. The air sweated despite the absence of a door or glass in the windows.

Jones made his move while Maria was laying out soup bowls on the two long trestle tables covered with damask tablecloths. Until now, although he'd frightened a couple of children with one of his exuberant welcomes, he had behaved himself, with athletic dexterity catching potato chips and peanuts thrown to him.

Suddenly he hurled himself between the builders' foreman and Pilar, knocked over a couple of chairs and, barking hysterically, disappeared through the doorway.

The enemy was at the gate—the woodman. "That dog should be shot," he said as Jones hurled himself against the wrought-iron bars.

"He lives here, you don't," I told him.

Diane joined me and spoke to him in Valenciano.

"He doesn't want to come to the party, does he?" I asked her.

"He wants you to know that if you order your orange and olive tree logs now they will be two pesetas a kilo cheaper than if you order later."

"Tell him to come back tomorrow at ten." Jones had my complete support in his dislike of this man—he was a hustler and an animal hater.

"Why ten?"

"Because I'll be in church. When he comes tell him we want them three pesetas cheaper . . . that's fair. If he doesn't agree threaten him with Jones."

The rain had stopped but a wind had sprung up, blowing leaves and grass clippings through the windows and doorway into the dining hall. I saw Ángel's sloe-eyed wife remove a pine needle from her glass of wine and drop it in the fireplace.

When the wind finally died down I heard a splash and a shout. I ran into the garden. A small girl was struggling and gasping in the deep end of the pool and two boys were stripping off to mount a rescue bid—they had probably pushed her in.

I thrust toward her the net, attached to a long pole, for skimming the surface of the water, told her to catch hold of it, and pulled her to the side of the pool. She sat on the grass and began to cry. "I didn't want to be rescued," she said between sobs. "I can swim."

She was taken home by her mother, one of the village hairdressers. Ten minutes later she was back wearing another party dress and threatening to jump in the pool to prove she could swim.

I was too distracted to take much notice of her because I had lost the Spanish flag that was supposed to be raised on the roof after lunch. As master of ceremonies I was a failure. It was beginning to look as if I didn't give a damn about anything, carelessly losing the national flag and displaying minimal interest in little girls dicing with death in the swimming pool.

I told the guests to take their seats, guiding them to their chairs and making sure that princes sat next to paupers.

Maria served the *gazpacho*. I poured wine—no one wanted my sangria. Nothing more could go wrong.

The crash registered only peripherally because I was deep into a debate with the policeman and the owner of the pharmacy about street lighting in the village. But a metallic thud followed by stifled cursing penetrated my consciousness.

Maria cleared the soup bowls, I refilled wineglasses while the guitarist played flamenco, coaxing wistful smiles from a couple from Andalusia, the home of the gypsy music. Through the doorway I could see blue sky above the cypress hedge.

From the terrace where we had seated five children—Jonathan could have stayed if we had known they were coming—came the sounds of giggling and barking. I went outside but nothing more serious than Jones embarking on a gecko stakeout was happening— he would sit for an hour at a time willing the small sticky-footed lizards to fall off the face of a wall.

In the barbecue on the far side of the lawn Ángel and Emilio were wrapping damp cloths round the two handles of the piping hot *paella* pan. Steam rose from the paddy field of yellow rice within its circumference. Often families sat round the pan eating directly from it, prospecting for the crisp *soccarat* beneath the rice. But this *paella* was on the heroic scale and we had brought a plastic table from the terrace into the dining hall to accommodate it.

Ángel and Emilio placed the pan on the table. Plates in hands, guests lined up to be served by Maria, returning to the trestle tables which, put end to end, stretched the length of the room, to await the go-ahead from the foreign couple with their peculiar ideas of protocol.

Diane forked a peeled prawn and everyone began to eat. The

chewing slowed, a faint grating could be heard. Paper napkins were applied to lips. Despair settled coldly on me as I realized that the crunchy morsel in my mouth was not a crispy vegetable, but gravel!

I removed a piece from my mouth, asked the guests to lay down their spoons and forks, and went outside to confront Ángel and Emilio, who were in the barbecue.

They confessed in a welter of recriminations. They had carried the *paella* pan to the front of the house, intending to bring it through the doorway of the dining hall but one of them had slipped on the rain-wet paving stones—I never discovered which—and they had spilt the contents onto the driveway where builder's gravel had been piled.

"And you put it all back in the pan?" I shut my eyes. "I can't believe I'm hearing this."

"We took it back to the barbecue," Emilio said. "We picked out as much gravel as we could. Then we smoothed it over."

I stormed back to the house. The dining hall was quiet, guests staring at their plates with awe and amazement. I told them what had happened.

Tears gathered in Diane's eyes.

It was Pilar who ended the crisis. "We're not blind, are we?" she demanded, addressing the other guests. "We can all see a piece of gravel and take it out." She took a spoonful of rice, removed a chip of gravel from it and began to eat.

One by one others followed. The *extranjeros,* the foreigners, had tried: that was what mattered.

Soon they were all eating as tentatively as hedgehogs making love. Relief surged through me and I too began to eat.

After that the party rallied. Doughnuts and pastries, bowls of fruit glistening with ice, Manchego cheese, brandy and more champagne were dispatched. I found the Spanish flag in the laundry basket.

Vicente tied it to the chimney, where it fluttered regally in the breeze.

I squeezed Diane's hand. She squeezed back. It was our first communal get-together and we sensed we were on the threshold of acceptance. It would take much longer—and we would always be the *extranjeros*—but the party had established that we wanted to belong, a sentiment not always evinced by foreigners. What had helped, of course, were the mishaps, which had dispelled any suspicion that we were patronizing: it was difficult to resent anyone who served a gravel *paella*.

The children played football in the dripping garden. One speared his arm on a rapier-tipped blade of a yucca that my shears had missed; his mother dabbed the wound with a scarlet antiseptic—he told the others it was blood and they touched it reverently.

The musician, black curls bobbing, fetched a piano accordion and played the latest pop music hits. I folded the trestle tables and danced with Ángel's wife. Other couples took to the floor, shyly at first, as if they had just met, then with nimble-footed abandon. Emilio sang robust songs.

At six o'clock the musician departed to play at his own saint's day party. But the festive spirit still pervaded the house so I grabbed the first cassette that came to hand and slotted it into the music center.

The tape whirred for a moment. Then I heard two familiar voices emerging from the loudspeakers.

"So what have you been up to, Diane?"

"Excuse me a moment, Jenny. Are you up yet, Jonathan?"

I pressed Fast Forward until "The Sounds of Silence" filled the room.

E I G H T E E N

The Gecko Blaster

The plasterer arrived on what I had hoped
would be a tranquil morning. The dog days
of summer had passed, stems of smoke rose
serenely from bonfires in the citrus groves,
smudges of white cloud drifted toward the sea,
almond pickers knocking nuts from their trees
with poles punctuated the daylight hours with a
drowsy clatter.

The tranquility was broken by the thump
of rock music. A white van pulled into the driveway; the driver, a young Spaniard with auburn,
shoulder-length curls, switched off the radio and
climbed out. A moment's peace. Then he switched
on a ghetto blaster or a boom box, a portable radio
and cassette player with twin speakers.

He smiled and shook my hand. He was, he said, the plasterer, an unnecessary introduction because his denim jacket and jeans were stiff with plaster. There were even traces of it on his bandit mustache.

I asked him how long it would take him to plaster the walls of the dining hall. The exterior was straightforward; what worried me was the interior, because we wanted an old-fashioned finish in which the plaster is applied with the heel of the hand, leaving slight hollows.

"Two weeks," he said. *"Mas o menos"*—more or less, the standard get-out for all Spanish estimates, as commonplace as *mañana*, which means tomorrow or any time in the near or distant future.

A minimum of two weeks pounding rock music when I was trying to beckon prospective readers into the quiet of the Siberian taiga? I had adapted to noise because it was as necessary to Spanish life as kicking footballs and kissing babies. The roar of cars without mufflers, the rasp of mopeds, the cannon fire of fireworks, the chatter and clatter of busy bars . . . but my skull would not be able to accommodate a relentless bass beat.

I told him to switch off the ghetto blaster.

"Sure man, why not?" He spoke hip with a Cockney accent—I learned later that he had worked as a waiter in London. He turned the blaster off. "But I must warn you—I can't do my best work without it." He smiled sweetly. *Why not live with it?*

Ghetto-blasting workmen are not uncommon in Britain, but in Spain they are symptomatic of the national disregard for noise—maybe it harks back to the cannon fire of their many wars. I once gobbled up my breakfast in a New York diner because the waitresses barking orders loudly, incessantly, into the kitchen were putting me off my sunny-side-up eggs: I discovered that they were all Spanish.

"I'm trying to write a book," I told him.

"A writer, huh? Cool, real cool." His hand strayed to the On button of his blaster. "Music would give you inspiration, you know."

"I've got plenty of that," I said. "My problem is getting it from my brain down my arms to my typewriter."

"Yeah, well, I dig. I write too, music. I've got my own group."

"You can write while you're listening to tapes?"

"It's the only way I know," he said.

"And you can't plaster properly without playing them?"

He stroked his drooping mustache. "I'd lose the rhythm."

"Could you play the tapes more quietly?"

"I could try, but rock music played softly . . ." He shook his head and his shoulder-length curls shook with it. "Music's got to take you over body and soul."

"Try," I said.

"Okay, man, it's your money." I had previously arranged to pay him by the hour and I got the message—the lower the decibels, the slower the work.

I left him mixing plaster in the dining hall, where Emilio was fitting window frames and an electrician was threading wires into cavities behind the walls. When the three of them had finished, only the door, window glass, minstrel gallery, and floor tiles would be needed.

I adjourned to the annex—one tiny bedroom and a bathroom—and tried to return to the Russian steppe, but the beat of the music still reached me. Frustration spilled over: I had to find a way to broker peace.

I returned to the dining hall. The plasterer was standing on a ladder slapping plaster onto a wall listening to the Rolling Stones, whose music I normally enjoyed. So apparently did Emilio and the electrician, who were both working energetically to the beat. Diane was in Denia, Jonathan was back at his kindergarten in Denia after the summer vacation.

I beckoned the plasterer onto the terrace. He followed, bringing the Stones with him. Emilio joined us.

"Be honest," I said. "What would really happen if you turned off the player?"

"Simple," Emilio answered for him. "Toni couldn't work."

I looked at Emilio suspiciously. "Toni? Is he related to you?"

"Only by marriage."

I sighed. "How closely?"

"He is my wife's nephew," Emilio said.

"Is there anyone in the village who isn't related to you?"

"My wife and I both come from big families."

Toni slotted another Stones cassette into the player. Jones, ears flattened, retired to the end of the garden. Even Ethel stalked away. A gecko fell off the wall.

I was tempted to throw the blaster into the pool. But if I did I would be without a plasterer and I had been warned by the builders that it was difficult to find anyone who was willing to render an old-fashioned finish on a wall.

Toni rolled a cigarette—maybe it was a joint. In the living room I could see Maria mopping the floor tiles to the beat. I was outnumbered.

I told Toni to carry on plastering and wandered round the garden. Ripe tomatoes hung from staked plants in the vegetable patch. Marrows and pumpkins nestled among dying leaves. Crickets jumped from the lawn into the pool and I rescued a few with the net.

The Stones reached me loud and clear.

I had experimented with earplugs in the annex, but although they could muffle the hammering and pounding of the builders, they couldn't extinguish drums and bass guitar. What could I do? Delivery date for the novel was the New Year and the Trans-Siberian hadn't even reached the bridge where it was going to be hijacked by Zionists.

Emilio joined me. He had a solution—I wasn't surprised. He knew of a room to let where, during the day, I could escape from Toni and his blaster.

"How much?" I asked him.

"Cheap."

"Is the owner a relative of yours?"

"Not exactly." He brushed sawdust from his silver-streaked hair.

"Yes or no, Emilio."

"My wife's brother-in-law's sister . . ."

The bass beat grew louder, dispatching a flock of swallows from the telephone wires. "Okay," I said, "let's have a look at it."

The room was an attic in a line of whitewashed houses next to a seamstress whom Diane had met in Pilar's. She made the traditional finery for girls and women in the *fallas* in Denia—brocade dresses with flouncing ankle-length skirts, gold-and-white, crimson, blue, or emerald green. (They wore coiled hairpieces at their ears and upright golden combs and they were all beautiful at these times of fiesta.)

The attic was furnished with a bed, a table, and a chair. On the table stood a jam jar containing stems of dead bougainvillea, the water stained mauve by fallen bracts. The window looked across a yard to another terrace house, painted pigeons in cages cooing on its roof terrace.

It was all I needed: it was quiet. I got it for the equivalent of seven dollars a week.

I arrived after breakfast the following Monday and worked through the morning, taking to the streets to brood if my characters refused to do what I had ordained for them. During these sorties I tried to integrate more, chatting to the priest, the traveling fishmonger, the simpleton with the knowing smile, the schoolmistress, and the policeman known as *El Pistolero* (the gunman) since he had loosed off a few shots at an unscathed but indignant bank robber.

At first *El Pistolero* treated me warily. I was a foreigner, a relatively rare breed inland from the beaches, and was probably a fugitive from the law in my own country.

So he played a waiting game, possibly hoping I would incriminate myself. He warned me instead of booking me when I parked illegally; reminded me when Jones, intimidated by a sighting of the woodman, escaped and went on the rampage, that he could be put to sleep because he hadn't been inoculated for rabies.

When he was finally convinced of my probity he gave me a ticket whenever I parked the car indiscreetly and fined me for Jones's misdemeanors. He had accepted me!

What forged our rapport as far as I could make out was my respect for the village bobbies in Britain, back in those far-off days when the police were more revered than reviled. He reminded me of that breed and my reverence must have been transparent.

He was paunchy, dark hair thinning, blue pants sagging with the weight of his pistol. But he was local; he knew if any crimes such as the theft of crates of freshly picked oranges waiting to be collected on the roadside, or a shoplifting spree, were brewing and aborted them before they got under way.

In his view, laws were merely guidelines and foreigners' respect for them never ceased to amaze him. The obedience of Germans exasperated him. Over a coffee and a brandy he told me one day that two of them had actually gone to the town hall in Denia and informed startled officials that their papers were out of order.

I thought *El Pistolero*'s finest hour had come one day when I was in Pilar's store buying ham and *chorizos* and blue Cabrales cheese packaged in leaves. Customers were discussing the dearth of bank robberies. The culprit blamed for this lack of initiative was progress, not a popular phenomenon with villagers who, having observed what disarray technical innovation had caused elsewhere in the world, had turned their backs on it.

No one was more vociferous than a woman with a chest like a bookshelf and a voice like a chain saw.

"We used to tell the cashier at the bank how much money we wanted and he would give it to us. Now he makes love to a computer and we have to wait until he's finished."

Like the others in the shop she spoke in Valenciano and I had to decipher what she said as best I could.

Pilar handed her a morsel of *jamon serrano*, salt-cured and wind-dried ham, and she chewed it angrily.

She had a point about the banks. A year or so earlier transactions used to be completed speedily to enable the staff to pursue their private businesses—the first bank I visited on the coast was in turmoil because the cashier was in danger of losing his deck-chair concession on the beach. Today, personnel were slaves of wayward microchips.

The woman helped herself to a slice of *fuet,* a sausage thinner and harder than *chorizo*.

"Once we shuffled beads on an abacus and all our sums came out right," she said. "Today we feed facts into an idiot brain and they come out fiction."

She accepted a strip of dried *bacalao,* cod, from Pilar. "Once we listened to plays on the radio and made up our own minds what the characters looked like. Do we have a choice on television?

"Fax messages? Poof! Isn't it better to listen to your daughter's voice on an old telephone on the wall?"

She shook a jar of pickled onions, making them bob like corks.

Diane knew the woman moderately well because with her voice she was difficult to ignore—she could have found employment as a drill sergeant—but her message was low key and logical. What place, she was asking, do microchips have in villages where life is orchestrated by the seasons?

Her ally was the policeman who maintained law and order in his own magisterial fashion. I hoped there were still such policemen and stentorian spokesmen in villages all over Spain to keep technology at bay. Progress is a remorseless opponent, but it was just possible they had got it licked in *pueblos* like ours.

A frail woman with faraway eyes stroked a mauve eggplant. "Yesterday a computer in the bank sent my husband fifty thousand pesetas," she said. "He would have been better pleased if he hadn't been dead for thirteen years." She smiled into the past.

An old man with an autumn-leaf face, reputed to have been a burglar until arthritis crippled his hands, tugged at his fingers, making the joints click. "Progress . . . That's what finished the good times for professionals like me at the banks. Alarm systems, hidden eyes, infrared cameras . . ." He pulled his thumb and it popped as loudly as a twig snapping.

Which was when a young housewife with her hair in curlers dashed into the store. "A bank raid—just now—" At long last, her tone suggested. "Gunshots—"

I raced into the street and grabbed *El Pistolero*. Together we ran to the bank, a modest establishment containing a counter, a safe, and a computer that was treated by the staff of two with profound distrust.

El Pistolero, gun in hand, shouted to the impassive gray-haired cashier: "Where did they go?"

The cashier looked surprised. "The thieves? How should I know? They didn't rob the bank."

El Pistolero faltered and glared at me. "You said—"

I turned to the cashier. "There wasn't a robbery?"

"There was an attempted robbery, all right," he said. "The manager's on the phone to police headquarters now."

"But—"

"The robber had a gun, an imitation I think, but he tried to rob one of the customers, not the bank. The customer's with the manager. He didn't have any money anyway—I should know, he's been overdrawn for months and I refused to give him any."

"What about the gunshots?" I asked.

"Fireworks. It's my father's saint's day. He lives above the bank. He loves explosions, the louder the better. These days he's a little deaf. All those bangs . . ."

I turned back to *El Pistolero* but he had disappeared.

The woman with the chain-saw voice turned on her heel in disgust. "The robber stole nothing? *Madre mia,* that's progress for you!"

I heard the gecko blaster—I had renamed it after it had blasted a gecko off the wall—one hundred yards from the house. I almost turned and drove back to the village, but Diane had promised to make *zarzuela,* fish and shellfish in a rich sauce, and I was hungry. She was in the kitchen snapping her fingers to the beat—I had no allies.

Emilio had fitted the window frames; a glazier with scarred hands was measuring them. Toni, perched on a ladder, was molding plaster on a wall with one hand.

I told Diane about the robbery. She nodded vaguely: Mick Jagger reigned. I returned to my attic in the afternoon and gave the driver of the Trans-Siberian a hard time.

Every day I wrote steadily, morning, afternoon, and evening. Then a couple of drinks in one of the bars, and home to supper beside the pool in the warmth of the late summer night, the scent of jasmine heavy on the air.

The routine lasted only a week. When I arrived at the attic the following Monday morning, three workmen were uprooting the street outside with pneumatic drills. By comparison the music from the gecko blaster was a string quartet.

Replacing my portable typewriter in its case, stashing the pages of the manuscript in my briefcase, I drove home, arriving just as Toni switched on the blaster, sending geckoes scuttering into the garden.

I took Diane's arm. "Are you teaching today?"

She nodded. "At eleven."

"Call up and say you're sick."

"But I'm not."

"Oh, yes, you are," I said. "You don't know it, but you're sick of this noise—it's addling your brain. And pack a bag. We're going shopping in Valencia. Jonathan can stay with Arturo."

I slotted a cassette into the player in the Jaguar. Gentle music, "Lara's Theme," from the movie *Dr. Zhivago* in memory of our days together in Moscow.

The road to Valencia, sixty miles to the north, followed the coast through the small towns of Oliva and Gandia, to the Albufera, a lake separated from the Mediterranean by a sliver of land, the haunt of 260 species of birds. So serene was the lake that day that reflections of palm trees and sharp-roofed Valencian cottages on the shore lay on the water as motionless as images in a mirror.

There was supposed to be a sunken village in the center so we asked a guide to take us to see it in his flat-bottomed fishing boat powered by an outboard engine.

The guide, weather-beaten and taciturn, undertook the mission and pocketed our money with canny fatalism. Birds took off ahead of the boat; fish—the lake is renowned for mullet and eels—darted out of its way.

When we reached the middle we asked him to point out the village, said to have been built on an island or small peninsula, before it was dispatched to the bed of the lake by an earthquake.

He cut the engine and pointed downward with his thumb. We peered overboard but all we could see was water. We had been told that when it was calm and clear the roofs of houses were clearly visible.

Diane looked at him shrewdly. "Have you ever seen the village?"

"It's down there," he said.

"But have you ever seen it?" she demanded.

"You don't have to see to believe."

"You told us—"

"You asked me to take you to see it. You could have been lucky."

"It just wasn't our lucky day?"

He conjured up a smile that cracked his face, pulled the cord on the outboard and took us back to the shore.

We drove on through the *huerta,* rice and vegetable fields, the kitchen garden of Valencia, where herons waded as cautiously as old ladies paddling.

As we approached Valencia I got stuck behind a truck spouting diesel fumes and lost my patience. The journey, Albufera apart, had already taken nearly two hours and I was hungry. As I swung out, an oncoming truck, horn blaring, emerged from a heat shimmer.

Diane yelled. I braked, just managing to pull behind the truck I was trying to overtake. I stopped on the side of the road and, head in my hands, waited for the glimpse of death to fade.

Near the center of the city a gypsy leaped from the curb at a red light and washed the windshield that I had only just cleaned at the Albufera. I gave him two hundred pesetas: by rights I should have been in a hearse.

We booked into the Reina Victoria, a dignified hotel just off the Plaza del Pais Valenciano, the main square. Its solid bedrooms were designed for serious sleeping, its paneled lounge and bar as hushed as a club in St. James's, London.

In the evening we strolled around the square, hemmed by lofty baroque buildings and streets swarming with fender-nudging traffic, its flower market blooming with late roses and chrysanthemums, its fountain tossing spray into the breeze.

We ate at a famous fast-food restaurant, the Barrachina, in the square and went to bed early. Twice during the night I awoke bathed in sweat as a truck bore down on me.

After breakfasting in our room on fresh orange juice, croissants, and coffee we went shopping in *El Corte Inglés,* the Bloomingdale's of Valencia. Peter Pateman, the designer of our dining hall, had sold us the bar made from an old wedding chest, an antique table seating eight, a bookcase, a wine rack, and a spinning wheel. What we needed just now were easy chairs, rugs, side tables . . .

After lunch in a dark bar in a street of tottering tenements in the old quarter—*arròs con fesols i naps*, a rice dish cooked in a broth with white beans, turnips, onion, pork and sausages—we drove home, giving way to all oncoming trucks.

It was dusk when we got there. Lights were on but the house was strangely quiet. I went into the dining hall, where Toni was moodily mixing plaster. He scarcely acknowledged me.

"What's the matter, Toni?" I asked.

"The cassette player, man. It's kaput."

"That's tough."

Rejoicing, I retired to the annex to do some work before supper. But the silence was oppressive—contagious too, because Jones and the cats all seemed to have lost their voices.

My ears were clogged with silence. I couldn't work; I was becoming Spanish.

I went back to the dining hall. "I'll do a deal with you, Toni," I said. "I'll lend you my cassette player on one condition—that you play it softly, but really softly. You dig?"

He held out his hand. "Cool, man," he said. "Real cool."

NINETEEN

Guests Galore

Forgotten acquaintances suddenly came back into our lives when word got around that we had bought a place in the sun. Real friends made contact with us before heading for Spain, but casuals phoned when they just happened to be in the area, anywhere from a ferry crossing the English Channel to a bar a few hundred yards down the road. We put the acquaintances in a narrow bed in the annex squeezed between my typewriter and my books on Siberia and they usually departed precipitously, complaining of night cramps.

One acquaintance, Ted, was undeterred by his nocturnal proximity to salt mines and penal camps and turned up for a second visit. So we then gave him the Aitor treatment, prolonged exposure to the menacing presence of the Basque restaurateur that depressed unwanted guests so comprehensively that they packed their bags and left. But Ted proved resilient even to this extreme measure.

He was a freelance wine correspondent who contributed mostly to magazines in Britain and claimed Bordeaux was his spiritual home. He was a large, florid man with soft white hair and was as boring as a carton of plonk. So much so that when he announced at a wine-tasting in the City of London that he had to leave to catch a plane to Bordeaux, someone said: "Give my regards to Monsieur Deaux."

He usually brought us a bottle from some obscure vineyard with a nose-wrinkling bouquet, an unhealthy color, and a flavor to match, and spent much of his stay disparaging Spanish wines despite the nectars of Rioja, the heady produce of Catalonia spearheaded by the Torres family, the sherries of Jerez, and the exquisite and expensive Vega Sicilia wine.

On the third day of his second visit Diane, normally patient with unwanted visitors, led me to the end of the garden and said: "He's got to go."

"Why?"

"Because he hides bottles of cheap wine under his bed, gets drunk, and scares the hell out of Maria. She's conscientious and honest and I don't want to lose her. Any suggestions?"

"Yes," I said. "We've got to poison him."

"Isn't that a bit extreme?"

"It's an extreme situation," I told her.

I had remembered from the days when I had met him as a reporter in London that he was a curry as well as a wine bore.

Over lunch on the terrace—cuts of cold meat and *chorizo* and chicory salad followed by Manchego cheese and crusty bread—I sounded him out.

"Still fond of curry, Ted?"

"Call me Teddy, more personal." He made an exhibition of tasting the run-of-the-mill red Valdepeñas wine. "Of course. All those years in India . . ."

"Like it hot?"

"Hotter the better. A curry isn't a curry until your head steams." He smiled boyishly. "Used to have it for breakfast, lunch, and dinner in Bombay."

"Good," I said, "because we're having one for dinner."

"The first I knew of it," Diane said later while Ted slept off his lunch beside the pool.

"I'll make it."

"You can't cook."

"Where Ted—sorry, Teddy—is concerned anything is possible. And I will serve it. That is very important."

Cookbook to hand, I spent the afternoon making an Indian curry spice mix. Red chili peppers, green chilies, black peppercorns, mustard seeds . . . Chicken Vindaloo powerful enough to blow a bridge.

I also made a less venomous mix for Diane, Jonathan, and myself and served Ted's separately in the kitchen with a minimal portion of rice.

He sniffed it appreciatively at the table on the terrace. "Hope it's got a kick in it."

"It's got that, all right," I said.

"Good man, no time for the sissy stuff. *And a woman is only a woman, but a good curry is a Feast.* Adapting Kipling," he explained. "Sorry, my dear"—to Diane.

Diane glared at him. I gave Jonathan permission to take his own bland curry indoors in front of the TV.

Ted stuck a forkful of steaming brown explosive into his mouth and chewed expectantly for a moment. Then the detonator exploded. He opened his mouth, clutched his throat, and croaked: "Water!"

I passed him a pitcher of water, ice cubes clinking in it like wind chimes. "Too hot for you, Teddy?"

He gulped water. I wondered if it would change to steam. He blinked watering eyes.

"Not *too* hot. Just a bit spicy. Caught me by surprise."

"Eat up, then. They say it gets hotter by the mouthful." I dug into my curry, which I had prepared in a different saucepan.

He took another mouthful of TNT and tried to sluice it down with water but fragments must have stuck in his throat, because he began to cough violently.

When the coughing spasm had passed he glanced at his wrist-watch, pushed aside his plate, and said hoarsely: "Great Scott, almost forgot—got to see a man about a crate of wine in Denia. Wants my opinion . . ." He began to cough again.

"Don't worry, Teddy," Diane said. "We'll keep it hot for you."

"And the good news," I said, "is that I've made enough for break-fast and lunch tomorrow."

We didn't hear him get up in the morning but he left a note say-ing the wine he had tasted in Denia was excellent and he was driving to Madrid to market it. He didn't return.

Tom, once known as the meanest man in journalism, was also a pro-fessional house guest—although how he had the nerve to invite him-self to our house when he knew I despised him beggared belief.

But there he was standing in the doorway of the dining hall one autumn day with a nondescript woman wearing a gray twinset who was presumably his wife. "All the hotels in Denia are full," he said. "Can you help us out for the night?"

"Shall I make a few calls?" I asked him. "No," he said hastily, "that won't be necessary—I've already phoned around and there isn't a room to be had."

It was lunchtime—so Diane, who didn't know how obnoxious

he was, invited the two of them to eat with us. She had been reliving her years in Rome and had cooked spaghetti Bolognese, which I had been looking forward to eating all morning.

"I'm sure Tom hasn't come all this way to eat Italian food," I said without much hope. "*Paella* is what he's lusting after, isn't that right, Tom?"

"Italian will be fine," Tom said. "Won't it, Bridget?"

"If it's not too much trouble," his wife said, twisting the worn wedding band on her finger.

Tom carried three suitcases from his rented car, dumped them in the annex, and took his place at the table on the terrace. "I bought you a bottle of wine," he said, "but it was broken in transit." After pouring himself a brimming glass of Campo Viejo red wine, he dug into a plate of spaghetti and meat sauce.

He was one of those people who, although endowed with the appetite of a starving hyena, never put on weight. Hollow-cheeked and sparse-haired, he always looked too skinny for his clothes. He smoked a pipe and his sweaters and shirts—a faded maroon one that day—were perforated with holes burned by smoldering shreds of tobacco.

His one redeeming quality was his journalistic savvy. Such was his tenacity, supplemented by a reluctance to spend money mixing socially with other journalists, that he was an accomplished reporter with a string of exclusive stories to his name.

He accepted a second helping of spaghetti from Diane, sprinkled it with the last of the grated Parmesan cheese, helped himself to another glass of wine, and told us he intended to take us out to dinner that evening.

Diane accepted eagerly but I didn't believe it. It was his habit, when pressed to eat in company, to discover when the check arrived that he had left his wallet behind. Invariably a young reporter in awe of his reputation offered to pay his share.

When he issued his invitation to us, I decided to do a deal with

Aitor, the moody Basque restaurateur. A deal with the devil, accord-ing to Diane, when I told her about Tom's reputation.

After he and Bridget had enjoyed a swim, a nap beside the pool, and a couple of cocktails, he put on a blazer, shiny with wear, and said: "Right, let's go out and have a bang-up meal. On me, of course."

Diane glanced at me. Was I right about him? the glance inquired. I nodded imperceptibly—trust me!

"I know a good place," I told Tom. "The owner's a bit of a charac-ter—you know, outspoken—but the steaks are out of this world."

"Lead the way," he said. "Money no object. Just like old times, huh, Derek?"

"Not quite," I said.

"Might as well go in your car," he said. "Bit more class than mine"—pointing at his threadbare automobile rented from a cow-boy outfit in Alicante.

I told him to wait in the car with Bridget and Diane while I locked up the house. As I'd anticipated, the annex was already locked; I unlocked it with a spare key and picked up his black leather wallet lying on the single bed—maybe Bridget would have to sleep on the floor—between my typewriter and a book about the Trans-Siberian Railroad.

In the empty restaurant, where a log fire fueled with pinewood burned and spat, a table covered with a red-checkered cloth had been laid for us.

The Basque, bleary-eyed and scowling as usual, brought us a pitcher of red wine from nearby Jalon that Tom immediately sent back. "We want the best Rioja you've got," he said.

After the thick tender steaks had been served with scalloped potatoes and canned peas, Bridget took a bite from hers and said, "Delicious," the only word I had heard her utter since lunch.

I ate my meal as swiftly as a stray dog, followed Aitor into the bar, and said: "Are you sure you're going through with it?"

"Quite sure," he said.

When I got back to the table Diane was staring at her empty glass, preoccupied presumably with what lay ahead.

"Anyone want coffee?" Tom asked brightly, lighting his pipe and brushing smoldering tobacco from his blazer.

No one did.

As Aitor approached with the check, Tom went into his famous pocket-slapping routine familiar to journalists all over the world.

"Oh, my God," he exclaimed, glancing pitifully at his wife. "My wallet . . . Have you seen it?"

"No, darling. The last time I saw it was when we stopped at a garage on the way from Alicante." She was obviously well versed in the deception but not, I suspected, happy with it.

Giving his pockets another chastising, Tom bowed his head in spurious defeat. "I'm sorry about this, Derek, but I've lost it. Maybe it's been stolen. I'm afraid you'll have to pay and I'll settle up with you when I can lay my hands on some cash."

"No time like the present," I said. "I found your wallet. Isn't that wonderful?" I fished the wallet from the back pocket of my trousers and threw it on the table. "There, I can see the money and your credit cards."

Tom stared at it as though it was a sleeping scorpion. "But—"

"You left your room unlocked," I lied. "That lock on the door needs repairing . . . I opened it and there was your wallet lying on your bed. I knew you needed it so, hey presto, I brought it along."

I beckoned Aitor, who was hovering near the table. "My friend would like the check," I told him.

Aitor placed it on the table in front of Tom. It was, I knew, the equivalent of $150, not a lot of money for such a meal in New York or London but a fortune for a restaurant in a Spanish *pueblo*. It was twice what it should have been.

"This is preposterous," Tom exploded, staring at the check. "There must have been a mistake." Sparks flew from the pipe clenched between his teeth.

"Come off it, Tom," I said. "Don't let the side down. We don't want the Spanish to think we're a nation of tightwads, do we? Didn't I hear you say, 'Money no object'?"

He counted out the bills as though peeling off layers of his skin.

"I'll take care of the tip," I said as he rose and, shoulders slumped, made his way to the car parked outside.

Confronting Aitor when he came to clear the table, I said: "You've made a good profit, double what you expected to get. You must be a happy man."

The scowl gathered around his bloodshot eyes lifted for a moment. He spread his hands. "*Señor* Derek, I am not a crook. I didn't want that money."

"So what are you going to do with it?"

"Give it to charity. What else?"

And I believed him. Retrieving the scowl, he picked up Tom's money, stuffed it in the pocket of his striped apron, and piled the plates on a tray.

I was walking down the driveway, having driven the car into the garage, when an ethereal figure emerged in the moonlight from the orange trees to my left. Tom's wife, Bridget.

"I locked our door before we went out to dinner," she whispered. "I tested it just in case it was still open. It wasn't!" She kissed me on both cheeks. "I want to thank you for making this holiday worthwhile. His face when he got the check . . . If only—"

If only what? I could only guess. She ran down the driveway and disappeared into the annex. The door shut and I heard the key turn firmly in the lock.

They left the following morning.

One other guest visited Aitor but the roles were reversed; this time Aitor the tormentor was tormented.

The guest was an octogenarian, Sir Rupert Grayson. Born into money and privilege, Rupert served in World War I as a second lieutenant in the Irish Guards. With him was Rudyard Kipling's son, John. Rupert was blown up but survived, John Kipling was reported missing, later presumed dead. Thereafter Rudyard Kipling treated Rupert as a surrogate son. And when he came to Spain more than half a century later, a fragment of the shell that wounded him was still embedded in the flesh of one hand.

His brush with death whetted his appetite for life. He headed for Hollywood where he became friends with, among others, David Niven, Clark Gable, and Shirley Temple.

Back in London he went into publishing and wrote a series of thrillers about a precursor of James Bond called Gun Cotton. During World War II he assumed Gun Cotton's derring-do mantle and became a King's Messenger, delivering secret dispatches all over the free world.

Rupert, whom I had met in a bar in Gibraltar, turned up at our house just as the swallows were leaving in September, crowding the telephone wires and congregating in the sky before flying to Africa for the winter. He stayed in a small hotel in Denia.

From there I used to drive him to Aitor's bar where, out of perversity, he set up office, taking over two or three tables for his books and papers. Bulldog chin lowered, exotic cravat knotted at the neck of a safari jacket, he became a local attraction as he revised his memoirs with a broken ballpoint pen.

I enjoyed his company, his ascerbic wit, and the whiff of aristocratic assumption that still accompanied him from a bygone age, but Aitor didn't share my enthusiasm.

Not only did Rupert occupy more than his ration of space, he usurped his authority, demanding a steady supply of Fernet Branca pick-me-ups, cracking a table with his stick if he didn't get them.

Aitor fought back. He discovered that Rupert hated noise, a quixotic aversion in Spain, and therefore created as much of it as possible.

Outside he employed youths to let off fireworks. Squibs that were lit and thrown; *tro de bacs,* which exploded when hurled against walls; strings of bangers known as *tracas;* fiery serpents' tails called *borrachos* (drunks).

But it took more than a few bangs to shift an old soldier who had been blown up in World War I and had a piece of shrapnel in one hand to prove it. When a boy threw a *masclet* into the bar, Rupert took a couple of wax plugs from his carpetbag, dusted them down, and stuck them in his ears.

I was reading my newspapers while he corrected passages about quieter locations he had visited as a King's Messenger, when Aitor, who had been steadily sipping absinthe, asked Rupert if he intended to eat.

Rupert cupped a hand to one plugged ear. "Could you speak up, please."

Aitor shouted: "Eat, do you want anything to eat?"

Rupert's formidable jaw rose. "Yes," he said, "I rather think I do," and took two cheese crackers from his bag.

Aitor ran his fingers through his tangled black-and-gray hair and returned to the bar, a wounded and dangerous animal.

I saw him grope under the bar. Was he going for the gun he was reputed to keep there? I wrote on a sheet of typing paper: *I think he's got a pistol.* Rupert smiled and offered me a cracker. No gun materialized.

Later that day when the bar was packed with orange pickers lunching off *fabada,* bean and pork stew, a specialty of Asturias in the north of Spain, fireworks blew up as I was returning to the restaurant.

No one ever ascertained how the fireworks, which had been stored for a fiesta in a shed in a field, were ignited. But thunderflashes exploded like grenades, Roman candles pumped balls of colored fire into the air, rockets took off as venomously as guided missiles.

The pyrotechnics finally broke Aitor's tenuous grasp on sanity. Just as I arrived he did snatch a gun from under the bar and aimed it at a recognizable enemy, Rupert. Not wanting to see Rupert, a reprobate from an age of chivalry and derring-do, blown away with a broken ballpoint in his hand and a packet of crackers in his bag, I vaulted the bar and tried to grab the gun—a rusty pistol that had probably seen service in the Civil War—that Aitor was aiming at him.

Aitor possessed the strength of a madman and we wrestled energetically. Before I finally overcame him he pulled the trigger, the bullet punching a hole in the window and narrowly missing a couple of orange pickers.

I was never quite sure whether Rupert knew that Aitor had loosed off a shot at him or whether he had confused it with the fireworks or whether he had thrust the plugs so firmly into his ears that he had heard nothing.

Aitor was locked in a police cell and could be seen through a grill in the surface of the sidewalk through which well-wishers passed cigarettes to prisoners.

He was later transferred to a mental home.

Rupert flew back to London on a whim and finished revising his memoirs in various watering holes where peace and quiet reigned and supplies of Fernet Branca and cheese crackers were inexhaustible.

TWENTY

Ángel's Last Stand

We had anticipated a pause in November before making the decisions about our future in the orange groves.

But Ángel sidetracked any such leisurely expectations; first by threatening to quit, then, indirectly, by involving me with a fugitive from Russia and a Mafia lieutenant.

He made his first move when I drove him in Diane's Citroën to a garden center on the other side of Montgo where he got a discount.

It was an untidy time of year, windows of sunshine opening onto periods of gloom, rainstorms filling the fields to overflowing. The wheels of the battered little car tossed up wings of spray as we forded a flooded crossroads; clouds obscured Montgo's flat brow.

When Ángel wasn't in communication with the clouds, he often consulted the mountain as though it was some prehistoric deity.

He wasn't alone in his reverence. Although it wasn't all that high—753 meters at its peak—the land on either side was so flat that it affected the moods of the inhabitants.

When it wore a wig of raincloud, the fingers of the grape-pickers moved nimbly and the old women in the village weaving and crocheting in their patios took their unfinished baskets and shawls indoors; if eagles floated above it in a blue sky, the pickers poured wine down their throats from *porróns*, wine bottles with long spouts, and took a long siesta and the old women stitched and weaved unhurriedly.

On its Mediterranean side Montgo was green and granite gray, on this its flank, it was the color of mellow red brick. From a distance it looked like a legless elephant, a cave for one eye, trunk reaching for the coast. It was also a clock: Spaniards could tell the time by the height of its shadows.

Badgers and wildcats lived on its slopes and a lake lapped a cave inside it. The fragments of an Iberian village thousands of years old stood clustered at one end. Herbs broke underfoot, their scents crackling in the nostrils—marjoram, camomile, rosemary, thyme, sage, anise . . . such a potpourri that in Moorish times the Great Caliph, Abd-ar-Rahman, ordered them to be officially listed.

Driving to the garden center a few weeks earlier, Ángel had pointed at Montgo's shadows. "It's eleven o'clock."

"No, it isn't," I said.

"*Mas o menos*, more or less."

"Wrong. Today is Monday?"

"And tomorrow will be Tuesday."

"Think about the time again," I told him.

He thought. "It's eleven."

"Ten. Summertime ended over the weekend and the clocks went back an hour."

It was one of my few triumphs over Ángel—his attitude encouraged pettiness—and on this sullen November day he was to have his revenge.

The plants outside the garden center were marshaled around a stone farmhouse with a long arched terrace where raisins had once dried before the vines were ravaged by phylloxera, the disease that arrived via France.

But there were no longer any vivid splashes of color among the climbers, bushes, and saplings. Bougainvillea, oleander, hibiscus, and plumbago; jasmine that made nosegays of patios in the summer, and dama del noche, which at night smelled of harems—all had faded with the passing of summer.

Only inside did plants bloom luxuriantly beside packets of seeds, bulbs, tubers, and corms. The glass-roofed center smelled of the jungle and cats employed to catch rats and mice slept in its humid warmth.

While I chose an orchid for Diane I told Ángel to buy tulip and daffodil bulbs, dahlia tubers, and seeds for bedding plants, anything except salvias because the prim red flowers were as common as sparrows in English parks.

I also bought one of those miniature watering cans with a long spout with which old ladies sprinkle hanging baskets of petunias—and themselves—because I am a softer touch in a gardening center than a hypochondriac in a pharmacy.

Driving home, we passed broad-beamed women hunting snails in a dripping pause in the rain beside ranks of leafless vines as forlorn as gravestones. Flannels of cloud hung over Montgo.

As soon as we pulled up in the driveway I escaped into the kitchen for coffee while Ángel retired to the garage with our purchases.

Diane examined the white-and-greenish orchid in its transparent package quizzically. "It's a sweet thought," she said, "but—"

"You don't like it?"

"Don't you remember me telling you they are my least favorite flower? They make me think of funerals, I don't know why . . ."

"I'll bring you weeds next time," I said and strode across the driveway toward the garage. Which was when a sudden gust of wind betrayed Ángel.

It picked up an empty packet from the garage where he was sowing seeds in shallow boxes filled with damp loam and deposited it at my feet.

Across the packet above a picture of a familiar flower, I read one damning word: *salvias*. I picked up the packet and showed it to Ángel. "I thought I asked you NOT to buy them."

"I thought you said buy them."

"No, you didn't, Ángel." I knew we had reached a crossroads in our relationship and I think he realized it too. "*You* wanted salvias. You'll have to empty the seed box and buy a packet of petunias out of your own money."

The confrontation was unseemly and trivial but ultimatums are rarely the causes of war: it's what precedes them that counts.

Two spots of red appeared on his cheeks, the only time I had seen him evince any physical signs of anger.

He picked up the box and placed it in the back of his van.

Sitting behind the wheel of his van, he wound down the window. "Did I tell you I have been offered a job in Granada?"

"No, Ángel, you didn't."

"I will have to think about it," he said.

"You do that, Ángel."

He nodded, adjusted his disgraceful hat, and drove away.

Ángel was also responsible for the next distraction. I was in the Bar Paraiso drinking coffee when I noticed him playing chess with a stranger, an old man.

Mid-morning regulars eyed them speculatively, because Ángel rarely lingered over his bottle of mineral water in the bar and, in any case, strangers were always the objects of conjecture, particularly this one who wore a *shapka,* a Russian-style fur hat. He was tall and skinny and his gray topcoat looked as though it contained an in-built clothes hanger. He reminded me of a superannuated spy.

When Ángel noticed me he whispered to the stranger, laid down his king in surrender—I had never realized his talents extended to chess—and hurried out of the bar.

The stranger smiled at me and held up a pawn, an invitation to a game, a common enough gesture in Moscow's Gorky Park. I joined him more out of curiosity than a desire to play, because chess makes my head ache.

While he set up the pieces I waded straight in. "Are you Russian?"

"No," he said, "Spanish." We shook hands across the board and its two armies of worn and chipped warriors. "My name's Enrique. But I've lived in Russia for fifty years." He spoke English carefully as though the vowels were made of broken glass.

"I lived in Moscow for a year," I told him.

"As a journalist?"

"How did you guess?"

"You don't strike me as a member of the diplomatic corps," he said, taking one of my pawns with a deftness not far removed from contempt. "Your friend—Ángel, isn't it?—tells me that you've had a disagreement."

"That's one way of putting it."

"A pity. When you reach my age"—he must have been in his eighties—"you realize that all dissent is a waste. I realized it almost too late."

"Almost?"

"I have come back to make my peace," he said, removing one of my knights. "You see, I fought in the Civil War—on the right side but the side that lost, the Republicans. So I went to the Soviet Union where I could still practice what I had fought for."

"And you still believe in Communism after all these years?"

"I believe in equality," he said with dignity, adding: "You realize I'm threatening your queen?"

"Of course," I said, withdrawing her masterfully as though I was working to a preconceived and Machiavellian plan. "But not Communism?"

"No political system is perfectly conceived: they all adapt to circumstance."

"At least you've acquired the politician's skill of never answering a straight question," I said.

I made a stupid blunder with a bishop, so confusing him that he removed his fur hat, as soft and black as satin, revealing a shiny bald scalp.

He stroked the hat lovingly. "When I bought it," he said, "it was full of fleas."

Three moves later he called "Checkmate," and I moved a respectful distance from his hat.

The return of this prodigal might have passed off more smoothly if another veteran, Ramón, hadn't arrived in the village independently two days later, singing the praises of the right-wing Nationalists who had triumphed all those years ago. Ramón had fled with his family to New York in 1938 when the Republicans were still in power in the region. Both émigrés, I suppose, had decided to make the journey to Spain this November in case another winter took them from this life before they could make the pilgrimage.

Ramón wore a fedora and dark glasses and polished his fingernails on the lapels of his coat like a card sharp, but when he took off his shades his old eyes watered. He was shorter than Enrique, his skin was dry and mottled, but he had a good head of cropped, stone-gray hair.

By mutual agreement Enrique, the old Communist, and

Ramón, the venerable Fascist, met the village elders beneath the acacia trees on alternate days.

"It's better that way," Ramón told me. "We don't want to start
fighting the war all over again."

The thought of the two ancients doing battle with their walking
sticks over a conflict that most Spaniards tried hard to forget seemed
ridiculous, but I kept my counsel.

Tuesdays, Thursdays, and Saturdays were Enrique's prime time
and I listened fascinated to his stories about life in Moscow, because
I had only experienced it through a position of journalistic privilege.

He turned out to be a stoic who viewed the injustices under the
Soviet rule philosophically. "You can't have equality in thirty degrees
of frost," he said. "Someone will always hog the fire."

He was a great believer in the effect of climate on national character. "Russians are impassive because frost freezes their tongues.
Spaniards are extroverts because sunshine reaches their hearts."

I put it to him that, in the final reckoning, there wasn't much to
choose between Communism and capitalism.

Surprisingly he nodded. "Communism is the equal distribution
of poverty, capitalism is the unequal distribution of wealth. Take
your pick."

"But you've dedicated your life to Communism," I protested.

"To its ideals," he said. "Not its abuses."

Enrique fingered his fur hat; I drew back in case it still harbored
fleas.

I met Ramón with the old men on Mondays, Wednesdays, and
Fridays—they all gave the acacia trees a wide berth on Sundays
when their womenfolk called the shots, attending Mass, parading
their grandchildren, soaped and shining in the village, ordaining
mealtimes.

He told me that when he first settled in New York he worked

the numbers racket in Spanish Harlem and became a lieutenant in the Mob. He saw nothing wrong in the activities of the Mafia. "Organized crime isn't as dangerous as random violence. Ask any cop."

He had earned good money—"Taking it from mugs"—bought a house with a front lawn and a poolroom in New Jersey, and married off two of his three daughters who now had sons "with prospects." In the Mafia, I presumed.

It was his unmarried daughter, Raquel, who had persuaded him to return to Spain. "A good girl but butch." Reared, I guessed, as the son he had never had.

I asked him about the Civil War.

"Disorganized," he said. Which was when I first detected a hint of reticence foreign to his nature. It made me curious.

I watched him speculatively as he was driven away in a hired car by Raquel, pouter-plump and bespectacled, to the house they rented in Denia.

The following day I questioned Enrique, who was staying in a bleak, cabbage-smelling hotel on the coast—it must have reminded him of Moscow—about Ramón. But I got the impression he was holding back too.

It was beginning to look as though I had another mystery on my hands. But before trying to solve it I had to attend to Hoppity.

The condition of his stump had deteriorated, blood and pus leaking from it, so we took off his splint—these days he was chewing through one a week—put him in a cat basket, and took him to the vet. During his nine-month residence with us he had become the most pampered member of the family—even Jones nuzzled him before trying to steal his food.

The vet, a caring practitioner named Juan, the owner of a mus-

tache as luxuriant as the fur of some of his patients, wasn't opti-
mistic.

He dressed the wound and prescribed medicine. "If he isn't better in a couple of days . . ." His mustache drooped.

We put Hoppity back in his basket and took him to the car
through a waiting room where a dachshund was inadvisably curling
its lip at a large dog, a German shepherd.

Back home Hoppity got to work on the bandage with his teeth.
We gave him milk in a saucer and filleted sardines but he ignored
both.

He spent the next day disposing of the remnants of the bandage
and sleeping. When we stroked him the following morning he barely
stirred and the wound was suppurating badly.

Diane and I took Jonathan aside and told him there was no point
in prolonging Hoppity's suffering.

Jonathan asked: "Why doesn't God do something about it?"

"He is," Diane said. "Through us. We mustn't let him down."

Eyes moist, Jonathan ran to his room.

I took Hoppity back to Juan, who gave him an injection. He died
swiftly and painlessly, tipping forward into Juan's hands as he had
once tipped forward when he tried to raise his healthy paw.

That night I heard him tapping round the house on his wooden
leg. But it was only a dream.

Two day's after Hoppity's death, still intrigued by Ramón's oblique
attitude to the Civil War, I again tackled Enrique and asked him if he
remembered his Fascist contemporary in those blood-stained years.

"Who knows? It was a long time ago, another lifetime," Enrique
said.

He was eating *churros* and drinking chocolate milk outside a
mobile café, part of a traveling market that assembled in the village
once a week.

I persevered. "You did live here at the same time as he did."

"Maybe," Enrique said. "But Ramón is a common name and sometimes the years do more than age people—they remodel them."

"You were about the same age."

Enrique swallowed the last mouthful of *churro* and licked sugar from his fingertips. Beside us women burrowed in heaps of second-hand clothes.

"We lived here half a century ago," he said. "He is now American, I am Russian."

"No, you're not," I said. "You're Spanish. And I don't think you're telling the whole truth."

He finished his chocolate milk and threw the plastic cup into a litter bin.

"The truth," he said, "is the shining light of civilization but sometimes it should be dimmed. Politicians know that if they are truthful all the time anarchy will prevail. The truth can hurt too. Why hurt people? Don't lie, just sometimes keep truth under wraps."

"You fought for what you saw as the truth in 1936," I said.

"That was an absolute truth. We Republicans fought against corruption, privilege, exploitation."

He stood up and put his fur hat on his bald head and we walked together through the streets filled with pale sunshine.

I didn't let up. "But after the war Franco brought stability to Spain."

"Stalin brought stability to Russia. Ask the legions he slaughtered, ask anyone who survived the penal camps."

"So what is truth?" I asked.

"It's what you believe in at a given time. Like fashion it changes."

"And you truly don't remember Ramón?"

"I told you, it was a long time ago." He stopped in the empty space beneath the acacia trees and smiled the wintry smile he had brought with him from Russia. "If you'll excuse me I should like to spend a little time in the past."

Convinced now that neither Enrique nor Ramón was being totally honest I made inquiries about both of them. These were complicated by the villagers' understandable reluctance to resurrect those barbarous years, but I was driven by a desire to see the two stubborn old men reconciled. To prove, as Enrique had said, that "all dissent is a waste."

Diane joined me in the quest one evening when we found Ramón standing outside the open-air cinema that in the summer was as popular as indoor movie houses had been before television. Families licking ice creams and munching popcorn watched Westerns and horror films under the stars; babies crawled beneath rows of fold-up seats; husbands retired to the bar behind the back row during tiresome love scenes. We enjoyed the informality of these evenings so much that we saw *King Kong* twice.

We took Ramón that evening to a bar where there was usually a movie showing on a flickering TV screen. Tonight it was John Wayne in *True Grit*.

"Helluva guy, the Duke," said Ramón, pointing his bottle of beer at the TV.

Diane sipped a *penalti,* a tiny beer. "You're a macho man, right?"

This pleased Ramón; he felt for his shades in the breast pocket of his black jacket. "Nothing wrong with that, ma'am. Macho men win wars. Patton, Churchill . . . Rommel if he'd been on the right side."

"But you were on the winning side in the Civil War," I said. "Why did you go and why didn't you come back?"

"Always regretted it. But this neck of the woods was Commie and even after the war it wasn't safe."

"How old were you?" I asked him.

"About thirty, I guess."

"*You* could have come back."

"And left my mom and dad to fend for themselves? Tough city, New York . . ."

Diane interrupted. "Macho men can forgive, can't they?"

"Sure they can," Ramón agreed.

"So why don't you shake hands with Enrique?"

"Up to him, I guess," Ramón said.

"The Duke would have done it," I said.

"Yeah, well—"

A fusillade of shots erupted on the TV screen; by the time they had spent themselves Ramón was on his way out of the bar.

"I think the final shootout is approaching right here," I confided to Diane.

"Why, are you pulling one of your journalistic stunts?"

I put one finger to my lips. "All will be revealed," I said.

There was only one arena in which I could envisage the denouement between the two veterans and that was in the open-air cinema where gunlslingers and vampires had enlivened the hot summer nights.

My suspicions about both of them had been confirmed by other ancients and I set the scene with the care of a Broadway choreographer. The fold-up seats had already been stacked for the winter; only a table and two chairs remained on the concrete floor below the high blank wall where the screen hung. There were two exits, one to the left and one to the right, leading onto different streets, and I made sure they were clear.

On the table I placed an open bottle of wine, and two glasses.

Happily the weather cooperated. A warm smoky evening with a few stars glimmering in he sky.

Ramón's daughter, Raquel, also happy to cooperate, had arranged to meet her father inside the empty cinema. I had summoned Enrique on a subterfuge—a nonexistent appointment to play another game of chess.

Deadline: five P.M.

Hidden behind the bar crouched a motley cast of extras, Emilio and the gas man among them.

4:57. Not a murmur from either of the adjoining streets, not even the bark of a dog or the splutter of a moped. Had the two protagonists been scared off?

4:58. A car drew up in the main street in front of the box office. A door slammed. I heard footsteps.

4:59. The confrontation, I reflected, was going to look pretty silly with only one participant!

Another automobile on the opposite side of the auditorium. Another set of footsteps.

I had calculated that, with only the one table, two chairs, two glasses and a bottle in view in the fading light, whoever arrived first would sit down, barely distinguishable from anyone else approaching.

Ramón approached hesitantly, glanced around, and sat down.

Five P.M.: A tall, sharp-angled silhouette advanced from the opposite wing.

As Enrique reached the table I snapped on the light beside the bar. He and Ramón stared at each other, frozen in its glare.

I reached them before either of them had time to escape—the extras were to emerge at a given signal—and spoke softly and urgently.

Stunned, they listened. Gratefully it seemed to me, Ramón in particular.

"In the first place," I said, "I know both of you lived in the village at the same time during the Civil War and that you knew each other. I also know that you"—prodding a finger at Ramón—"were *not* a Fascist, you were a Republican just like Enrique. Am I right?"

Ramón sat down and poured himself a glass of wine. "My family couldn't emigrate to America as losers, refugees. We had to have . . . a bit of style."

"As if it mattered a damn," I said. "Spain lost the war, not the Republicans or the Fascists."

"It mattered to me," Ramón said. "Things like that matter if you're a Spaniard. Why do you figure Enrique went to Russia? Pride is why."

I turned to Enrique. "What I don't understand is why you haven't told anyone that Ramón was a Republican."

Enrique took off his fur hat and massaged his bald head with the tips of his fingers. "What's the point? For thirty years he has been Fascist, he has convinced himself he's one. Let him stay that way, we are all what life makes us. The people in the village don't care what he was."

"They would have once," I said.

"Once is a long time ago."

I pounced. "If it's so long ago why don't the two of you shake hands?"

They stared at each other in the twilight remembering, perhaps, the futile passions that had divided the land.

Slowly their arms rose, the limbs of old-fashioned toys freshly wound up. The palms of their hands brushed together, their fingers tightened in a frail grip.

Which was when the supporting cast burst cheering from behind the bar, embracing them and producing more bottles of wine and beer.

As the party got under way I noticed Ángel standing in the shadows watching. When he saw me he nodded almost imperceptibly and made his way out of the cinema into the street.

For the next few days Enrique and Ramón took their places on the benches beneath the acacia trees on the same days telling the other old men about life in Moscow and New York. Then Enrique flew back to Moscow, where he had a Russian wife and a married daughter.

"Will you come back?" I asked him as he waited in Denia for a bus to Valencia. "Settle here with your wife? After all, the Socialists are in power in Spain."

He examined his fur hat. "No," he said. "That would be betrayal.

I believed in Communism in the thirties. I still do. One of these days it will prevail. Christianity didn't catch on overnight, did it?"

As the bus picked up speed he smiled at me and from the backseat raised his *shapka*. In the distance I heard what sounded like a burst of machine-gun fire, but it was only fireworks.

Ramón didn't return to the United States. Raquel flew to New York and sold their house in New Jersey. With the proceeds they bought a new house with sharp edges and marble steps in a village near Denia with views of the coastal plain and, in the distance, the Mediterranean.

From time to time Ramón returned to the benches beneath the acacia trees and told stories about organized crime. When he confessed he had never killed anyone the old men looked so disappointed that he treated them to accounts of beatings with baseball bats and rubber hoses filled with lead.

Once I met Raquel, on her way from the hairdressers to pick him up, her brown hair stiff with lacquer.

Life, I ventured, must have been daunting, living with a hard man like her father.

She laid a dimpled hand on my arm. "Has he been telling you all that stuff about the Mafia? Shame on him. The only time he ever saw a gangster was in a movie house—his favorites were James Cagney and George Raft."

"He didn't work the numbers racket?"

"Are you kidding? What he did was open a corner store in Queens. He sold Spanish food. *Fuet, chorizo,* Manchego cheese . . ." She licked her lips. "He sold the best potato tortillas in the whole of New York City."

When I got back to the house after putting Enrique on the bus to Valencia I found Ángel in the garage sowing seeds in a box.

I asked him about the job in Granada.

"My wife wouldn't have been happy there," he said.

I pointed at the packet of seed in his hand. "Petunias?"

"Pansies. I tried to buy petunias but I couldn't find any."

I doubted this but at least they weren't salvias.

TWENTY-ONE

The Fat One

D ecember, we had been in the house for nearly a year, and the deadline I had set five months earlier was nearly upon us.

What we had to decide when the twelve months had expired was whether we were truly here to stay or whether our tenure in the orange groves had been a folly we could write off as experience. To do so we had to establish if we had adapted sufficiently and if we had been accepted.

Even more pertinently we had to calculate if we could survive economically and that depended on the reactions of publishers in London and New York to my Russian thriller, which I had finished as autumn settled into winter. So far the response had been acknowledgement followed by silence as unfathomable as the Siberian taiga.

But first Christmas, *Navidad*. The build-up to December 25 was complicated by *El Gordo*, the Fat One, as the annual national lottery on December 22 is known, and a belated christening—Jonathan's.

He should have been baptized years earlier but a couple of priests, one in Ireland and one in England, had refused to officiate because he wasn't resident in their parishes and we had been so absorbed with getting him settled in Spain that we had overlooked our spiritual duty. If we left it much longer he would be so old that he would have to duck when he was ceremonially admitted into the House of God.

We might have left it until after Christmas if his prospective godmother, Sally Goddard, hadn't arrived from England. Sally, the beautiful and bubbly daughter of two of our best friends in the United Kingdom, who harbored a deep sense of responsibility beneath her exuberance, was staying for only two days; as she wouldn't be returning to Spain for a long time, it was imperative that we act promptly.

We had already decided that Jonathan should have a Spanish godfather and we had chosen Miguel Ferrer, the swashbuckling property developer who had sold us the house. He was married to Janet, an attractive and savvy businesswoman, who was the daughter of the former motorcycling champion of Britain, Roger Frogley.

There was a snag: Miguel didn't know he had been chosen.

In Spain all Christian rites are approached at a meditative pace, all except funerals, when no time is wasted in slotting the corpse into the cemetery wall. We approached Miguel in his office in Denia and he considered our request with dawning pleasure. Ahead lay a lot of planning . . .

"When is the christening to take place?" he asked.

A moment's hesitation. Then Diane told him. "Tomorrow."

His smile wavered momentarily but he was an entrepreneur accustomed to converting adversity into achievement and he recovered swiftly.

"Where?" he asked warily.

"In the church in La Jara," Diane told him.

"And the reception?" An integral part of most holy rituals.

Improvising wildly, Diane named a restaurant, the Cova del Mero, on the beach at Las Marinas, an extension of Denia, owned by the father of one of Jonathan's friends, where fish leaped from the sea into the cooking pot.

He nodded approvingly. Despite the unseemly haste the occasion was being conducted with decorum and celebratory indulgence.

We drove to the restaurant while the morning was still yawning itself awake. The sea was milky calm; seagulls cried and a crescent moon left over from the night hung in the sky.

"A christening lunch? We would be honored." The restaurant owner, stocky and nautical, sat on the terrace and gazed at a cargo boat on the horizon. "How many?"

"About thirty." It was surprising how many friends we and Jonathan had acquired.

"Perfect. When?"

Diane stared into her coffee, fisted her hands, and said: "Tomorrow."

"Tomorrow?" He jerked back in his seat.

Stirring her coffee as though it was a pot of glue, Diane nodded.

"Impossible!"

But we knew it wasn't, because in the final reckoning a Spaniard always accepts any challenge in love, war, or gastronomy.

"What do you want me to serve?" he demanded.

"Seafood," Diane said.

He spread his hands. *You might as well ask for the nectar of the gods but we will see what can be done.*

Next the priest. We found him in his little church in the village standing in a pool of yellow-and-orange light shining through the tinted panes of a window, staring forlornly at a crack in a stone arch.

"When?" he asked, after he had agreed to conduct the ceremony.

"Tomorrow," Diane said.

"Impossible."

"But God," Diane said, "wouldn't want to deny a child entry into his Kingdom."

"But it's such short notice. And Christmas will soon be here." He gestured toward the Nativity tableau.

"The loaves and fishes . . ." Diane began.

"What about them?"

"That didn't take long to arrange."

"Very well," he said, "tomorrow." Head bowed, he walked toward the altar dragging his scuffed boots.

We went to bed early but we couldn't sleep. Suddenly we heard the cries of Jonathan's godfather, the restaurant owner, and the priest: "Tomorrow? Impossible!"

The morning dawned with pockets of mist lying in the orange groves. The only flowers left in the garden were a few frostbitten roses—Ángel's mysterious amphora plant, still unidentified, had stopped blooming weeks ago, its white blossoms replaced with prickly seedpods—but aloes and poinsettias were burgeoning.

The dining hall was now plastered inside and out; glass had been fitted in the window frames; all we lacked was the minstrel gallery—Emilio was visiting a sick relative in Murcia, south of Alicante—a floor, and a door.

The geckoes had hibernated and Jones was chasing low-flying blackbirds instead. Ethel slept.

While we ate breakfast without appetite, both brooding on what could go wrong on this auspicious day, Jonathan, unaffected, sorted his collection of picture cards of Spanish footballers.

At ten-forty-five we drove across the dangerous intersection, sparkling with frosted glass from a recent accident, and parked the car opposite the church. There waiting for us was Jonathan's godfather, Miguel, glossy-haired and immaculately suited, with his wife, Janet, and Sally, his godmother—her devilment replaced by an air of dutiful responsibility. Like us, she believed in the rituals of religions, which are the staging posts of any life in which God is respected.

Jonathan was duly cleansed from sin with holy water, while the priest smiled proprietorially as though he had instigated the impetuous ceremony. Miguel, Sally, Diane, and I adjourned to the vestry, where we solemnized Jonathan's entry into the Church with our signatures. It seemed to me that the ceremony also acknowledged his presence in the community.

I drove to the *pasteleria* to collect the cake for the reception.

It was already in progress when I got to the Cova del Mero. A vastly different affair from the roofing party—fancy catering, more foreigners invited, not so much village involvement. The feast began with slices of tuna roe and soft black olives. Salad as crisp as frost. Succulent prawns, crab claws, crayfish, and swordfish. Ice cream in hollowed oranges. Red and white Rioja wine, followed by coffee, brandy, and champagne.

"And now, *señor*," the owner of the restaurant said to me as the climax approached, "please bring in the cake."

The cake! I turned to Diane. "Where did I put it?"

"How should I know? You brought it—I came with Miguel and Janet."

"I must have left it in the *pasteleria*."

Pointing at Jonathan, who was preparing to cut it, Diane said: "So what are you going to do?"

"Buy another one?"

"All the shops are shut," she said, adding: "I took care of everything else." True—she always had while I labored with the novel in the claustrophobic annex.

Guilt and failure settled heavily on me. I walked out of the restaurant and stared out to sea. The father who had lost his son's christening cake . . .

But I *had* paid for it. It *had* been packaged in white cardboard. I *had* walked out of the *pasteleria* holding it carefully in both hands. Then I had reached into the trouser pocket of my suit for the keys of the car, after placing the cake on the roof.

On the roof!

But surely it must have fallen off on the way. I ran into the parking lot. The cake had shifted to the middle of the roof and a small boy, wearing ragged short pants and a torn blue shirt, thumb in his mouth, was staring at it.

"Would you like a slice?" I asked him.

He removed his thumb from his mouth and nodded.

Together we entered the restaurant with theatrical aplomb, partners in an exquisitely timed finale. Jonathan cut the cake and I gave the little boy two slices.

When we got home, dusk was beginning to settle. After Jonathan had gone to bed Diane said: "I think it was a success."

"I could only happen like that in Spain."

"With a little help from God," she said.

The other impediment to a smooth build-up to Christmas was *El Gordo,* the Fat One, the biggest lottery in the world in terms of total investment and cash payouts—the top prize, at today's exchange rates, was $300 million, and the winning number could be bought many times over in different series of the same digits. There were also hundreds of lesser prizes.

But it was communities rather than individuals that shared the top bonanzas—a city neighborhood, a village, a factory, or even a bar and its patrons could share the winnings.

The reasons for this were complex. But basically one full ticket costing about $200 could be divided into *decimos* (tenths) and some of those decimos were split into even smaller fractions. So if one authorized vendor in a community sold the number that won the top prize, worth all those millions of dollars, then a lot of ticket holders who had bought *decimos* or even smaller investments could share the money and a poor hamlet could become El Dorado.

These authorized vendors, all officially handicapped mentally or physically, sold tickets for *El Gordo*, drawn on December 22—also the lesser lotteries staged every week—on the streets and in bars and restaurants. They were allowed a markup on the price and the winners of big prizes gave them handsome tips. In our village there was no official seller—tickets were sold mostly by bar and shop owners.

Tickets were also available from official bureaus—one named Bellos in Valencia was supposed to have the Midas touch—and organizations such as the *fallas*, which also made a profit from a markup.

If *El Gordo* failed to make you wealthy beyond the dreams of working men then there was always the possibility that another lottery, *El Niño*, the Little One, not as corpulent but chubby just the same, might redeem your losses in January.

Sales for the Fat One began in late summer, reaching a frantic climax on the eve of the draw when hopefuls scoured the country for numbers predicted by clairvoyants and stargazers or combinations linked to dates of births, deaths, and marriages.

The winning numbers and accompanying prizes were laid like golden eggs from two spinning Bingo-like cages on a stage and chanted by children from an orphanage in Madrid. Throughout the morning of the twenty-second their voices could be heard on television and radio throughout the land.

When a big prize was sung out conversations froze, a rare phenomenon in Spain, while ticket owners checked their numbers. When the Fat One itself, the jackpot, was chanted, the country went into shock.

As soon as the location of the big win was made known, con men and ambitious panhandlers leaped into their cars or boarded planes if the winner lived in maritime Spain—the Canary Isles in the

Atlantic or the Balearics in the Mediterranean. In a village near us where a substantial prize was won householders splurged on electrical appliances: they overloaded the current and the village was plunged into darkness.

My compulsion to doodle the figure eight was the catalyst in my problems with the Fat One. At times of stress or preoccupation I scrawled eights on notepads or, recently, on pages of typescript when the narrative of the Russian novel lost its way.

Three days before the lottery was to be drawn Emilio came into the annex where I was rereading a typed copy of the manuscript of the book. I had come up with a twist involving the detonation of a bridge on the Trans-Siberian Railroad but I wasn't sure about its plausibility. As I agonized, my eights proliferated—and Emilio saw them.

"Your lucky number?" he asked.

"I hope so," I said.

I asked him how the minstrel gallery was coming along. Progressing satisfactorily, he said, his voice uncharacteristically distracted. He hoped to finish it by New Year's Eve. (A minstrel playing *Auld Lang Syne* on the mandolin sounded promising.) He was on his way now to his workshop in the village to fetch nails and screws, he said.

What he did instead was buy every fraction of a ticket ending in eight he could lay his hands on.

By evening word had got around about my numerical preoccupation and villagers, apparently believing that foreign authors were blessed with serendipity, were traveling far and wide to buy tickets ending in eight. (Even if you didn't win *El Gordo* you got your money back if the last digit in your number corresponded to the last digit of the Fat One.)

Ángel even drove to Valencia and bought a *decimo* from Bellos with three eights in it.

Neighbors crossed themselves as they walked past our gates; patrons in El Paraíso competed to buy me drinks. I couldn't sleep and took Jones for nocturnal walks although after ten P.M. he was a reluctant companion.

The odds against winning the Fat One itself were so astronomical that I didn't even consider buying a ticket. But if only the village could win one of the smaller prizes. If not . . . I knew how fickle human nature can be. I envisaged a lynch mob storming down the driveway.

December 20 was a Wednesday. Two days to go before the draw. In the evening we pinned up festive paper chains in the dining hall, festooned a Christmas tree with baubles that Diane had brought from Montreal, and hung greeting cards from loops of twine in the living room. The preparations intrigued Maria, the dreamy girl who helped Diane with the housework, because the Spanish didn't celebrate Christmas as rapturously as the New Year and Three Kings (Epiphany), when they exchanged presents, drank the champagne-like *cava*, and devoured *turrón*, almond and honey candy made in Jijona near Alicante. On New Year's Eve they gobbled twelve grapes while the clocks struck midnight.

I noticed Maria counting the Christmas cards.

She smiled. "That's lucky, thirty-*eight* of them."

"Supposing we get more tomorrow," I said.

"Don't open them until after the draw for *El Gordo,*" she said.

That evening we lit our first fire in the open grate in the dining hall with twigs of wild rosemary, kindling wood from a timber merchant, and logs delivered by Jones's enemy, the woodman.

The twigs caught fire; flames hovered round the sap-spitting logs. We toasted the baptism of the fire with *cava*.

Finally the logs caught fire.

Flames with dragons' tongues leaped up the chimney. Plaster above the hood of the grate cracked. Nuggets of cement fell into the flames. Panic!

I ran into the darkened garden and turned on the hose. It had been mended but the jet couldn't reach the outside chimney, which was now glowing even though it was lined inside with firebricks. Sparks flew like flaming moths. Jones barked at them. Ethel emerged from the dining hall and disappeared regally into the night.

The sound of plaster cracking finally faded and the last of the fiery moths flew away as the flames inside died down. I went indoors and told Diane not to worry: new chimneys always took time to settle, I explained.

Only Jones and Jonathan, who was eating chocolate-coated *turrón*, seemed disappointed that the danger had passed.

We drank another glass of *cava* and roasted chestnuts in the ash beneath a layer of smoke suspended across the dining hall.

We were interrupted by the appearance in the open space, still waiting for a door, of Beryl Kranz, the American painter, who had just returned from a trip to London.

"Boy oh boy," he said. "Was I ever lucky."

Diane handed her a glass of *cava*. "Why?"

"I bought a lottery ticket ending in eight at Valencia airport and I just heard that's your lucky number."

December 21, the eve of judgment day.

As the sun rose I walked around the garden with Jones. The poinsettias and the long buds of aloes, as smooth as snakes, were almost in bloom. The red-and-russet fruit on a pomegranate bush, packed with sweet-sour seeds, had split into grins. Leaves floated on the swimming pool—I had swum until mid-November, when a cold snap froze my blood.

But today the sun was warm enough to eat breakfast on the terrace, grapefruit juice squeezed from fruit from the garden, *ensaimadas* (snugly curled rolls dusted with ground sugar), and mugs of hot chocolate. We must have looked like archetypal foreign crazies eating in the open in midwinter.

"Have you packed?" I asked Diane.

"Packed? What for?"

"You realize the whole village has staked its future on a number which I just happen to scribble in moments of stress? If they don't at least get their money back we'll be as popular as a pair of barracudas in a tank of minnows."

"We? You mean you. I always thought there was something Freudian about those eights. They look like handcuffs. Did your mother handcuff you to a tree?"

"A lamppost," I said. "But seriously, I think we should go away for Christmas. We haven't got a door in the dining hall, the chimney looked as though it was waiting for blastoff when we lit the fire, and no one here gives a damn about Christmas except the cops."

Policemen directing traffic were inundated with gifts—wine, whisky, cigars, cigarettes, and *turrón*—that mounted so inexorably around the platforms on which they stood that motorists became dangerously disorientated.

"Has *El Pistolero* bought a lottery ticket?" Diane asked.

"Of course."

"Ending in eight?"

"Naturally," I said.

"And the priest?"

"He's bought a whole bunch," I told her.

"I know Pilar bought a few."

"Don't buy sugar from her after tomorrow—it might have powdered glass in it."

"The village could win the big one," Diane said hopefully. "Someone's got to."

"Pigs might fly. I haven't even bought a ticket."

"I have," she said, "ending in you-know-what."

When Jonathan came onto the terrace from his bedroom, blinking in the bright light, I asked him if he'd like to spend Christmas in a hotel.

"Will we get our presents there?"

"Of course," I told him. "We'll share a room, buy a little tree, hang up stockings . . . We'll leave a note here for Santa Claus telling him where we are."

"Can he read your writing?"

"He always has."

"Okay, let's go to a hotel."

Later I went into the village. The latest developments there were intimidating.

In a bar, Jesús, the gas delivery man, had bought three of the game-of-chance triangles of paper containing numbers. One of them had contained the figure eight and he had won five hundred pesetas.

The priest had taken eight confessions.

The debt collector had recovered 800,000 pesetas from a debtor.

Hope and cupidity stalked the streets.

On the way home I saw a white Seat lying on its side beside the crossroads, glass on the road sparkling in the sunlight. Its license plate ended in eight.

On the morning of the draw frost sparkled on the lawn. Ambrosio arrived to clean the pool and I switched on the TV: reporters were setting the scene for the drama that would continue through the morning.

By nine the smartly uniformed orphans chanting the numbers and prizes on the platform were well into their stride. One sang out a number, the other a prize, each picking up a ball bearing the relative information as it fell from a spinning cage.

Soon there was a commotion among the audience in the hall as the first two orphans to do their stint took the balls that had just dropped to referees to be authenticated—a big prize had been won by a hamlet in Extremadura, in the southwest, one of the poorest regions of Spain, but it wasn't the Fat One.

Prizes came and went. Other angelic orphans took over. At eleven I went for a stroll in the garden. The frost had melted, Ambrosio was vacuuming the pool. I was filling a plastic bag with oranges when the chanting on the TV stopped.

Jonathan appeared on the terrace and shouted: *"El Gordo!"*

I ran back to the house.

"What was the last digit?" I shouted to him.

"I don't know—I think it was eight." So most people in the village would at least get their money back. Maybe *El Gordo*. I would be a benefactor, a hero, a saint!

But the last digit wasn't eight. It was three.

Ambrosio drove away in his van. A middle-aged couple walked past the gates, heads bowed. I switched off the TV and called a kennel and a cats' home where I had made provisional reservations for Jones and Ethel.

When Diane got back from teaching I said: "Okay, let's get out of here today before the hangman arrives."

We drove inland toward Albacete, a cold and inward-looking city 150 miles away, where the International Brigade had been quartered at the beginning of the Civil War. We hardly spoke; even Jonathan was affected by the sense of anticlimax. We stopped for tea in the beamed lounge of the Albacete *parador*, one of a chain of state-owned hotels, many of them palaces and castles. In gloomy silence, we ate hot buttered toast and cakes made with ground almonds and oranges.

I paid the bill and we returned to the car like a family on its way to a funeral. And it wasn't until the key was in the ignition that Diane and I came clean.

"We shouldn't have left home," I said tentatively.

"I know." She still possessed the ability to surprise me.

Jonathan also looked surprised. "I thought——"

"Supposing," I said, "there isn't a chimney in the hotel room for Father Christmas to climb down."

"Let's go home," he said.

"As a matter of fact," Diane said, "we've got to go back—I forgot my overnight bag. Our money and traveler's checks are in it."

"I was ashamed," I said. "Losing the villagers' money for them was bad enough but skedaddling . . ."

"I enjoyed the drive and the tea," she said.

"A long way to come for hot buttered toast and cakes."

"It will be quicker driving back. It always is."

The receptionist in the Albacete parador canceled the booking we had made in Cuidad Real one hundred miles further on and we drove home, much faster than we had departed.

It was dark and cold when we arrived, the sky glittering with stars. Diane hurried down the driveway with Jonathan and I nearly bumped into a massive door blocking the entrance to the dining hall.

I stepped back. "That wasn't there when we left."

The door opened. A feast had been laid on the antique table I had bought from Peter Pateman. *Tapas,* roast lamb, fruit, cheeses . . . Lights winked on the Christmas tree. A log fire blazed in the grate. The floor was laid with terra-cotta tiles. Emilio and Ángel and their wives were waiting for us.

I turned to Diane. "You knew about this, didn't you?"

"That's why I left my bag and the money behind. I did know we had to come back but first I wanted to see if you felt the same."

I kissed the two wives on their cheeks and began my apologies. "I'm sorry—"

Emilio interrupted. "*El Gordo?* Don't worry about it, Señor Derek. Did you know that the numbers on the winning ticket add up to eight? That's good luck for *El Niño.* We have to buy tickets ending in eight all over again. Everyone in the village is very happy."

Not as happy as they would have been if they had won, but I realized later that the hard times they had endured in the past had left a legacy: it had made them grittily philosophical.

"Are you happy, Ángel?" I asked.

"January will be a lucky time," he said. "It is written in the clouds. And if *El Niño* fails us then there is always *El Gordo* next December."

The admission that the January lottery might not bestow riches was the only time I heard him admit that the clouds could be fallible. He also confessed that he had bought the derelict lemon grove at the end of the garden while I was still negotiating for it with the owner. A familiar fury assailed me but he had timed the announcement well: it wasn't an occasion for recriminations.

Next day we picked up Jones and Ethel and I rekindled a fire in the dining hall from the still glowing ashes, and it burned without threatening the chimney.

That afternoon I received a cable from my London publisher congratulating me on the Russian thriller. A REAL PAGE TURNER STOP UNDERSTAND ON GRAPEVINE NEW YORK FEELS LIKEWISE STOP CONGRATS.

I surveyed the dining hall, finished except for a few nails and a lick of varnish. I remembered last night's banquet. I reread the cable. I grinned idiotically at Diane and Jonathan. *"Feliz Navidad,"* I said. "Merry Christmas."

For Christmas lunch Diane cooked a turkey followed by plum pudding that we ate in the dining hall. We might have been in London or New York except that later that evening it was just warm enough to drink wine on the terrace beneath the stars.

The following day we emerged from our festive cocoon. We had been in the house a year, give or take a few days. Orange pickers were having an exuberant breakfast in the orange grove next door, a carpet salesman, hair as glossy as duck's feathers, was laying out rugs on our driveway.

On New Year's Eve Diane and I each ate a dozen grapes as the clocks chimed midnight and wished each other a Happy New Year.

On New Year's Day Emilio banged the last nail into the minstrel gallery. "Now all it needs is a few coats of varnish," he said.

"The painter's a relative of yours?" I asked.

"On my wife's side," he said.